CW00507012

ARTHUR BRYANT
Portrait of a Historian

By the same author

My Father, A. G. Street
Portrait of Wiltshire

ARTHUR BRYANT

Portrait of a Historian

PAMELA STREET

COLLINS
St James's Place
1979

William Collins Sons and Co Ltd
London · Glasgow · Sydney · Auckland
Toronto · Johannesburg

First published 1979
© Pamela Street 1979
Set in Monotype Bembo
ISBN 0 00 216663 1
Made and Printed in Great Britain by
William Collins Sons & Co Ltd, Glasgow

TO MY SUBJECT

Sometimes I thought I knew him well,
Oftentimes not at all;
Save for his work: a Pimpernel
Hidden behind a wall.
'Only portray,' he seemed to say,
'That which outlives life's span;
Leave me alone to write today –
I am a working man.'

'He is a writer who, more than any other I
know, has applied his historical imagination
and knowledge to a criticism of modern tendencies
most penetrating, and combined with true vision
and constructive power. His writings are a
bridge not only between past and present but the
statesman and the artist. The power and style of
his writing would alone lift him above the flux
of things, but the thought behind them will make
him remembered when England is herself again.'

H. J. Massingham, *Remembrance*

Contents

Preface

In attempting this portrait of a historian, my subject both helped and hindered, although the scales finally came down firmly on the helping side. I am indebted to Sir Arthur Bryant, not only for allowing me *carte blanche* to quote from his books, articles and private letters, but for all the infinite and meticulous trouble he took to put me right about anything over which I had gone wrong, especially the details of his work during those many years when I neither knew him nor found sufficient quotations of a personal kind to guide me.

For someone who has no pretensions to being either a literary or historical critic and has only written two books, to write anything about someone who has written nearly forty must seem an act of great impertinence. But after working for Arthur Bryant for only a short time, he became for me – not just because of all he had done but more because of his sheer individuality – someone who needed to be portrayed. He was quite unconscious of this. He was not an easy sitter. Often I felt I had to catch him 'in transit'.

But once he realised I was in earnest – persistence, though by no means knowledge, was something we both shared in common – he gave me information far beyond anything I could possibly have expected. Several rough drafts of this book were made some years ago. Because they all seemed to end quite naturally in the same place, I have not attempted to carry the final version further, particularly as in 1973 – the year he wrote *A Thousand Years of British Monarchy* – he moved to the cathedral close at Salisbury and later gave up his London home altogether, after which I no longer worked for him to anything like the same extent.

In the summer of 1977 he became seriously ill and cancer was diagnosed. He received this news just before he was due to give the annual 'One People' Oration in honour of Silver Jubilee Year at Westminster Abbey on Monday, July 18th. That at the age of 78, he survived and recovered from two serious operations, afterwards refusing to allow any such occurrence to interfere with his work or way of life, was, I think, testimony both to his own courageous determination and the skill of an outstanding surgeon. The 'One People' Service in the Abbey, which took place immediately prior to his first entering hospital, was deeply moving, all the more so for the very few of us in the large congregation who knew what he was about to undergo. The Oration itself was delivered with all his usual eloquence:

'A hundred years ago, in the heyday of Britain's naval, commercial and colonial ascendance, the poet Swinburne wrote of her,

"All the past proclaims her future,
Shakespeare's voice and Nelson's hand,
Milton's faith and Wordsworth's trust
In this our chosen, chainless land
Bear her witness. Come the world against her
England yet shall stand."

Is it still true in the very different circumstances in which England, and the British people, find themselves today? And is it true what William Pitt declared a century earlier, when Britain stood alone, facing across the narrow seas a revolutionary nation in arms with three times her population, with all western Europe aligned against her, with her own industrial districts starving, Ireland in rebellion and even the Fleet in mutiny? "I am not afraid for England," he said, "we shall stand till the day of judgment."
To answer that question, one must first ask what England – or Britain – is. And I, who am no prophet, politician or social reformer, can only answer it as a historian. Our past made us . . . *we must go back to the past to find an answer. . . .*'

South Street,
London, W.1.
1978

PART ONE

I

Man at Work

'Britain was not a land
where men could be both
comfortable and idle.'

*The Story of England:
Makers of the Realm*

'What is needed in this country,' he announced, peering at me over the top of *The Times*, 'is for everyone to work harder, look forward and stop belly-aching.'

'Yes,' I said.

'The greatest forces threatening to destroy our civilisation today,' he went on, 'are too many motor-cars – and too many politicians, civil servants and business men who have been promoted above their mental and social ceilings.'

'Yes,' I said again.

He was lying in bed recovering from an injury to his back. It was 10 a.m. and he had already been working for almost six hours. He was surrounded by newspapers, books, his writing-pad, a brief-case, two overflowing hold-alls, a jam-jar full of pencils, his private telephone, a wireless, a half-written article for *The Illustrated London News*, the remains of breakfast, three dozen copies of *The Great Duke* awaiting his signature and a personal letter, a packet of slimming biscuits, a beloved wooden mascot known as 'Bear', the morning's post, a bible, three pairs of spectacles, the core of an apple and a long, seventeenth century duelling sword. In his right hand he held a red and blue crayon poised ready to pounce on any provocative item of news which caught his fancy and he would later want cut out for reference.

'Look at this,' he exclaimed, feverishly outlining an article entitled 'The Three Day Week', 'we seem to have become a nation of holiday-makers and long-weekenders.'

'All except you,' I said, diving under the bed to rescue two cheques and a telegram signed 'MONTGOMERY OF ALAMEIN' which read: 'SO VERY SORRY TO HEAR YOU HAVE BEEN IMMOBILISED ON YOUR BACK. I WOULD EXPECT SUCH THINGS TO HAPPEN TO ME BUT YOU HAVE A LONG WAY TO GO BEFORE YOU ARE AS OLD AS ME. AT ANY RATE DO PLEASE BE CAREFUL.'

By the time I had reappeared his telephone was ringing. 'I hope,' he said, reaching out a broad arm across the grand miscellany, 'that it isn't the *Sunday Express*.'

'So do I,' I answered fervently. I knew just what that meant and I didn't see how he could do it, what with the appalling arrears of work with which he was faced since his illness and the exhausting task of getting *The Great Duke* into print against time. It *was* the *Sunday Express*.

'They want me to do an article on murder,' he said, after putting down the receiver. It was just after Blackpool's Chief Superintendent of Police had been shot.

'When do they want it by?'

'This afternoon. I think I'll get up. I might find it easier than trying to write in this semi-prone position.' He was looking very white and drawn, and I knew he was still in considerable pain. A few weeks ago he had undertaken the almost Herculean task of rearranging all the books in his library and, maintaining that only he could do it, had torn a muscle in his back. With reluctance (because I doubted the wisdom of the procedure) I tried to help him out of bed but it proved too much, even for him. For a moment I thought he was going to pass out altogether, but I had reckoned without the incredible strength and persistence of the man. He was under contract with Beaverbrook Newspapers and I should have known that he would write the article standing on his head if need be, and that by the end of the afternoon, having been typed and retyped (some pages as much as half a dozen times or more) it would be on the Editor's desk as requested.

Eventually, he agreed to remain in bed, and having made him as comfortable as I could, sharpened his pencils, supplied him with fresh sheets of pink foolscap, collected as much of his post as I could lay my

14

hands on without actually delving under the bedclothes, and received instructions to find any relevant material pertaining to 'Crime', I left him alone. Once outside the door I could hear the other telephone ringing in the secretary's room. In order to get to the latter I had to use the special security key with which all the doors in his house, except the library where he worked, were kept permanently locked. In my hurry to get the secretary's door open, the letters slid from my hands, scattering themselves over the landing floor, all except two, one from a Tory peer and the other from a Socialist back-bencher which, after dealing with the caller, I was intrigued to find had become amicably stuck together by a large blob of honey.

Having re-assembled the post, removed the excess stickiness and hastily written down the names of all the morning's correspondents in the Letter Book in case any further calamity occurred to their respective missives, I set about searching for references to 'Crime'. Although I had been working for Arthur Bryant for about six months, I was only just beginning to get the hang of his filing system which, like the man himself, was complex and unique. In his six-storied house in Rutland Gate there were letters and papers everywhere: in cellars and a strong room in the basement, in cupboards and chests on the ground floor, in antique bureaux and tallboys on the landings, in cardboard boxes and cabinets in the official filing room next to his library, in suitcases underneath book-shelves in the library itself, in disintegrating yellow envelopes stacked in the second filing room, in chests of drawers in his bedroom, in little wire trays which seemed to move about with a velocity of their own and which suddenly presented themselves in the most unexpected of places, and in vast tea-chests in his attics.

For some unaccountable reason 'Crime' appeared to have infiltrated into several areas: a small drawer on the first landing, a larger drawer on the second, and in a new-looking envelope which I myself had placed for safe keeping under the table in the secretary's room. In rash, energetic moments such as these, I believe I had hopes that I would one day try to change the whole set-up. I would streamline it in rather the same way as I imagined experts in time and motion studies might do, when they undertook a detailed survey and came up with the astonishing information that it would save a housewife one hundred and thirty-five minutes, twenty-eight seconds of walking-time per day if her sink was ripped out and shoved next to her cooker. All 'Crime', for instance, I would safely imprison in the secretary's room. 'Prime Ministers' I would take out of their murky little hideaway in the second filing room and somehow promote them to the library. At the risk of doing my lungs permanent injury, I would burrow under the layers of dust in the attic and give the reviews and notes pertaining to poor Charles II (the book which first brought Arthur Bryant fame), a justifiable airing. But at the end of the day, when I was tired and typed-out, I knew such a feat would be impossible. For one thing, I would never have the time or energy to go through with it; for another, it might make my employer unhappy. His system was too remarkable, too established, too individual to him. It was like the British Constitution. It had evolved down the ages and, after its own fashion, it worked.

Arthur Bryant was 72 when I first started my secretarial duties for him and I was then 50. There were forty-one stairs between his library on the first floor and the secretary's room on the third, but he took them in his stride with a nonchalant disregard for any attendant effort or inconvenience. Admittedly, he did not have to perform this mountaineering feat quite as often as I did, because when he was writing at full spate I would have to go up and down them like a Jack in the Box, first of all typing his manuscript in rough with very wide spacing so there would be room for him to make balloons and squiggles all over the page. The result, when handed back to me, seemed almost like a coded message for starting a Third World War. Then I might possibly be asked to do it in rough again, on which the corrections would be less numerous but still almost indecipherable. Then on the third lap we would, with luck, 'go into fair' as he put it, with one, or more often two, carbons into the bargain.

When I first became his secretary my spirits rose at this stage. I used to feel the battle was nearly over and I took great pains with my typing. Then I would trot down the forty-one steps with what I felt to be quite a presentable offering in my hand which I laid, reverently, in all its unsullied glory, on the top of his desk. But I had yet to learn what a perfectionist he was. Page after page would gradually become subjected to a formidable array of pencilled hieroglyphics. One or two might be found faultless enough to scrape by with nothing more than a sausage-shaped balloon and the correction of a literal for which, to my horror, I found I was the culprit. Other pages came in for stricter censorship: the ruthless slashing of half a paragraph, the transposing of sentences, the obliteration of the unnecessary word (something about which he was most particular), or the insertion of an idea which had only just come to him. Sooner or later, with a diffident and disarming smile, he would pass me the revised sheets with an 'I'm so sorry, but I think these will have to be done again,' and back I would go up the forty-one stairs to retype something which I was beginning to know by heart.

And now, this morning, here was another *tour de force* about to take place, albeit with a difference. For my employer, it would be more difficult because he was in pain and working to one of the tightest time-schedules I had known. For me, it would be that much easier because his bedroom happened to be on the same floor as the secretary's room and there were no stairs to compete with.

After I had sorted out all references to 'Crime' which I felt might be of use I took them in to him. He thanked me in an abstract way and went on writing. Judging by the amount of scribbled-on sheets which had already accumulated on his pad, I doubted that he would require any references at all. He had obviously got the bit, or rather the pencil, between his teeth. He really did bite his pencils, and the harder he concentrated, the more ferociously he bit. Occasionally, fearing for his inside, I devised ways of making the ends more unpalatable, such as wrapping little bits of sticking-plaster round them or painting them with bitter aloes. But it was to no avail. Biting pencils was a lifelong habit, impossible to stop. Sometimes he asked me to soak the ends in peroxide for hygiene's sake, but if left there too long the liquid evaporated and the ends became corroded with a bluish powder which I felt constituted the greater of two evils.

Today, he was fairly massacring his pencils and I was just about to leave him to it when he suddenly became more aware of my existence, unclipped what he had written, marked the pages which he wanted done separately with a red cross inside a circle, and the pages which could safely be merged to their predecessors with a cross only. Then he passed them to me with a charming request for 'Rough'. It was now about 11.15 a.m., and throughout the rest of the morning pink foolscap passed between us at astonishing speed. By 1.30 p.m. we were well away and actually 'going into fair'. I was also rather hungry. But I had learnt that lunch with Arthur Bryant was a question of 'When in Rome. . . .' It was never before 1.30 pm and was much more likely to be two or even three o'clock. Moreover, he himself never seemed to want it. He ate a large and rather late breakfast and maintained that a mid-day meal was not only an interruption, but that anything heavier than a glass of orange juice, two little squares of cheese and some fruit had a disastrous effect on the afternoon's work. He often despaired of the occasions when he was obliged to attend formal luncheons and seemed genuinely surprised that most people did find it necessary to take time off in the middle of the day in order to eat and even felt better for so doing.

Sometimes he would ask me to get through to his publishers between 1 and 2 p.m. Until I knew him well enough to suggest tactfully that perhaps this was not the best of times to try, I would attempt to do as requested. Then, with my hand over the mouthpiece, I would say from the other end of the library, 'Sir William's at lunch.'

'Then get me Adrian.' There would be an uncomfortable pause whilst a skeleton staff at Messrs. Collins intercommunicated with themselves. Finally I would be told that the same disgraceful fate had befallen Mr. House.

'He's also at lunch,' I would venture, nervously.

'Try Michael.' There would be a further silence during which I could sense him becoming steadily more impatient.

'He's out too,' I was finally forced to admit, after eliciting that poor Mr. Hyde had likewise succumbed to temptation.

'It's incredible,' my employer, who dearly loved them all, would then boom. 'All at the Dorchester, I suppose, eating quails at the expense of their hard-working authors.'

On this particularly harrowing day Arthur Bryant – or A.B. as I had come to think of him – missed out on lunch altogether. He drank his orange juice, but the little bits of cheese and dish of peeled grapes which I took in to him remained untouched alongside 'Bear' and the unopened second post. I myself ate a sandwich and a banana in the secretary's room and went on typing. About 4.15 p.m. I heard him telephoning the *Express* to say that the article would be ready in three quarters of an hour's time if they would send a messenger down for it. I always became acutely anxious at this stage, because A.B.'s conception of time and my own were completely different. I think it must have been something to do with the historian in him that made him feel there was so much more of it than I did. He thought in terms of centuries whereas I thought about minutes. Somehow I felt time to be a commodity I might easily run out of, like sugar, and therefore I wanted to stock up with it, allow myself plenty of extra, rather like the Chinaman who managed to arrange a spare ten minutes for himself whenever he was going on a journey in order to let his soul catch up with him, thus preventing any panic. As soon as I knew the messenger from Fleet Street was probably on his way, I began hurrying and hitting the wrong letters on the rather ancient typewriter, locking the keys and striking chords as a bad pianist might do in a frenzied attempt to speed up the Grande Finale. At the risk of having to have pages retyped, A.B. simply went on correcting and perfecting to the last minute, regardless that a man on a motor-cycle or a girl in a taxi might be on the last lap down Knightsbridge and the Kensington Road.

Possibly his optimistic attitude to time and my own apprehensive one resulted in a happy compromise because usually, when the door-bell of No. 18 rang loud and clear throughout the whole house, the article, if not actually in the envelope, was all but. Today, the crash-helmeted motor-cyclist was only kept waiting a few minutes. For the last time I pounded out the final paragraph:

> 'The tragic murder of Blackpool's Superintendent Gerald Richardson and the resultant resort to arms by the police in the London streets to capture his alleged murderer has spotlighted the deteriorating values – and security and peace – of our society. It is time for Parliament to undo what, in mistaken kindness it did, and to give expression to the wiser instinct and convictions of the great majority of those whom it serves and represents.'[1]

A.B. read it through, nodded, and asked me to clip all the pages together. For once, to my great relief, his pencil remained firmly in his

---

[1] *Sunday Express*, 10th October, 1971.

mouth. At last I was able to run downstairs and deliver the article safely into the messenger's hands, carrying up the tea-tray on my return journey. I felt there could be nothing better than a strong cup of tea at this stage and I poured A.B. out a cup and handed it to him.

'Tea,' he said, in surprise.

'It's almost 5.30,' I replied.

'Really? Well, I suppose I might lose my secretary if we don't have it.' Reluctantly, he laid down his writing-pad. I took a quick look at it. He never let up. With that incredible facility he had for 'switching' from one task to another without a moment's respite, he was now finishing his article for *The Illustrated London News*.

2

The Horse's Mouth

'Little, bright, hurting, jewelled memories
may sometimes jerk one out of the present
into the past.'

Illustrated London News,
3rd June, 1939

Somewhere amidst the wealth of material with which A.B.'s London
house overflowed, I happened to come across an essay he had written
for *The London Mercury* in 1934, entitled 'The Art of Biography'. It
was an art in which he had made his name in his early thirties with
Charles II, his short life of *Macaulay* and the three volumes of the
definitive life of *Pepys*. These had led to his being asked to write the
authorised biographies of some of the most famous figures of the
time – King George V[1] by the Palace, Cecil Rhodes by the Rhodes
Trust, and Kipling, Lord Roberts, Beatty and Wavell by their families.
Having by then embarked on the more difficult task of writing general
history, his commitments to his publishers had made it impossible for
him to accept these opportunities, much as he would have liked to have
done so. 'Had anyone told me,' he once said to me, 'that I should one
day be given the chance of writing the lives of my boyhood's heroes –
Lord Roberts, Rhodes, King George and Kipling – and not taken it, I
should have thought him mad!' In the case of the last it was a source of
much additional regret to him that his recommendation to Kipling's
family that the late Lord Birkenhead should undertake the task he had
had to decline, should have led to the tragedy of the latter's brilliant
biography remaining so long unpublished.

I sat on the floor of A.B.'s attic reading what he had written about

---

[1] A.B.'s *King George V*, published in 1936, was a short tribute to him written immediately
after his death, a decade before he was asked to write the official biography of the King,
subsequently undertaken by Sir Harold Nicolson.

biography, and became so absorbed that I forgot to feel guilty for not doing whatever it was he expected me to be doing. I suppose, somewhat presumptuously, the idea had dimly formed in my mind that one day I might write something about him, myself. There was a particular passage which held my attention, in which he reasoned that a biographer should be animated by a twofold passion:

'. . . desire for truth, and instinct for art. "Here is a man" he should say to himself, "I must find him"; and again, "Here is a man, I must make him live". To find him, he must comprehend the direction of the man's work, for it will be along this line in the main that the man's character will advance; and whether his hero succeeds in keeping to that path or is driven from it, his desire to follow it will provide the key to his soul. Yet though a great man's work is the ultimate purpose of his life, it is by no means the whole of his life; as we have already seen there will probably be many vital influences and occurrences which have nothing to do with his work, which are often at cross-currents to it and of which in most cases no trace remains to the biographer. It is the biographer's business to try and find as many of these as he can. To do so he must collect every fact on which he can lay his hands, not because all these facts are in themselves useful, but because any one of them may, in conjunction with some other, provide one of the essential clues for which he is seeking.'

There was also one brief sentence elsewhere in the article which stuck in my mind. It followed a much longer one where A.B. had been listing the materials, or 'dry bones' as he put it, with which a biographer works. Having wound up this with a reference to photographs, letters, books and even furniture which the subject had loved, he then wrote three words which made me think: 'The rest – silence'.

I began to realise that in attempting to write anything about A.B. I was both at an advantage and a disadvantage. On the credit side, especially in his reference to silence, the advantage was enormous. My subject – or would-be subject – though self-admittedly an extremely secretive man, was not exactly silent. In fact, occasionally he 'opened up' to me in a way which he inferred he never normally allowed himself to do. I was also surrounded, even overwhelmed, by the 'dry bones', so indispensable to any biographer whatever state of rapport he or she may have with his or her subject, always providing that my particular subject gave me enough time to look at them.

But on the debit side there were many imponderables. Biographies of living people, as A.B. pointed out, are seldom satisfactory. This he confirmed again in a long letter which I subsequently received from him during one of my attempts to put my idea into practice: 'If whether before my death or after it – by far the easiest time for an author to write a biography – there is sufficient public interest in me to justify a commercial publisher to commission a Life of me, I would far rather you wrote it than anyone else. . . .'

But after these unexpectedly encouraging words came the most awful warnings: restrictions, prohibitions, plans of his own, the strict necessity of chronological sequence, lists of enterprises completely unconnected with writing about which I knew nothing, references to personal battles: to prevent the 'high-handed annexation of Sarawak, preserve the independence of Ashridge Bonar Law College, alter the placing of a High Tension Pylon Line over a particularly beautiful part of North Buckinghamshire'. This was followed by daunting, detailed descriptions of all the various papers, letters and memorabilia packed away like dried-up sardines in dirty old boxes all over his two large houses, intricate instructions as to where to find what – 'Alanbrooke, big chest in strong room' – and finally, the words: 'The preliminary work of assembling and arranging such a vast mass of material would inevitably take a long time. From my own experience of preparing and writing biography I should say, even for a quick worker like you, three years. And I therefore doubt . . . whether you will ever wish to undertake such a long and wearisome task.'

He was right, of course. Just looking at the dreadful dilapidated conglomeration was sometimes enough to make me feel tired. Besides, he had become categorical about the necessity for concentrating not so much on his life but his work. 'You must remember,' he said, 'that the lives of most writers are dull ones. They aren't like men of action such as soldiers, statesmen or even administrators. A writer is so much of an onlooker; it is an unromantic trade and there is only one means of attaining perfection in it: hard work. The only interesting thing about writers lies in what they produce. . . .'

Yet although I appreciated all he said, it was the character of the man himself I found so intriguing. He may have been a great historian – exactly how great I did not feel I could, or should, attempt to assess – but he was also the most fascinating, eccentric, enigmatic personality I had ever come across. It was this, more than anything else, that made me long – rather, I imagine, as a painter longs to portray some striking face or figure – to write about him, this man whose life, only towards the end of it, touched mine.

I hardly knew him prior to the time when I became his secretary in the spring of 1971. I should probably never have got to know him at all had he not been kind enough to write a Foreword to a short book which I had written about my late father, A. G. Street, whom he had known through mutual professional interests. I should certainly never have come to work for him had he not extended a helping hand to me at a time when I was alone in London and particularly wanted something with which to occupy myself. His offer seemed like a lifeline. But I was by no means a trained secretary and, knowing the importance of his work, felt diffident of accepting. Realising that I was nervous, he made allowances. First of all I began by simply fetching work to take home with me; when this 'passed' I began going to his house for an hour or two in the mornings; gradually this extended into the afternoons and evenings. Almost without knowing it I had a full-time job on my hands, perhaps more of a one than I had bargained for.

Because around my new employer there seemed to revolve a ceaseless ferment of things to do: books waiting to be written, letters hoping to be signed, proofs crying out to be corrected, telephones demanding to be answered. Only occasionally, as if by some miracle, came the unexpected respite, when the book which had been waiting was finished, the letters in the post, the proofs with the printers and even the telephone quiescent for a while. His library would cease to look like a battlefield and everything – or at least a good part of it – seemed to have come right in the end. Then he would say, with one of his most charming smiles, 'How about a visit to the zoo? I should like to see some of those little furry animals. Wouldn't it be nice if we could take one out for a walk?' He adored all animals, especially dogs, whom he considered to be far superior in many virtues to human beings.

24

Yet for all his kindness and loyalty to those people whom he knew and loved, he was strangely suspicious and even cynical of others, attributing this anomalous streak in his character to the departure, when he was nearly four years old, of a nurse known as 'Other Nan' to whom he was deeply attached, and the arrival of another in her place who appeared to reject him in favour of the new-born baby and, in consequence, for some years made his life a misery. Whether these particular years held the key to much of his subsequent behaviour is something on which, perhaps, only a psychologist would presume to comment. I only know that A.B. himself often referred to this 'unloved' period, advancing it as a reason for his secretiveness, moodiness and general mistrust.

It seems important to go back to those early days, especially the influences in them which gave rise to years of so much achievement, before writing of the time which, by and large, I shared with him and which was the original inspiration for this book. My father invariably admonished me to 'write about something you *know*'. I did not really know Arthur Bryant until 1971. Because I have not attempted a biography but simply a portrait of him as a historian, I have depicted the *terra incognita* by quoting many of his own words as illustration, either through conversations I had with him or through his writings.

For in the passages which I have extracted from his articles in *The Illustrated London News* – the magazine in which, in 1936, he succeeded G. K. Chesterton as the weekly writer of 'Our Notebook' – it has been possible to link together a great deal of information which A.B. has revealed about himself in the course of this unique journalistic marathon. Nothing that I can write about this man with whom, in his seventies, I was so often in daily contact, can compare with that which I have been able to record 'straight from the horse's mouth'.

That he was a dark horse, often an obstinate one, always an eloquent one and certainly one with an overwhelming force of personality, makes it seem all the more imperative that he should be able to 'speak for himself', and with that astonishing power for recreating both scene and atmosphere, take his readers – and listeners – back with him in time by those strangely moving personal reminiscences, many of which I found hidden in the dusty piles of magazines stored in his attics.

3
Father to the Man

'By birth . . . I belong to the same
century as Macaulay and Mr. Gladstone
and Benjamin Disraeli. That dates a man.'
Illustrated London News,
19th August, 1939

'To my youthful brain . . . Queen Victoria
was the august lady who listened entranced
to the beautiful poems of Lord Tennyson
and invented electricity and the tricycle.'
Punch, 22nd September, 1920

Arthur Bryant was born on February 18th, 1899, in a house on the
royal Sandringham Estate in the parish of Dersingham. 'I happen to be,'
he wrote, nearly fifty-three years later,

'a late, very late Victorian. . . . Born into the world of the hansom
cab and the bowler-hat, of W. G. Grace's closing days and the
crowning, heavily gilded glories of the Victorian Empire, I have
witnessed two world wars, the coming of the aeroplane, the
submarine, wireless and atomic bomb, the loss of that Empire,
the virtual elimination of the British aristocracy, haute bour-
geoisie and the country gentry, the disruption of Europe and the
socialisation of Britain. . . .'

At the time of his birth his father, Francis Bryant,[1] was an official in
the Prince of Wales's secretariat. When Queen Victoria died in
January, 1901, and Edward VII succeeded to the throne, he accompanied
the King to Buckingham Palace and was given, as an official residence,
a Regency house in Lower Grosvenor Place on the Palace wall adjoining
the Royal Mews.

For almost four years A.B., or 'Boy' as he was called in the family

---

[1] Sir Francis Bryant, CB, CVO, CBE, ISO, JP. (1859–1938.)

circle, was virtually an only child, cared for devotedly by his nurse, 'Other Nan', with whom, as was the custom in that stratum of society at the turn of the century, he was firmly relegated to the nursery quarters on the top floor of the house. His mother, described by him as 'delicate, a poet and dreamer', nevertheless succeeded in managing a well-ordered household, one which, despite the necessity for thrift, consisted of a resident cook, two maids, a part-time laundress, as well as a nurse for her young son. Until the birth of his brother, Philip, he seems to have led a happy, secure existence.

But just before his fourth birthday, changes brought about by the arrival of his younger brother, the disappearance of 'Other Nan' and the installation of her sister as successor, turned A.B.'s safe, secluded little world upside down. Surprisingly, perhaps, it was not the new addition to the family whom he resented. Between Philip and himself, despite widely differing temperaments ('Philip[1] was a saint,' he used to say, 'I'm not'), there grew to be a deep bond of affection and friendship. But it was the new nurse against whom all his passionate young being rebelled. For not only had she deprived him of the loving relationship he had hitherto enjoyed but, in its place, engendered another of an unfortunately antagonistic kind.

How this state of affairs could have gone so long unnoticed by a mother who, according to A.B., was very far from neglectful or unloving, seems strange, save for the fact that in those days the subtle invisible barrier between the world of the nursery and the grown-up one below was much more inviolate than the flight of stairs and wicket-gate which physically separated them.

In his own reminiscences about his childhood which have appeared from time to time in *The Illustrated London News*, and of which the best have been reprinted in *The Lion and The Unicorn*, there is no reference to this unhappiness, only an expression of deep love for his family and home. His father, brought sharply into focus in a few sentences, was

'a man of great method and integrity, whose word was his bond and whose life was governed by unchanging, inexorable rules based on work. Except on holiday his routine never varied –

---

[1] The Reverend Philip Bryant, for many years chaplain of his old school, Harrow, where he was greatly loved, died in 1960.

breakfast, after a cold bath and exercises, at eight and never a minute later; a short walk in St. James's or the Green Park with my nurse, my brother's pram and me before crossing the Palace courtyard to his office, a small upright figure dressed in the regulation top hat and frock coat of his calling. . . .'

Of his much younger mother, he wrote,

'once a week, on her At Home day, I used to descend to carry on halting and reluctant conversation with her visitors, or sometimes, when she was alone and I was allowed a brief escape from the nursery, to pretend to help her with the accounts of the St. Peter's, Eaton Square, choir school, to feeding which . . . she devoted much of her time and talent for frugal and wholesome housekeeping which she had so improbably, in the light of her temperament, acquired from my father.'

But the city in which he was brought up, A.B. brings back to life with a picture more vivid and poignant than any:

'. . . I should like to revisit the London of my youth. I know there was much squalor and tragedy in it: the drab dirt of the slums, the destitution of those who had failed in the hard, strenuous race of life, the pathetic beggars and crossing-sweepers and ragged children, the sight of whose poverty wrenched at one's heart as one walked the thriving, confident streets of the world's greatest metropolis. Yet, on the whole, it was a London with conviction, faith and, with what comes from these things, vitality and energy. I should like to see and hear again its familiar sights and sounds: its horse-buses and jingling cabs and carriages, its tinkling hurdy-gurdies, the gleaming, varnished shop-fronts and striped awnings in the Bond Street sunshine, the fine brown of horse-dung eddying on the dusty summer pavements, the parade of men and women and horses at Hyde Park Corner on June afternoons, and the quiet of the royal parks of Kensington and the Pimlico squares before the first motors invaded them and the long Victorian peace, which lasted from Waterloo to Mons, came to an end.'

At the same time as a youthful A.B. was absorbing so much of the world around him, there were certain other factors which influenced his young mind, directing it, unconsciously, towards the past. From his great-grandmother he inherited some little wooden blocks, the front of each bearing a picture of a king or queen of England with their respective dates and characters, summed up in a single word, on the back. Then there were the books which were either read to him or which he read himself: *Little Arthur's History of England*, Mary Synge's *History of the World* containing brief and simply-written accounts, with poetic headings, of every famous global character, which helped to give him a sense of the vast sweep of human history. After this came Kipling's *Puck of Pook's Hill, Rewards and Fairies* and, as a passion for soldiers developed, Napier's *War in the Peninsula* and Alison's *History of Europe*.

But perhaps the most important reading was that which he undertook in his father's library, as he pored over the enormous bound volumes of *The Illustrated London News*:

'More, I think, than any other circumstance, even than my father's habit of reading history aloud to me, this implanted in me a feeling for the past and ultimately made me a historian. . . . It was my wont to lie for hours in front of the fire reading old volumes of *The Illustrated London News*. It was a symptom, I suppose, of mingled idleness and curiosity; it was occasionally frowned on as a habit by elder persons. But it was very persistent, and once in front of a volume it was hard to get me to move: I would turn the pages for hours, gazing with fascinated eyes. . . .

There is a great deal of history in those old nineteenth-century folios. Here is the day-by-day chronicle, in picture and letterpress, of a past age. What is so valuable about this kind of study, if it can be called such, as I think it should be, is that one is hereby led to see the past not as a carefully selected train of events leading up to some fashionable modern hypothesis, but as the spasmodic day-by-day affair it seemed to our forefathers. When one comes to think about it, it is just so that the events of our own day present themselves to us. Posterity will no doubt see them in a different light, just as we see the events of the past in a different light to that of those who actually experienced them. But then, what sort of a picture will posterity, by doing so, form of our motives and state of mind? Which picture . . . is really likely to be nearest the truth? That neat, simplified one which our descend-

29

ants will master from their textbook histories, or that more complicated affair with which we are so painfully, if confusedly, familiar?'

Writing later in this same magazine which captivated his interest so long ago, he has provided an even more revealing self-portrait as he was at that age, by humorously pointing out the contrast between his brother and himself as they played on the nursery floor of Lower Grosvenor Place, each according to his developing personality and interests. He described the games on which they embarked, with the aid of tin personages and an old rocking-horse, in the days when his sole ambition was to become a general and his younger brother merely wanted to simulate an existence of a much cosier kind, that of their next-door neighbours, the King and Queen of England.

For Philip, brought up with the love which the new nurse withheld from his elder brother, was a 'peaceful soul'. . . .

'He partook far more of the character of Mr. Chamberlain (in his umbrella days) than of the German Führer. He liked an undisturbed routine; he very much disliked wars, revolutions, parliamentary broils, street riots and even fires. It may be asked why, in this case, my will was allowed to predominate, and why my brother's more pacific and therefore righteous intentions did not triumph as they so plainly deserved to. The answer, I fear, is that I was four years older, and therefore bigger and stronger. . . .

'My brother confined himself to the life of the Royal Family, whose tastes were as orderly, as well conducted and pacific as his own. They resided in a large, stationary rocking-horse in one corner of the nursery, surrounded by a courtyard, as similar as possible to that outside Buckingham Palace, and a walled park. Within these confines they did their best to carry out a life of their own – a life, that is, of regular habit and slow and elaborate routine such as satisfied my brother's gentle and orderly mind. This little household of bearded station-masters, bowler-hatted travellers and hospital nurses, who, for lack of more appropriate toys, represented the King, the Queen, the Prince of Wales, and all the Royal Family and their retainers, pursued with great dignity and deliberation the even tenor of their way. Or perhaps it would be more true to say they tried to. For, like the peace-loving democracies in recent years, they were subject to outside disturbances of a most tiresome and incalculable nature. Those disturbances emanated always from a restless and romantic mind which, unhappily for them and my brother, controlled powers and forces which they could never for long ignore. It was not Hitler, then a homeless waif in the slums of old Vienna, but I who was the bane of their existence.

'For scarcely had the under-housemaid at the Palace started the undeviating routine of the royal day by calling the footman who carried the shaving water to the Prince of Wales's apartment – somewhere between the rocking-horse's ears – and the black-bearded, frock-coated Prince of Wales had proceeded according to hallowed custom, across the saddle to the broad area above Dobbin's tail where Majesty itself slept, when the sound of a galloping courier could be heard approaching the Palace gates. A moment later the intruder would be hammering on the front door, and, though only admitted after every possible expedient for refusing to open the door had been tried, his tidings would prove of a nature which it was almost impossible for royal personages to ignore. Either the Prime Minister had been assassinated, or a revolution had broken out in the streets, or an invading army was – without the least warning – approaching the capital. On other occasions the entire town was in flames and given over to furious fire-engines. For, unhappily for my brother, it was I and not he who controlled the army, the politicians and the civil population beyond the Palace wall. And the day's routine of a conscientious monarch could scarcely be pursued without some relation to their troublesome vagaries and misfortunes.

'None the less, my brother made a brave attempt to minimise the effect of such disturbances on his household. His ambition was always to get through the entire twenty-four hours of Palace life without a break in his comforting, domestic routine, and with no more serious interference than some minor domestic mishap, such as the disappearance of one of the Royal Family down a hole that led to the hollow centre of the rocking-horse. It was an ambition that was rarely achieved, for wars, revolutions and tumults surged round the Palace without cessation. . . .'

31

And around A.B. seven decades later it seemed to me turmoil of one sort or another was still surging. He thrived on it. He grew up a loner, a larger-than-life man with larger-than-life ideas, a person with, for want of a better expression, personality plus. He seemed to fill a room, sometimes – except when he was on his best behaviour – to disorder it to an alarming degree. He was a man of extremes. Having always taken on more than most men could ever contemplate, he was invariably overflowing with enormous optimism, deep despair, urgency and strange, unaccountable articles of clothing or equipment which would temporarily become disengaged from the magnetic force to which they were attached and lie, limp and abandoned, until such time as their owner (or more often their owner's friends or associates) would sweep them up again in order that they might accompany him on another foray.

Sometimes, pondering on the imponderable, I wondered to what degree nurture or nature really *had* played in his strange and compli-cated make-up. On the occasions when I floundered along beside him, trying both to understand him and keep pace with the incredible speed at which he walked during our sorties into Hyde Park – which salutary habit he felt necessary for us both, despite the amount of work waiting at Rutland Gate – I felt I was with as complete an 'original' human being as it would be possible to find. His mind was fecund, mercurial. Being in daily contact with it was rather like being gripped by an interesting novel, one which one was unfortunately only able to read in fits and starts. I was never quite sure what he was going to say (or do, for that matter) next, but I was always anxious for the next instalment.

And, although at the beginning of my acquaintanceship with him his past life was no more than a blurred negative, gradually, as another isolated little vignette was presented to me, either during the course of conversation or through something he had written, everything became that much clearer. A picture of his earlier years when he and this century were both nursery-young began to take shape in my mind, and I felt that another piece of a rather mysterious complicated jigsaw had been slotted into place.

*   *   *

'I always wanted to be a soldier,' A.B. said to me. 'It seemed inconceivable that I should ever be anything else.' It was not difficult to understand how this ambition had come about. For there he was, a small and obviously very impressionable child, to whom the Changing of the Guard was part of daily life. Brought up in the shadow of Buckingham Palace, where he lived alongside all the King's horses and all the King's men, the desire to become one of the latter seemed a natural outcome. 'Earth,' he wrote in later life,

'might have held things more fair to show than a battalion of red-coated infantry lining a London street in the grey of the dawn or a squadron of Lancers – all blue and cherry and gleaming silver – but my youthful eyes had not beheld them. What was good enough to guard the King of England and do him and (with polite reserves) his royal guests honour was good enough for me. At that time I believe I knew the facings of every regiment in the British Army. The drab dishonour of khaki – the herald of a shameful pacifism – was still in the unguessed future.'

London in those days, according to his own words, 'did things in style'. On the day before the actual arrival of foreign potentates he was usually taken for a special tour of the decorated streets to view their completed glories. 'That night,' he wrote, he would go to bed in

'a state of excitement that made sleep impossible. Even if slumber came for a time to tired eyes, it was soon broken by the tramp of urgent feet passing under the window. Squads of garnished and highly polished police officers arriving in Central London from some outlying suburb would swing along the still-darkened street; . . . a gilded carriage with scarlet-jacketed footmen would glide over a golden-sanded roadway . . . and, most thrilling of all, a little later the sound of distant martial music would be borne to eager, straining ears. . . .

'I would creep, flannel-pyjama-clad, to the forbidden window long before I was called, silently lift the blind and peep out at those intriguing sights in the gas-lit street below. . . . I would listen eagerly for the chimes in the familiar church beyond: chimes that would herald the coming of my own approaching hour of calling. For, my father having an official position at

Court, I was, so far as processions were concerned, though in nothing else, a privileged urchin. It was my happy lot, on such occasions, to rise early and, conducted by my nurse, to make my way through the streets, crowded with others hurrying in the same direction, towards the Palace. Just where the throng began to grow thickest and the way become seemingly impassable, we stepped aside and, by a kind of talismanic process, found ourselves inside the side gate of the Palace. Then followed what I think was the most exciting moment of all – the passage of the Palace from one end to the other along its underground corridors till we emerged into the daylight and the quiet serenity of my father's office. And so, as Mr. Pepys would have said, out into the forecourt and down the Mall, between lines of scarlet soldiers to out allotted place. . . .'

It seemed surprising to me that A.B. always maintained he lacked a good photographic memory, for all such commemorative and spectacular occasions – especially the great military pageants of King Edward VII's funeral and the coronation of George V – made a lasting impression on him. Sometimes I felt he was rather like a seismograph. He seemed to sense immediately, with what he referred to as his 'antennae', the atmosphere in a roomful of people, the responsiveness of an audience in a hall or the feeling behind a national movement. His mind was forever reaching out and spanning the community in the same way as it spanned the centuries.

Yet for all his compassion and loyalty to his nearest and dearest, he remained singularly unaware of the day to day life going on around him. Whereas his younger brother, Philip, endowed with a calmer, gentler nature – happily fostered by his nurse's affection – grew up to become sociable and intensely interested in people as individuals (which eventually led him to take Holy Orders), the elder brother was always too concentrated on the task in hand to be concerned with domestic trivia. Gossip bored him. He had, as he himself admitted, absolutely no small talk. In his schooldays he described himself as having been a 'lazy little beggar', disinclined to apply himself to anything that did not interest him, which therefore only left military history and cricket to have the full focus of his attention. 'While my self-sacrificing parents,' he wrote, 'though not my schoolmasters, who quickly sized up my titanic capacity for inattention and scholastic idleness, thought that I was acquiring knowledge in the most expensive form available, I was in reality drawing elaborate maps of battles, real and imaginary, and planning invasions of every country on earth. Long before Hitler turned his attention to war, and while he was still sentimentalising over architecture in Vienna or splashing paint on window-frames in Munich, my plans for global conquest were complete. I knew all the answers long before the First World War. If winning wars consisted only of drawing up clear-cut plans, which it doesn't, I could have beaten Hitler with my eyes shut!'

There was one early episode in his schooldays which had made him bitterly ashamed, so much so that it was only in later years that he had been able to laugh or talk about it at all. It occurred when he was six years old on his first day at the mixed kindergarten of the Francis Holland School for Girls in Graham Street, to which he was taken daily by his nurse. Already pent-up and distrustful, 'I believed it to be,' he said, 'not just for the morning, but for ever.' Like others before him who had found themselves in the same unhappy circumstances, he cried. But A.B. never did things by halves. He cried and he cried and he went on crying, with the same kind of persistence which permeated other, more creditable ventures throughout his whole life. Having been passed from one teacher to another who had all done their best to put a stop to such disruptive behaviour but without success, he was finally put into a cupboard which happened to be on the platform of the main hall of the school. And there, apparently, he was forgotten.

Worse was to follow. Nature gained the upper hand, first in the form of comforting sleep, but later in a much more urgent fashion. When the school assembled at the end of the morning for the beginning-of-term address from no less an august personage than Canon Scott Holland, an unmistakable trickle began to appear from the direction of the cupboard. The door was hastily opened to reveal a small boy who had disgraced himself in front of the whole school. A.B. was overwhelmed with shame. Horrified and mortified by what he had done and ostracised by his fellow pupils, who held their noses at his approach, he spent the rest of the week in indescribable loneliness and fear, terrified lest his nurse – whom he knew to be a friend of the nurse of two little Jewish girls in the school – would learn from her what had happened and expose his shame to his parents, whose disgust and revulsion at such a breach of decent civilised behaviour he could not bear to imagine.

On the following Saturday, when there was no school, what he feared came to pass, and the two nurses with their charges met in Hyde Park and started to exchange gossip. Hoping not to be noticed, the little pariah hid behind a tree. Then what seemed a miracle happened; a warm hand crept into his. It was that of the elder of the two sisters who told him that she felt he had been cruelly treated and that, though she had not dared to say so at school, she felt terribly sorry for him. A.B. fell wildly in love.

* * *

By the time he was eight years old, he became an altogether happier child again. 'Other Nan's' successor had departed; another young woman had arrived to take care of his younger brother; he himself had become a pupil at Gibbs's fashionable but then *avant garde* school in Sloane Street. Here he found a satisfactory outlet for his excess energy by becoming captain of the junior football team. But it was Mr. Gibbs's advanced ideas on education which appealed the most:

'If one complained of a headache, the kindly Headmaster – a man of true reforming zeal and bursting with ideas for the amelioration of the human lot – would be summoned, and would subsequently, if it was a fine day, take one for a row on the Serpentine, instead of leaving one cooped up in a stuffy, boring classroom, or, if it was wet or in winter, accompany one to a matinée. The cost, I suppose – though the Headmaster was a man of such benevolence that this may not have been so – was charged to one's parents, much as today it would be charged to the tax-payer, in other words to someone else. If, on the other hand, I felt so low that even the Headmaster's efforts seemed irksome, I had only, I discovered, to blubber and howl and I was despatched home in a taxi. It was all very comforting and reassuring and helped one to develop a strong expectation that the world was different from what it was. Unfortunately I was taken away from this liberalising establishment after a year and sent to a school of a much sterner kind. . . .'

For now he was unable to escape the fate of nearly every young boy brought up in such circumstances. At the age of nine he was sent away to a preparatory school. The usual unhappiness suffered by all small children at such a time was, in his case, intensified. Partings throughout his life always brought about great lowness of spirits and, as each holiday drew to a close and he knew that he would soon be returning to Pelham House at Sandgate, he sometimes considered throwing himself over the banisters. Nor was the situation helped by the fact that the Headmaster, an appropriately intimidating figure with a huge white moustache – though in reality a kindly and good man – used to come to lunch in the Bryant household on the first day of every term, changing, like some chameleon, from affable sociability in the dining-room of Number 17 into a seemingly terrifying martinet before the arrival of the Kentish coast.

'I remember with what sense of unpitying doom and finality the day came to return to school: the last hours among the loved familiar things of home, the parting with one's parents on the bleak, inescapable platform, the chilling comfortless aridity of the barrack life to which one returned put a term to all hope of future happiness. . . . In those days one knew grief as Lear or Oedipus or Desdemona knew it. . . . Presently, of course, we learnt philosophy. . . . Even in those first desperate days of term, amid the heartache of the cheerless, rowdy dormitory, or in the hopeless perplexity of Latin unseen, one would become conscious that in the fulness of time these Promethean sufferings would be succeeded by the bliss of faraway holidays. And the knowledge would make one speculate a little curiously on the nature of time that could seem so inescapable and eternal, and yet presently and imperceptibly transform one's circumstances and life into something utterly different. . . .'

Presently, as he moved up the school, time did make life a great deal more tolerable. He was also heartened by the presence on the staff of a retired army matron of the Florence Nightingale tradition. For, being passionately interested in all things military herself and knowing how much he wanted to be a soldier, he became somewhat of a favourite of hers. And there were invariably occasions which, being associated with fighting men, lifted him temporarily right out of the humdrum into a world which had always fired his imagination:

'One of my great treats was to be marched on a Sunday afternoon in crocodile . . . to Shorncliffe a mile or so away, there to file through the lines of soldiery and see the British Army taking its sabbath rest in the famous camp where a century before John Moore had trained the Light Brigade to be the finest fighting corps in Europe. It was still an army recruited mainly from the plough and the gutter – the army which Kipling sung and Florence Nightingale had sought to humanise and which cloaked the hardships and rigours of existence beneath uniforms of scarlet, gold and gleaming pipe-clay. To see it was an aesthetic as well as a martial experience, and I think it was the former, even more than the imaginary glamour of war, that made me – an untidy, slovenly, ill-co-ordinated child – passionately resolved to be a soldier, so that at that time it scarcely seemed conceivable to me that my future life could ever take any other course but the conventional military one of crammer, Sandhurst, a regiment of the Line, India, and, if I was fortunate – for wars were then rare and supposed to be on their way out – a participant in some glorious charge or heroic forlorn hope in which, contrary to all probability, I would distinguish myself and win the notice of my sovereign, promotion, and one day, for I spent much time studying the campaigns of Napoleon, a major-general's plumed hat or even a field-marshal's baton! . . .'

Little was he to guess, on the day at Pelham House when he witnessed Blériot perform the then astonishing feat of flying the Channel, that within another eight years he would have learnt

'equally inconceivably, to fly myself in a kind of aeroplane called a Maurice Farman, not all that different to the primitive machine in which that pioneer French aviator did, in the space of half an hour, what Napoleon and his Grande Armée had tried so hard to do a century before and, because of Britain's command of the stormy, tidal waters below, failed to do. Indeed, the reminders of that failure were still very present to a little boy whose school playing-fields contained a circular Martello tower erected in 1804

38

or thereabouts to prevent that very Napoleonic invasion. . . . On special occasions, I remember . . . the whole school used to climb the narrow, dark, winding stairway which led to the roof of the Martello tower and there, while the Union Jack was run up to the top of the flagpole give, at the Headmaster's bidding, three cheers for the glorious past, present and, as we believed, the future of our country. A good many of us, indeed, were to die in that belief on the battlefields of two world wars. It is worth, perhaps, bearing in mind that at that time I and my contemporaries were almost exactly the same distance in time from the Crimean War as we were from the mechanized, rocket-haunted, computerized, patriotism-despising and permissive age which we now, such of us as still survive, inhabit. . . .

'My own dawning interest in politics, as I stood proudly with the prefects to cheer the memory of Lord Nelson on Trafalgar Day, or see Blériot fly the Channel, was focused on more distant scenes: on our new allies, the dear little Japs, helping us, as I supposed, in the Pacific, and on the threat of the Kaiser and his ﾠHigh Seas Fleet to our naval supremacy. About the latter – for I was a thorough-paced little imperialist – I felt very strongly. In this, indeed, I appear to have been not only abreast of the history of my age, but a little in advance of it, for by the time I had passed on to a public school, looking down on the still unbuilt-over clayey fields and elms of the Middlesex plain, public interest in Britain had shifted to the "Dreadnought race" with Germany and the "rebellion" of Protestant Ulster against the dominant Liberal Party's proposal to concede Ireland home rule: these and the suffragettes. All these great matters impinged excitingly in a slight manner on my personal life. I was entertained in our first Dreadnought by her captain as she lay in Weymouth Bay; I paddled the Ulster champion, Sir Edward Carson – a great hero of mine – round my uncle's lake when he was fishing there; while a great friend of my mother's used to support the suffra-gettes and entertain the leaders, a circumstance which mildly endeared them to me, though I had little sympathy with their claims, sharing my mother's old-fashioned view that women's genius lay in the home rather than on the hustings, a view, reactionary and deplorable though it must seem, in which later experience has tended on the whole to confirm me. . . .'

At the end of each term, the longed-for familiar routine took place: Christmas holidays in London, Easter ones in the country, summer ones again in the country or at the seaside, once the thrilling ritual of the great cockney August Bank Holiday saturnalia had taken place, the annual Surrey *v.* Nottinghamshire match, to which his father – a member of the Surrey Cricket Club – always took him:

'To be part of that enormous crowd which sat, packed like penguins, round the Oval ground on an August Bank Holiday to see A. O. Jones's Nottinghamshire challenge Lord Dalmeny's Surrey was to comprehend the greatness of England. . . . Those were the days of county cricket's high Edwardian splendour; the names of the champions ring across the years like the warriors of the Iliad: MacLaren, Fry, Jessop, Barnes – surely the greatest bowler that ever lived – Woolley, Hayward, Gunn, Spooner, Hirst, Rhodes. I never saw Ranji in his lithe, panther-like prime: only the Rajah-like figure of the Jam Sahib, returned for a brief season to play in the Elysian fields his genius had made immortal. Nor did I ever behold on the field – though several times in the pavilion – the greatest cricketer of all: the bearded, Jove-like Doctor. But the others I saw by day and dreamed of by night, and I shall go to the shades, when my time comes, the richer for their presence. . . .'

Some part of nearly every country holiday was always spent at what A.B. referred to as his 'second home', a Regency country house belonging to an aunt and uncle in a secluded valley of beechwoods, park and lakes, on the borders of Dorset and Wiltshire which, in later life, for a time became his own. Wincombe, as it was called, was

'. . . the daydream of many an exiled hour in city street, in school, in camp. Here all the journeys of my imagination ended. I used to lie awake at the beginning of a new term at school, conquering in fancy the stubborn miles and interminable weeks that separated me from my heart's desire, speeding the imagination between the dusty hedgerows of a still unspoilt England towards the spired cathedral town in the West and the cool avenues and winding lanes of ancient cultivated valleys eaten out of the chalk through the centuries by sparkling trout-streams, each more sacred to me than the one before, because nearer the place I sought. I saw in my dreams the grey Norman church on the hillside, where one day I hope to lie, the high hazel hedges between which slow horses dragged enormous loads of hay or mangels in bright-coloured, curved wagons of antique design, the little Gothic-windowed lodge with its brightly painted white gate at the entrance to the beech woods, the drive whose every bend and tree and bush were symbols of boyish adventure, romance or dream, the sudden gasp of excitement as the woods began to drop away into space and that ever-new, never-changing vista of enchantment came into sight. . . .'

One of the most endearing traits in A.B.'s character was his enthusiasm and delight with which he looked forward to something. It almost seemed as if he had the same capacity for this at seventy as at seven, the only difference being that the looking-forward as he grew older was so much more the enjoyable part. It was a state of mind confirmed in his own words written in later life: 'I have had my little successes, and have enjoyed them, I dare say, as much as any man, but they have given me no joy to compare with those of sweet, romantic, unrealised anticipation.'

Nevertheless, in those far-off days at the beginning of the century, it would have plunged one would-be holiday-maker into unmitigated despair had the date of departure for the seaside been postponed, even for twenty-four hours:

'. . . There was the excitement of waking early, knowing that the great day – the climax of summer happiness – had at last come; the spades of many sizes which I carried like golf clubs in a bag; the two – or was it three? – blasts of the whistle which I was allowed on this splendid day to blow at the street door to summon a "four-wheeler" and, most thrilling of all, the long, dark, lamplit tunnel under the railway by which in those days horse-drawn vehicles from York Road approached Waterloo. The next half-hour – for we always went very early to secure our seats – passed in a delirium of joy that I can no longer recapture, though I can still savour the pungent delicious smell of Edwardian trains – something they have lost with the coming of diesels and electrification – and the sense of triumph with which I sunk into my corner of the carriage, when the train had at last backed down the crowded platform and the pandemonium for seats was won.

'I did not read in the train in those days; I glued my nose to the window and kept it there. There I remained in a kind of ecstasy, seeing the fields and hedges flying past like milestones to paradise. For the next hour or so I seemed to be in another world. Like little Thomas Traherne, "I was entertained like an angel with the works of God in their splendour and glory; Heaven and Earth did sing my Creator's praises, and could not make more melody to Adam than to me." Even the crumbly egg sandwiches, eaten out of a bag between Salisbury and Yeovil junction, scarcely broke my trance.

'Later, as the slow train between the main line and our destination wound its way, puffing heavily, down some deep green western valley, I would lean out of the window to catch the first whiff of the sea. Every now and then a smut from the engine would make me withdraw my head until the first sight of blue horizon told me that my goal was near. I remember that I always used to run behind the trap which bore both my parents and their luggage from the station to our lodgings, too excited to finish the journey in any other way. . . .

'Do children still, I wonder, enjoy their departure from the town to the seaside at the start of the summer holidays as much as they used to when I was a boy? . . .'

4

Harrow

'God give us bases to guard or beleaguer,
Games to play out, whether earnest or fun;
Fights for the fearless and goals for the eager,
Twenty, and thirty, and forty years on.'

Edward Bowen,
Harrow School Song

'The cumulative effect of these songs on the
youthful mind, sung week after week and term
after term . . . is profound. I have long
been convinced that they affected my own
outlook more than any other single factor in
my schooldays.'

Illustrated London News,
1st January, 1949

'I'm going to Harrow for the end of term Songs,' A.B. said to me.
'Would you like to come?'

'Thank you very much,' I replied. 'I should love to.'

'It's going to be a bit of a rush,' he continued. 'I've got this committee meeting at the Mansion House this afternoon. Would you mind
going ahead to Baker Street about 5 o'clock and buying the tickets?
I'll do my best to meet you there by then or soon after.'

I can see him now, hurrying down the station steps, a flying figure,
urgent, slightly anxious. 'Ah, there you are. Good. I think we can just
make it.'

We fled through the barrier, brandishing our tickets like criminals,
jumping alarmingly on to a crowded, point-of-departure train, strap-
hanging for most of the journey until we reached our destination, a
place where he had spent four and a half years of his youth, a place of
which he wrote in 1943:

'The railway station of late Victorian or Edwardian days has been replaced in the name of progress by a concrete fabrication harsher to the eyes, harder to the foot and seemingly less convenient to the traveller than the old, since it involves the unavoidable climbing of many steps. The place where my running shoes used to be sucked off my feet by wet clay is now a concrete street; the site of the old smithy left over from an earlier equestrian age is a pseudo-palatial cinema. The old village and school, with its quiet Georgian houses, timber-framed cottages and spreading chestnut-trees, is now an anachronism – a backwater of the past forgotten in the wilderness of progress.

'So, many people would say, is the school itself. . . . The old school tie, a snobbish adornment in the days of my youth, is become a badge of shame. . . . I still on non-official occasions wear mine. It gives me the same prickly and glowing feeling that a sober eighteenth-century squire must have felt when occasionally in loyal Hanoverian days he sported – after dinner – the white rose in Shrewsbury market-place. For I am still, in defiance of the triumphant spirit of the age, very proud of my old school. . . .'

And he was, that wintry evening, obviously very proud of it. He pointed out the various features, standing outside looking across towards a lighted London and, once inside the Speech Room, eager to see which of the songs would be sung, later joining in each with enthusiasm and talking afterwards about incidents which had occurred during his time there. It was the same pride evoked by these songs which had caused him to write of Harrow during the egalitarian and spartan days of the war:

'Even by the standards of today its record seems no bad one. Winston Churchill and General Alexander are names of which any school in the Old World or New might feel proud. The wise and kindly old man who struggled – largely, I fear, in vain – to teach me mathematics, had struggled in an earlier stage of his career to impress the same verities on our present Prime Minister. . . . This excellent man used, I remember, to tell with great affection a story of a class whose inertness one sleepy summer afternoon wrung from him a despairing "Oh, what can I do with you boys?" – a rhetorical question which elicited from the cherubic-faced future Prime Minister the unanswerable rejoinder of "Please, Sir, teach us!" The good pedagogue and his brethren seem to have taught their apt pupil to good advantage. If the school on the Hill has had any share in moulding Winston Churchill's genius, it can claim to have earned its keep in the world with the most progressive school in the land.

'Expensive keep, I dare say someone will say! Broken top-hats on the parched sward at Lord's, scandalous fees, a prodigious consumption of strawberries and ice-creams – "dringers", we used to call them – in the school tuck-shop on summer after-noons. True, and yet the life, as I remember it, was Spartan enough, and I fancy in Mr. Churchill's time it was even more Spartan than it was in mine. These eighteenth century public schools carried into the cushioned world of twentieth century Westminster and Mayfair a much-needed robustness and tough-ening. Their historic function, as I see it, was to make those born into life's sheltered crannies feel early the whip of the tempest that the plain man has to face on his exposed rock all his days. In a world in which favoured inequality of some sort seems ineradic-able, even if it only be that of the Commissar and the good Party member, it is something to make sure that the offspring of the privileged shall learn what it is to be kicked in the pants before the moral arteries harden. . . .

'I can see no good reason for abolishing a good school merely because it differs from the average. The sensible course, it would seem, would be to make the average approximate to the good. Leaving aside the top-hats and the "dringers", which don't matter, I can see nothing to prevent the State, if it wishes, supplying every boy in England with the same spartan fare as I enjoyed in the most expensive school in England 30 years ago. In a properly planned community . . . it should cost no more to feed and educate a boy in a boarding establishment than at home. . . . Whether a boarding-school really produces better educational results than a day-school is a matter of opinion, but there is no doubt that the majority of parents who could afford to exercise any choice in the matter in the pre-war world thought that it did. Personally, though I have an open mind on the matter, I sincerely hope the same freedom of choice will still be allowed after the war. But I also hope that the freedom of choice will not be confined on financial grounds to the rich, or even to the ideologically elect, but that it will be open to all. . . .'

Once, after a similar journey to Harrow in order to listen to its songs, he wrote:

'I do not pretend that I was very happy at school: I was not, perhaps, the kind of boy who would be. The return from the holidays was always a nightmare whose shadow still haunts my occasional dreams. Yet I came to love my school, more, I fancy, than I ever did my College at Oxford, where I was infinitely happier. And analysing this curious idiosyncrasy of the mind, I believe that my love for the school was made and fostered largely by these songs. This was the more curious because I was not, in the accepted sense of the word, a musical boy. . . . But then, as now, those songs, enshrining the life of a school where I had small wish to be, made an enormous impression on me. I think it was because in a scholastic world where there was little room for beauty, they alone were concerned solely with beauty – beauty not perhaps of outward form, but beauty of character and ideal, of loyalty, love of friends and wonted place, and of a nameless understood chivalry.

'And I see now that my unhappiness at school was not due to being bullied, for I was not bullied, nor even to my longing for my own home, which was considerable although only temporarily painful, but to a certain aridity and absence of colour and light and consequent inspiration that were then, and possibly still are, the inevitable concomitants of public-school life. And then in the midst of that drab and barrack-like wilderness of each successive term of twelve or thirteen interminable weeks came this burst of song. . . .

'One realised as in a flash of vision in darkness the meaning of life around one, its purpose and guiding unity. One knew oneself to be part of a tradition greater than oneself, that gave meaning, beauty and hope to all that one could do or endure. . . . Of this I am sure, that such a legacy of transmitted poetry and music, interpreting the daily round of familiar school life and, through it, the wider life to be, is something not lightly to be discarded. It is an educational factor beyond the measure of examinations, text-books, and educational conferences. . . .

'I have always felt convinced that these songs must have played some part in Winston Churchill's subconscious mind when, out of his transcendent courage, he compiled those wonderful speeches, so simple and so eternal in their youth and faith, in 1940. The spirit that runs through them is the same spirit that, through Churchill, fired England and turned that year of disaster, peril and humiliation into her "finest hour". . . . A year later – at an almost, if possible, darker moment – at the beginning of the desperate winter of 1941 when our hopes had been dashed in Africa, when Russia seemed to be facing imminent defeat with the victorious Germans at the gates of Moscow and Leningrad, and when the Japanese were about to strike at our defenceless rear, Churchill visited Harrow to hear again – and sing – those songs. It was then he used the words: "This is the lesson: never, never, never – in nothing great or small, large or petty – never give in except to convictions of honour and good sense". And he went on – referring to an extra verse which had been added to one of the songs in his praise: "You sang that extra verse in my honour, which I was very greatly complimented by and which you have repeated today. But there is one word in it I want to alter. . . . It is in the line,

> Not less we praise in darker days
> The leader of our nation.

I have obtained the Headmaster's permission to alter *darker* to *sterner*. Today we praise in sterner days. Do not let us speak of darker days; let us speak rather of sterner days. These are not dark days: they are great days – the greatest days our country has ever lived. . . ." '

Almost one of the first articles I ever typed for A.B. was written about his old school.

'It imbued me and thousands like me with the belief that whatever was to be enjoyed had first to be earned; that only by taking thought for the morrow could the morrow be what one's hopes would make it; that "waste not, want not" was an inescapable law of the universe and that, by hardships cheerfully and bravely undertaken, one could alone hope to reach the stars. . . . Our heads were cropped, our bottoms were tanned, our pride was humbled and the mickey kicked out of us before we were allowed a chance to swagger and suppose ourselves, as foolish youth is inclined to do, lords and sole judges of the universe. . . . We served an apprenticeship in the valley of humiliation. . . .'

The annual event at Lord's between Eton and Harrow was something which, having acquired a love of cricket through his father and predisposed towards all ceremonious occasions, he appreciated more than most:

'It is more than half a century since I first watched the Eton and Harrow match. It was then a terrifying ordeal for any little boy who was inclined to be untidy or whose parents were not well endowed with this world's goods. For the smartness, not to say dandyism of attire expected by even the youngest fourth-former, the flummery, the snobbery and dazzling fashion of the occasion are something which can hardly be envisaged by those who do not remember it as it was in the days before the First World War. Long before the great day one was expected to try out patent-leather shoes – and they had to be new and of the highest fashion – to acquire a new top hat, a fancy waistcoat, a cane adorned with ribbons and rosette of the right colour, and one's turn-out when the great day arrived and the London exeat began had to come up almost to Brigade of Guards' standard.

'As for Lord's itself, it was like the Royal Enclosure at Ascot – every seat was taken, and in the outer circle and on the ground itself during the intervals one could scarcely move for the crush.

'That was the outward form of the Eton and Harrow match in the thirty or so years that preceded the Kaiser's war, when imperial Britain was sitting pretty on top of the world and what today would be called the "Establishment" – and it was then a real Establishment far too strong even to be criticised, let alone mocked – sat resplendent on the coach box; . . . proud women in wonderful black and white concoctions with peacock trains, long ribbons and flounces, parasols and bonnets of the most elaborate millinery, attended by lordly looking men in shining black top-hats – the day of the white or grey topper had still to come – immaculately square-cut frock-coats, enormous button-holes and collars as big as horse-halters, while between them walked little be-caned dandies, every whit as smart, who a dozen years later were to perish leading their companies or regiments at Ypres or on the Somme and among the tawny Gallipoli hills.'

* * *

It was not really until his final year at Harrow that anyone suspected that there might be more to this quiet, hitherto undistinguished boy than had been apparent. Curiously enough, until then, despite his earlier love of history, he had not shown any particular aptitude for this subject. But now he came under the influence of George Townsend Warner, the Senior History master, one of whose earliest pupils had been G. M. Trevelyan. Although when invigilating on some occasion during A.B.'s first term, Warner had described him as 'the grubbiest little boy I have ever seen', as soon as he began to teach him and read his essays, he became interested.

In the summer of 1916, owing to Warner's perception of his new pupil's potentiality, the latter made a momentous decision. He was then 17 years of age and had intended going into the Army Class at Harrow the following winter, prior to a year's training at Sandhurst and then: the war. If, however, he was to attempt the scholarship for Cambridge which Warner – a Cambridge man – was urging him to do, it would mean forgoing this idea. Realising that he might, in fact, get to the war earlier by trying for the scholarship and then joining the Flying Corps after his 18th birthday instead of undertaking the statutory training at Sandhurst for a regular commission, he took Warner's advice and settled down to concentrate on history.

As he had already done the previous year, he spent his summer holidays with an aunt and uncle in Ireland, in a world, as he put it, 'as remote from the England I knew as any place on earth . . . of rolling Atlantic breakers and far horizons and mauve mountains and grey rocks . . .' and also of 'bright-eyed, carillon-tongued Irish cousins', who forced their dreamy and seemingly slow-witted guest from England to live at their own chattering pace and with the oldest and prettiest of whom he fell in love.

His uncle – a daring small-boat yachtsman – was a Lt. Commander in the R.N.V.R., carrying out the dual trust of supervising anti-U-boat detection measures on the Connemara coast and administering the vast poverty-stricken estates in Galway and Clare for the Congested Districts' Board. In his company A.B. visited the isolated peasant communities of Atlantic islands in their fever-stricken hovels, trudged at his side over peat moors and mountains and glimpsed something of the old peasant Ireland, with its despairing poverty, superstition and inertia and of the forces that were beginning to transform it and give it new hope and purpose. But what he found most exciting of all, was cruising with his uncle and watching at night for suspected German sympathisers running supplies to German U-boats. Once at dawn, having anchored in a storm the previous night, he woke to see a squadron of grey battleships momentarily sheltering from submarines on that wild and lonely Atlantic coast.

With so much fascination on all counts, coupled with his habitual aversion to partings, it was a world which he must have found more than difficult to leave. And his return to Harrow resulted in still further sadness. On the first day of term it was given out in Speech Room that Townsend Warner had died. His pupil was then pledged to two things: the scholarship (with little aid from the stop-gaps who came to take Warner's place), and the Flying Corps.

But with the persistence and dedication with which he invested anything on which he had set his heart, A.B., to his own surprise and everyone else's, gained an Exhibition at Pembroke College, Cambridge, that winter and joined the Flying Corps the following summer, acquiring, into the bargain, the St. Helier school prize for essays and a Harrow leaving scholarship. Warner had been right. Not only did this particular pupil become a distinguished historian. He also became, in later life, President of the Harrow Association, something which gave him more pleasure than any other honour ever conferred on him.

5
Flying, France and Oxford

'Each human mind sees the whole of God's
creation as the background of a gigantic
ride for its own peculiar hobby-horse.
Historians are not immune from this curious
trait. They see contemporary events not so
much as the uncertain, pulsating stuff of an
all-absorbing present, but as the raw material
of history.'

Illustrated London News,
14th June, 1941

'I wasn't really suited to the Flying Corps,' A.B. once said to me. 'I
would probably have done better in the Army provided I'd had a good
batman to keep me tidy. I was far too clumsy and unmechanical to
make a good pilot. When I first went up solo to loop the loop I nearly
killed myself.'

Before sending him up on his own his instructor made him repeat
carefully what he had taught and shown him. After reaching the
required height, in order to gain additional speed to carry the "'plane' –
as they called them in those days – round the loop, he was to push the
joy-stick forward so that the nose dropped and, as the machine dived
and gathered speed, pull the joy-stick hard back so that the nose shot
up in the air, continuing to hold it firmly against his stomach while he
turned upside down, at which point he had to remember to switch off
the engine so that the nose of the 'plane fell and it automatically came
out of its loop and righted itself.

'But I forgot,' he said, quite simply. 'I'd done all the right things up
till that moment but there I was, engine full on, 'plane upside down
and all the dust from the bottom of the cockpit beginning to pour onto
my face. I wasn't strapped in and started to fall out. To keep myself in
I let go of the joy-stick and clung to the sides of the fuselage. Merci-

fully, I suddenly remembered, managed to wriggle my hand along the edge to which I was clinging, reached the switch and turned off the engine. The nose then fell, and, several hundred feet below where I began, I came out of the loop. To this day I can remember exactly what my instructor called me when I reached the ground!'

Before he had joined the Flying Corps, A.B. had felt that, because he was fond of map-reading, he might make a tolerable observer. When, however, he found himself actually in the R.F.C. – at that time a Regiment of the Army – any preconceived ideas about his own part in it quickly came to nothing.

'There was little map-reading to be done, though as a gentleman cadet, a great deal more drills. . . . There were, in a minor way, plenty of hardships and scarcely a hint of the stars. But what at least seemed certain was that, should the day of apprenticeship ever end, the thing to be was not an observer, but a pilot; not to be flown by someone else, but to fly oneself. For, though in the German Air Force the pilot had first begun as a kind of super-chauffeur and the place of commissioned honour had been the observer's – a mistake subsequently rectified – in the R.F.C. from the very first the tradition had been the other way round. The man who flew the machine was the man who mattered. . . .'

'Or,' as he frankly put it to me, 'I was a frightful little snob and soon realised that a pilot was the thing to be.' And so, after an initial apprenticeship as a private at the Royal Flying Corps Depot at Farnborough where, for one incredible afternoon, he played cricket in the same eleven as Hobbs, followed by a longer spell at an Officers' Training Corps at Hursley, he graduated into the School of Military Aeronautics at Oxford, where

'in a high, streaky-bacon. Betjemanic goblin-market villa in the Banbury Road I studied, with patriotically-tempered boredom and distaste, the nobbly internals of Lewis and Vickers guns and the theory – a very different thing I was soon to discover, to the practice – of military aeronautics. . . . I lived in a sixteenth-century College, rowed in leisure hours in an eight on the Isis past emblazoned if rather shabby wartime collegiate barges, a d enjoyed for a few strenuous weeks, in uniform, the delights of an undergraduate's life.'

Being totally unmechanical and therefore unable to understand the working of any engine, A.B. passed his technical examinations simply by memorising what he was expected to know. Ultimately, after a prolonged and expensive apprenticeship for his country – which had to replace the machines he broke as stunting made him dizzy and high-altitude flying sick – he learnt to fly without either killing or seriously injuring himself. But by the time he had gained his wings and at long last reached France, his boyhood's dream of a permanent military career was finally at an end, for he was no longer a soldier but a temporary officer in the Royal Air Force into which the R.F.C. had by now become absorbed.

'How long ago it seems,' he wrote twenty years later, just before the outbreak of a second World War. 'One would not have missed for anything the honour of having served, however inadequately, in those early days of a great institution.' Yet, though only able to play a minute part in the great struggle now nearing its close, what he saw during his few months' service in France left a deep and abiding impression. The sense of historical perception which Townsend Warner had recognised in his schoolboy essays was already at work, unconsciously shaping what he was to write in years to come.

'I remember so well a November day just after the Armistice. I had been to Bethune on squadron business and was driving back in the late afternoon to Lille, where we were then quartered. Before it became dark we passed La Bassée, the point where the muddy, pocked pavé of the highway crossed the devastated areas. Here was the quintessence of annihilation. For four years the line at this point had remained almost constant. Horror had become static; pain, suffering and devastation were entailed upon this desolate estate. The town was no more than a pattern of stunted walls, battered almost down to the ground and in many places disappearing altogether in shapeless and charred rubble. Beyond was No-Man's Land, already fast merging, like Hardy's Egdon, into the approaching night which seemed its home. A cold wind came down from the North, and I made the driver stop, and stood for a while with my back to the highway and my face towards that outer cold darkness. Before me was the place of Golgotha and dead men's skulls.

'History was in it. I was only a boy, less than a year from England, and stood but on the fringe of that great era in which the experience of many centuries was crowded into a compass of time such as clocks cannot measure. I was the silent witness of heroism which had been and in which I had no share. The battle-field was still naked: neither man nor nature had yet done anything to deprive it of its awful and dread character. Here courage and patient endurance, despair and tortured anguish lay side by side, their gaunt flanks hidden in the night. The air was tainted yet clean; there was storm in the wind, and the spirits of the dead moved with speaking silence round rusted wire and deserted trench and those ghostly sentries of that lost land – the stripped skeletons of what in some unattainable distant past had once been trees. There is no describing it in this age, for only a great poet who had lived through it all could have done any justice to it. And in the end it is only through the poets that it will have any existence at all. . . .

'In a thousand years' time, the battles that were fought on Ancre and Somme, Lys and Yser, may be remembered not for the victories and defeats in which they resulted – the loss of this empire and the gain of that muddy, blood-sodden acre between the parapets – but for the sweet English words which some lieutenant or humble sergeant, rendered articulate for an hour by supreme stress and suffering, scribbled with a stumpy pencil on a scrap of paper torn from a field pocket-book or the back of an envelope.

'This legacy of English poetry which the war has left has scarcely been recognised. Most of the singers were in no sense professional writers, but ordinary citizens turned soldier, who felt impelled to express an amazing experience; many left behind them only a single poem; and only one or two survived the conflict that made them immortal. For, so far as transitory literature of man can confer immortality on its creatures, such poems as Julian Grenfell's "Into Battle" and Edward Wyndham Tennant's "Home Thoughts from Laventie", are likely to be read as long as literature is studied and English speech preserved. And the great struggle that inspired and engulfed them will, because of them, be sometimes remembered too. But it will not be its material achievements and results that will be recalled, for the reader will find no mention of them in these fragmentary and, as it were, accidental verses. Their theme is neither national victory nor defeat; reading them one would be at a loss to know who won the war, who fought it, or even what it was about. Anger, hatred, malice against the foe, even fear, have no part in their stanzas. For their subject is something greater than the war of man against man. They are concerned with another war, an eternal one, which is waged in every human soul between the powers of good and evil, between man's strength and man's weakness. They bear witness that, though man under suffering may be a poor, whining, cringing thing, helpless and utterly afraid, he also has it in him to rise above his doom and his own weakness. And that, after all, is the eternal theme of all great poetry – Othello in his hour of agony recovering his deluded sight, and his courage, and Samson bringing down the walls of Gaza and finding peace and quiet mind at the close. It was just this that these dead poets of England, and the inarticulate legions they spoke for, did. . . .

> "The blackbird sings to him, Brother, Brother,
> If this be the last song you shall sing,
> Sing well, for you may not sing another,
> Brother, sing!" '

*　　*　　*

Two months after the Armistice A.B. returned to England to continue studying, more or less where he had left off.

'As the grim year of 1918 gave place to 1919, it was peace and release and freedom from the drab enslavement of khaki – though also, one remembers, of comradeship and dedication – and the sad, grey devastated, wintry landscape of northern France and Flanders. And I was still not 20, with the world before me, and all the hopes and romantic illusions of youth. I travelled back to England, home and beauty, in January 1919 in a cattle-truck from Lille in a long night and day journey to a demobilization camp outside Boulogne in temporary and rather uncertain charge of 50 cheerful but near-mutinous soldiers and airmen from almost as many different units, and, leaving them there after a two-day wait, I crossed the Channel as an intending student under what was called Group 43, and, following some perfunctory administrative formalities in a station waiting-room at Folkestone, became a free man. A few hours later I was at home in London, a home-coming slightly marred by a difference with my meticulously honourable father – a model of the Establishment correctitude of those unpermissive days – over an Army blanket which I had brought with me and which had proved an invaluable adjunct during my rather chilly and uncomfortable journey, and which he insisted, to my ill-concealed scorn and indignation, should be packed in a parcel and returned to His Majesty's Government via, if I recall rightly, the War Office in Whitehall. What the inmates of that high and remote Valhalla made of this disreputable and tattered piece of military equipment when they undid the parcel in which my mother had tied it up, I have no idea. I can only remember that, half under my breath after my altercation with my father, I expressed, in military parlance, what I hoped they would do with it!

'This petty contretemps with a much-loved father – symbol, I suppose, of the eternal "generation gap" – and the strange wartime existence which had preceded it, were soon forgotten in the new life of Oxford which I found myself sharing with several thousand other demobilized students, many of whom, for all their scanty years, had commanded companies, and even, in some cases battalions and brigades, in battle.'

It may seem strange that, having won an Exhibition at Cambridge when he was still expecting to make the Army his permanent career, A.B., who had now abandoned that career, elected instead to go to Queen's College, Oxford, but he had certain links with the latter, where his maternal great uncle, uncle and cousin had all been famous rowing men. Going to Oxford was made possible by the fact that, with his passion for independence and determination to make no further demands on his self-sacrificing father, he had saved up enough from his Army and Air Force pay to enable him, with his demobilization gratuity, to support himself without the need for his Cambridge Exhibition.

What was perhaps more strange was that, though during his five terms at Oxford he read for History Honours and obtained them, as at

Harrow he showed comparatively little interest in the subject for which he had had so much liking as a child. He spent most of his time there – and it was, for him, a very happy one – reading literature and writing poetry, thousands of lines of which he committed to memory, as he had earlier done when learning to fly. Above all, he made friends, many of them lifelong, and nearly all with young men who, like himself, had served an apprenticeship in war before resuming their education at a university.

'I and my fortunate comrades were released into a still austere but infinitely welcome January England: free of every military restraint and obligation, heirs of victory and unassailable, eternal peace, young uncrowned lords of the Turl and High and of an Oxford which, it seemed, had been waiting and growing for us for six centuries. It was all ours: the grey quadrangles, the flowered gardens, the towers and domes; the learned men at their lectures and orisons; the gay lunches and suppers – when we could afford them – of salmon mayonnaise, ices and steaming chocolate sauce; the willow-shaded afternoons in Cherwell punt and canoe; the gala, parasolled visits in Eights Week and Commem of lightly-chaperoned, cousinly young ladies who opened, for romantic and unreckoning hearts, vistas of eternal, breathtaking happiness; the endless talk, wit and glow of friendship while St. Mary's deep-tolled bell proclaimed to unheeding ears the midnight hours.'

It was delight in the aesthetic rather than the scholastic and intellectual from which A.B. derived most benefit at Oxford. At long last, he was able to enjoy to the full something he valued so highly all his life and which had been so lacking in his previous time there as an R.F.C. cadet: liberty, the liberty of a world freed, as it was then hoped for ever, from war and khaki.

'Ours was a goodly heritage . . . those of us, that is, who were fortunate enough to return from war to a life of communal study and ease instead of the drab, harsh life and struggle of the industrial towns and factories which were to be the lot of so many of our wartime comrades. It was a land in which gentlemen of the older-fashioned and more decorous sort still went about in top-hats, in which ladies of all classes and conditions wore skirts which were a discreet half-way between maxi and mini, in which vicars presided over garden parties, and bathing-dresses for both sexes were wetly clinging and two-piece; in which parlour-maids in cap and apron provided a kind of domestic chorus to the social intercourse of their "betters"; in which garden chairs were made of wicker, not plastic or steel; in which motor buses were roofless. . . . Its social cement . . . was the upper middle class, professional and squirearchical, depicted in *Punch* by Lewis Baumer, with its unassuming, self-restrained, easy-going men, fresh from the Flanders battlefields, in well-cut sloping-shouldered lounge suits, neat bow-ties and Homburg or what were to become Anthony Eden hats. Beside them were wives and sisters with broad-brimmed millinery concoctions, kiss-curls and long, sloping breastless dresses widening out towards the base. . . . Beside it, mingling with it in the street, bus and tube and on village cricket greens and at meets in the rustic shires, the working-class, still in cloth cap and corduroys pursued an independent life of its own, while between the two there flourished, if that is the right word, a lower middle class – for the most part placidly unresenting and inarticulate – of black-coated clerks, small shop-keepers, and farmers clad in the shapeless but stout-wearing clothes of the closing years of Queen Victoria's reign.'

Though he had chosen and loved his time at Oxford, he made it no more than a brief resting-stage between demobilization and the start of an active career. He came down at the end of five terms, having gained Distinctions in the Shortened Honours Course for Ex-Servicemen, equivalent to a First[1] or Second.

'Foolishly or, perhaps, wisely, I felt the spur of the lost war-years, and impatiently wanted to storm the workaday world. I soon found myself in it, and the Oxford of the young released captains who had so gaily thrown their Sam Brownes over the moon became only a precious memory. . . .'

For all his many Oxford friends, he had still not lost touch with those with whom he had served during the war – many of them from a far less favoured background than his – and he felt deeply the unfairness

---

[1] A.B.'s tutor, R. H. Hodgkin, the historian of the Anglo-Saxons and later Provost of Queen's, told him afterwards that had he taken the longer course, he would, almost certainly on his papers, have been awarded a First.

of their having to return, as some of them did, to the world of the unemployment queue and the slum.

'There is nothing exceptional in a sensitive lad being appalled by what he finds the world to contain. It is happening all the time: it probably happens to all of us. The world is full of injustice, ugliness and brutality, and always has been. It is natural that generous and ardent young men, filled with a hopeful sense of what life might be, should be horrified and indignant at what so frequently is. . . .'

'An idealist, with an unorthodox itch to practise what I preached, I upset my poor father a good deal at this time,' A.B. recalled. 'He had recently been knighted for his services to the Crown, and I remember he told the King that he feared he had some kind of Bolshevik on his hands!'

It was with a vague idea of improving mankind through teaching that A.B. now set to work. Having rejected several possible openings – the editorship of Burke's Peerage, entry to the Foreign Office, the offer of a job as A.D.C. to a colonial Governor and a schoolmaster's post at Winchester – still intent on bettering the lot of the less privileged he began putting his beliefs into practice. Spending, like many of his contemporaries, two or three evenings a week in the boys' club of his old school mission in the Notting Dale slums – about which at this time he wrote and published, in a slim paperback, his first historical work, a history of the Harrow Mission – and realising that such efforts were rather like dabbling at a sea of destitution with a sponge, he decided to do something more constructive. He applied for and obtained a teaching post in a London County Council School, something which in those days seemed for a young man with his educational and social background a little unusual and unconventional.

Shortly after he started teaching he caught mumps from his pupils and developed double pneumonia. When his temperature, which for five days had been alarmingly high, fell suddenly, he became delirious and remained so for a fortnight. With five nurses – two of them male to hold him down – his life, during those days before antibiotics, hung precariously in the balance.

Miraculously, the crisis passed. Youth, the glorious early spring of 1921, and a remarkably resilient constitution, led to 'a summer of wonder: the best, so far, I think, of this century or of my lifetime. I was a young man then, on the threshold of life, with school, war service and university behind me and a future wholly unpredictable ahead. So much happened to me that summer that was the foundation of what came after: not so much material achievement, but of friendship and the knowledge of places that were to be woven into the texture of my heart. It was a summer that began for me with a convalescence from a dangerous illness; after four weeks of pain and delirium, poised between almost indistinguishable points of life and death – entered upon on a bleak, pneumonia-haunted winter day – I rediscovered a world bathed in early spring sunshine. . . .

'Only a few weeks after I emerged from the shadows, I was sparring in a Wiltshire meadow with a retired prize-fighter turned yeoman farmer. I did on one occasion, to his and my immense surprise, inadvertently knock out this ex-professional pugilist, a man of mighty sinews and straight carriage, whom I can still see silhouetted against the orchard blossom of that lovely spring. I used to walk home through the wood above the infant Nadder, wondering at the glorious heritage of country England into which I had been born and reborn, and counting wild flowers that belonged to June bejewelling the hedgerows of late March and early April. All that summer the sunshine and warmth continued, while I taught by day in a school in North London and spent my evenings coaching boys at cricket or learning myself – for I had nothing to teach them except clumsy enthusiasm – in the nets at Lord's. . . .'

During this period he added to his commitments by working voluntarily on several evenings a week for a children's library in a slum at Somers Town, in a house where Dickens had once lived. There, when his teaching at Holloway was done, he would spend an hour or two on his way home reading poetry to ragged little London boys and girls, who used to clamber all over him while he regaled them with Masefield's *Reynard the Fox* or Walter de la Mare's *Peacock Pie*. Afterwards, having changed for a dance, he would try, usually with success, to recruit one of his débutante partners to help with his next day's labours at the Dickens Library. He also wrote to Masefield and de la Mare (neither of whom he knew), to be rewarded by both poets paying a visit to the Library, where, amid much enthusiasm, they read their verse to the children.

Of the dances in those days, he wrote,

'I can still recall a very grand lady of the *ancien régime* standing at the top of a staircase receiving the guests with a grace and dignity which even then belonged to a world which had vanished – and much sitting-out on balconies overlooking leafy squares beside one dazzling creature after another, all wonderful to my sisterless vision, and all, I should imagine, looking back on it, profoundly bored by my shy, romantic and tensely dumb adoration. It is doubtful whether, as I prattled on about my North London boys or my views on poetry or cricket, they were even aware of it, and most of them, I think, though they did not seem so to my undiscerning eyes, were almost as shy as I. . . .

'At that time programmes were never seen at fashionable London dances. . . . Actually, of course, the absence of programmes was extremely inconvenient; young ladies, approached for a dance, used to say "missing three", or, if they were very sought after, or oneself a very poor and clumsy dancer – as I was – "missing seven". And as, particularly as the evening wore on, encores were frequent and it was sometimes impossible to tell when a new dance had started, this led to a great deal of confusion and, on occasion, to very embarrassing situations. Having a poor memory and small talent for arithmetic I used, in a furtive way when no one was looking, to enter surreptitiously on the back of a scrap of paper in my pocket, the name and promised dance number of any young lady in whose arms I particularly wished to walk or shuffle . . . round the crowded room.

'But though the nymphs of that far Arcadia were insubstantial, the summer that enshrined it was substantial and all-pervading, and when the school term and the *rus in urbe* evenings of chandelier, fiddle and saxophone ended, I plunged into the wonderful countryside that I knew was awaiting me, and, in the company of a new friend[1] first encountered during three days of shimmering heat on the beaches of Dymchurch, I made my acquaintanceship in two walking tours with the South Dorset of Hardy's novels and the Cotswolds and Severn Valley of Housman and Elgar. . . .'

---

[1] Walter Dunlop, later to become Arthur Bryant's brother-in-law.

'How vividly that is imprinted on my memory,' he wrote, many years later, 'striking southward over Win Green and the South Wiltshire downs.' And subsequently, recollecting the Cotswolds:

'I remember taking leave of them on a morning so lovely that I can still see the chestnuts and the cornfields and the rich peace of the Vale of Evesham, bounded by the Malverns, as I paused for breath at the top of Stanton Hill for a last glimpse westwards before striking across the high wolds for Moreton-in-the-Marsh. ... The morning paper had brought the news over breakfast that Middlesex, then bidding for the cricket championship, was embattled in a final contest, and the notion suddenly struck me that I should strap my scanty luggage on my back, stride the eight or nine miles that divided me from the nearest main-line station at Moreton-in-the-Marsh and return to London to see the afternoon's and the next day's play of what could plainly be a thrilling and historic match. I had just under two hours to cover the distance, so I did not hesitate a minute, but paid my bill, bade adieu to my kind and astonished landlady, and departed. Half walking, half trotting, I made Moreton station with ten minutes to spare, quenching my thirst with a vast flagon of cider in an adjoining tavern. I had to stand, I recall, in the corridor of the holiday-packed train, but it was worth it. By mid-afternoon I was in the Pavilion at Lord's, watching Middlesex in a nobly matched game gradually go up as Surrey, fighting magnificently, went down. ...'

Such was the kind of world which a young A.B. experienced and was to experience after the First World War.

'The so-called West End during the season ... the world of the Bright Young People and the night club, the mists of Cambridgeshire and the Fens, the rolling hills and skies of North Buckinghamshire, the Temple, the mountains of North Wales, the view over the Severn Valley from the Cotswolds, all in turn provided the point from which I looked on the changing contemporary scene, the history of my time, to which I was so inextricably bound. Looking back on it all, the latter seems to have dissolved so soon, almost before my youth was done, into the winter rigours of a Second World War and a great social revolution not yet complete.'

6

Teaching and Learning

'If I were asked what I considered to be
the country's first priority today, I
should reply in a single word: education.'

Illustrated London News,
4th January, 1969

As a result of attending and speaking at sessions of the *New Ideals in Education Conference*, and articles he wrote on his teaching experiences in the old Liberal *Daily News*, A.B. attracted the attention of the young, dynamic and *avant garde* Director of Education for Cambridgeshire, Henry Morris. Founder of the so-called Village Colleges, Morris's purpose was to transform rural adult education. Just before A.B.'s 24th birthday, he appointed him Principal of the newly renamed Cambridge School of Arts, Crafts and Technology,[1] and also Principal for Further, or adult, Education in Cambridgeshire. He thus became the youngest headmaster in England.

Morris wanted someone who leant not too heavily towards either the Arts or the Technical side of education. 'There was a gulf between the two at that time,' A.B. explained. 'Those on the art side tended to be fervent disciples of William Morris. They wore long hair and believed in hand-printing. Their opposite numbers were passionate advocates of machinery and bristled with clockwork precision and waxed moustaches. I was neither.'

Finding Cambridge enervating, A.B. moved outside the town to a bungalow half way between the villages of Trumpington and Shelford, accommodated by a landlady who had once been housekeeper to Rupert Brooke in the old vicarage at Granchester. Most of his travelling was done by motor-bike, on which he also managed to ride fifty-six

---

[1] Formerly the small William Morris Art School and now the Cambridge Technical College, one of its wings being named after Arthur Bryant.

miles to dances in the West End several evenings a week, before violating the silence of the Cambridgeshire countryside as he returned at full speed in the early hours of the morning.

It was, perhaps, an unusual state of affairs, but he was an unusual young man. In the same way in which he was forever losing everything yet discarding nothing, side by side in his strange make-up there were divers extremes: understanding and intolerance, generosity and thrift, impatience and procrastination, compassion and callousness, wisdom and impracticality, trust and suspicion, deception and artlessness, determination and vacillation, altruism and selfishness, method and untidiness, arrogance and diffidence, love of home and desire for freedom and, over all, like an enveloping mantle, lay what seemed to be his *raison d'être*: perfectionism at work.

'I believe we are put into this world not so much to enjoy ourselves – that is only an incidental happening and one which by the very nature of human consciousness cannot be continuous – as to realise and fulfil ourselves. Like plants, we are creatures of growth; our function is to develop according to our highest natures. And it would seem that human beings only grow as and when they forget themselves. Hard work and hard play are mighty educative forces; so are love and friendship. So, too, is great art in which man loses himself – great books and music and painting and architecture. So also even is war for those who give themselves selflessly or wholeheartedly to their country's or humanity's cause: the better the soldier – so at least my experience has taught me – the fuller the education . . . activity or inactivity, in the final resort and reckoning, is valuable or the reverse only so far as it helps to create character. . . .

'We need a world in which there is ample opportunity to forget ourselves in one complete and satisfying task. I have never met a good craftsman who was economically free to devote himself wholeheartedly to his craft who was not happy. But the moment a man allows the need for money, the ambition for social distinction, the craving for variety to distract him from his task, he is driven, like Adam, from his paradise. . . . Men and women are seldom *consciously* happy when they so lose themselves; it is only afterwards that they recall and realise such periods as times of exceptional blessedness.

'A hundred or more years ago boys were apprenticed to the trade or craft of their own father – of the man, that is, whom a boy, other things being equal, naturally most wishes to copy, help and emulate. In no instance that I can recall is there a suggestion in any of these that the boy disliked such work or regarded it as anything else but a matter of intense pride and self-congratulation that he was learning to excel in it. In other words he acquired with the knowledge of how to work well, the habit of enjoying work: in a material sense, and perhaps a spiritual one, too, the most valuable habit in the world . . . the foundation of all wealth under a free economy is a nation of men and women who have learnt to love, and have so become habituated to, hard work. . . .'

Throughout A.B.'s twenties, before he began to earn his living by writing history, no one could have worked harder as a teacher. He remained a passionate believer in education all his life. He practised it in turn as schoolmaster, headmaster, extension and adult education lecturer, producer of pageants, broadcaster and, ultimately, as an author of articles and books. In a sense, his histories and historical biographies, simply and lucidly written for all their underlying scholarship, have principally all been attempts to educate his country-men, young and old alike, in the realities and ideals of their national heritage.

'The task of teaching youth is probably the most far-reaching of all tasks to which a man can put his hand. . . . The supreme object of education, it seems to me, should be to make a child realise, in some way or other, his or her part and purpose in the vast, bewildering drama of human existence. For that child has been born with the power of decision: the power to decide at every moment of his or her life the actions which will surely and inevitably shape that life. That power of decision has to be exercised in a world over which he will continue to have virtually no control even if he grows up to be a dictator or a millionaire.

'We are creatures placed on an earth governed by mighty external forces which we cannot resist: time and death, for instance, are two of them which have us as irresistibly in their power as a floating feather is in that of an Atlantic storm. And yet, born into such a world, we have throughout every conscious moment of our existence that mysterious, inexplicable freedom of choice: of choosing, in great and small affairs alike, between courage and cowardice, love and hate, effort and sloth, self-control and self-indulgence, endurance and surrender. And as we choose at one moment, so will our choice at another be rendered easier or more difficult. Nor does it seem easy to avoid the conclusion that this business of personal choice by the individual is the only rational explanation – the only one, that is, that can satisfy our fallible, limited reason – of the purpose of our existence. . . .

'Self-mastery, for each of the countless millions of souls passing through the world is, so far as we can judge, the only explanation of the supreme mystery of all – that of personal consciousness. The world, the whole universe for all we can tell is, in Keats's words, "a vale of soul-making". We are each of us here for a brief while, blessed or cursed, as we use it, with the creative capacity – the will or freedom of personal decision – to manufacture our own individual soul and character. For what end we do not know, but in ourselves we experience, and with every year more fully, the extent of our success or, far more often, failure. At the end of life we are left with nothing else but what we have made ourselves by the exercise, for good or bad, of that power of decision. We make our own bed and lie on it. . . .

'To help a child to realise this, therefore, seems to me the supreme purpose of education. All the other things we teach him, knowledge of facts, culture, technology, accomplishments, rightly considered are merely means to help him in life to achieve this great end of ruling and shaping himself – the only real freedom the world offers. A child, of course, can only be taught to realise this little by little; he has to learn by experience far more than by precept. But to be shown, in little things as later in great things, that he has the power of decision over his inner self and that on the exercise of that power, now and hereafter, in ever growing measure his happiness in this world – and many of us believe in another – will depend. This is surely far the most important lesson anyone, parent or master, can teach a child. To fail to do so is like launching a boat on an ocean of storms without a rudder.

'For this reason I believe education without religion to be a contradiction in terms. When Wellington, a realist if ever there was one, remarked that the only effect of educating children in literature, mathematics and science without religion would be to manufacture so many clever devils, it was of this he was thinking. . . .'

* * *

Between 1923 and 1925 A.B. threw himself wholeheartedly into the task of turning an old-fashioned art school into what it has since become: the principal technical college of East Anglia. Having with great difficulty secured the Cambridgeshire County Council's agreement that the Art Classes should be allowed to draw from the nude ('the *nude*? Mr. Bryant,' said one astonished lady governor, who had gone to a great deal of trouble to find what she considered would be a suitably-clad one), he overcame the resistance of another governor, a pillar of the town's nonconformist community, who had objected that the presence of a naked model would cause unseemly sniggering among the younger students. For A.B. suggested to him that no such indecorum could occur if this anxious old gentleman could find time to attend one of the classes himself. 'This,' he recalled, 'he did, and thereafter attended every session of the life class, sitting at the back of the room with every appearance of approval.'

Cheerfully and persistently the new headmaster dealt with every obstacle and in two years had multiplied the college's numbers tenfold. Classes were started for every conceivable subject from motor engineering and plumbing to mothercraft, the cradle and plastic baby for use in the latter being housed, for lack of space, most incongruously in a corner of his own office. Soon his work began to be noticed. His forceful, magnetic personality made itself felt, not only in the educational world but also in that other world in which he spent his leisure time. Although 'leisure', perhaps, was hardly something synonymous with his character. He had to be continually doing something and that which he did always seemed done with panache. There was a kind of aura about him, which often left those who came within its orbit slightly bemused and exhausted. Tall, dark, handsome and possessed of great charm, it was inevitable that in those days women found him dis-

67

turbingly attractive. He, in turn, found all attractive women irresistible. Although, brought up in such a strictly orthodox Victorian fashion, he felt, as he put it, 'if you so much as kissed a girl, you had to marry her.'

At the age of 25 he married Sylvia Shakerley, the daughter of Sir Walter Shakerley of Somerford Park in Cheshire. During the summer holidays of that year, pledged to a round of country house visits, he was due to stay with her family for a dance. 'Sylvia was so pretty,' he said, 'like a piece of Dresden china, and what with this dance and the moonlight and my kissing her, we suddenly found ourselves engaged, and that was that!' The engagement was not without reservations on the part of both families. The Shakerleys, an old county one, had a vague distrust of anyone as clever and go-ahead as their prospective young son-in-law; whereas the Bryants, with some justification, felt that their headstrong elder son was not yet ready to settle down.

Arthur Bryant and Sylvia Shakerley were married at the end of the summer term in 1924 and took possession of their first home, the Reeded Barn Farmhouse, which they rented near Cambridge. Although the doubts of their respective families were ultimately to prove correct and the marriage was not to last, during the twelve years they lived together he learnt from Sylvia something for which he remained eternally grateful: her appreciation of beautiful furniture and of the visual arts, of which, for all his passionate love of poetry and landscape, he had been until then strangely blind. Kinship with the Shakerley family also brought him another uncovenanted and deeply-valued benefit. It put into his hands, as he afterwards said, 'the stuff of which history is made'.

'One grey December day in 1923, a concealed door in the wall of the Somerford library, decorously camouflaged by an eighteenth century hand with the names of books that were never written – Bishop Allworthy's *Sermons*, Lear's *View of the Stage*, Dr. Maggott on the *Hereafter* – was opened for me and I found myself standing in a vast stone cell, with shelves all round me loaded with almost all that remained of the life record of countless Cheshire men and women.

'I did not, of course, know this at the time. All I saw were bundles and bundles of documents, tied in dirty grey parcels, and on tables round the walls an indescribable litter of parchments and papers. There were also some great seals of England lying about on chairs as though they were waiting to be thrown away as too old to keep. And the whole floor was powdered fine with the dust of broken seals.

'Such was my first introduction to the Shakerley MSS.[1] As casually I began to turn a few of the papers over, something of their meaning came dimly to me. Here was the actual past, of which I had read unimaginatively in books. I could touch it and peer into it and savour its musty, faint but vivid perfume. Curiosity gripped me.

'After my first discovery I asked to be made free of the muniment room. Every day during that Christmas holiday I turned the great silver key, pushed back the heavy door and then closed it after me and sat down in that cold storage chamber of the past. The living life of the house without, the misty trees in the park and the sodden landscape of wintry Cheshire beyond receded: I could only hear the whispering voices of men and women who, after the silence of centuries, had found a listener and were trying to speak. And gradually I learnt to attune my unaccustomed ears.

'At first I did little more than follow an idle curiosity, picking up such letters as lay on the surface and tasting rapidly wherever the unfamiliar handwriting admitted of such easy reading. . . . What began as a relaxation from the monotony of a winter holiday in a lonely country house soon became a regular hobby. When I returned to my professional labours in southern England, I took a few of the bundles with me and fell into the pleasant habit of occupying my evenings by copying the more interesting parts of the letters they contained into a large exercise book which I bought for the purpose. When Easter again released me, I hurried north to renew my acquaintance with the muniment room, silent and unvisited during my three months' absence – that tiny pin-point of time in its long generation of oblivion. The letters I had copied during my absence had aroused my curiosity to pursue a dozen different trails, and my blood was whetted for the chase. . . .

---

[1] Some of which are reprinted in *Postman's Horn*.

'Many of the bundles, I soon found, revealed only legal documents. . . . There seemed at first something uncanny in turning over and fingering conveyances of land in places like Stockport, Wigan and Macclesfield, made in days when King Henry II sat on the throne of England and whose minute pendant seals bore the devices of long-vanished monasteries and of semi-fabulous beings like the seven palatine Earls of Chester. . . . But what I sought and learnt to treasure were not the deeds. The jewels which lay thick to my delving hands were the letters, still folded as their long-dead recipients had left them, the very sand from the stand-dishes of their first writers glittering in their folds, so that often my fingers and wrists were stained with minute dust. . . .

'A casually opened letter would give a glimpse of some – to me – thrilling intimacy: a Jacobean elopement, the scrapes of an Elizabethan undergraduate, a harassed Governor of Chester receiving royal orders from James II to admit a priest to say mass in defiance of law in Chester Castle . . . Until one became used to it, it was often confusing to find intimate friends and lovers concluding their letters: "Your humble and obedient servant", while tax-gatherers and other officials almost invariably ended their unpalatable communications with "Your loving friend. . . ."

'When at last the letters were all sorted and the year-files placed in a vast oak spice-chest with innumerable drawers – made by a Welsh carpenter for the writer of many hundreds of them in the early eighteenth century – the education of a historian had begun. . . . The sweet, regular labour of it taught me what school or university – though they laid the foundations of it – had never taught, a craft: to do one thing thoroughly without evasion or omission. It is a lesson learnt by most men who practise a handicraft in their own way, but seldom provided by the rather "slap-dash" and desultory reading of modern literary education. Yet it is well worth attaining, for though it may not increase a man's moral stature, it tends to give him a sense of balance and values, makes him love quality and shun shoddy, and teaches him to judge men and things. . . .

'Here were real lives that had once meant as much to their possessors as mine to me. One got a queer, almost godlike, sense of being able to see the future of these long-dead beings as well as the past, of being able to feel and yet to be unswayed by feeling. And with it a sense, too, of humility, for even as one now beheld these, so might one also be seen and judged hereafter. . . . No man can live for ever; neither can his work. To read the lives of the ancient dead over their own shoulders is to con that mournful lesson; they lived, desired and strove.

> And all their hopes and all their tears
> Be unknown things of other years.

Yet, as I read, I found that even that had in it some sense of quiet satisfaction and companionship; the gulf of loneliness which divides man from man is bridged in that enchanted moment; one knows the nature of one's lot on this dream-visited planet, and accepts it with all its implications:

> I know my life's a pain and but a span;
> I know my sense is mock'd in everything;
> And, to conclude, I know myself a Man –
> Which is a proud and yet a wretched thing.'

And suddenly, after reading what he had written about the Shakerley MSS, I realised what this monumental self-imposed task had meant to the man for whom I now worked. Not only was it an exciting, absorbing interest for one already dedicated to the past; not only was it a revelation that the past was so real; not only was it a stroke of great good fortune that fate had placed these relics in such appropriate and appreciative hands. It provided the unconscious groundwork which was to make him not only a lifelong student of the past, but a dedicated scholar.

* * *

In 1925 A.B. was offered a lectureship by the Oxford University Extension Delegacy. He accepted the post gladly because, having achieved what he had set out to do at Cambridge, he wanted to get back to teaching in preference to educational administration and also because, having political ambitions, he realised that Extension lecturing would give him time, especially during the summer when lectures were in abeyance, to read for the Bar.

He therefore left Cambridge and leased from his friend, Sir Harry Verney – a colleague on the Harrow Mission Council – the White House at East Claydon in North Buckinghamshire, where he was to live for the next twenty years. It was a small, early 17th century manor house, for long a farmhouse, just outside the village which, right from the start, meant much to him.

> 'I can still see the glittering white of the newly-distempered walls and the beautiful brown oak of the beams stripped of their many coats, the shining elm staircase, the vast fireplace we undug in one room and the carved Jacobean stone overmantel of another, the ancient walnut and mahogany furniture we had brought with us which fitted into their places in their new home as though they had been made for it, and the seventeenth and eighteenth century ladies and gentlemen in their gilt frames who seemed to accept, so surprisingly and naturally, their new and humbler home as if it was part of the eternal order of things. They looked down as though they were happy, and as though the serenity of that enchanting, welcoming little house had won their hearts, as it had ours.'

In his new post as University Extension lecturer, he soon became aware that 'whatever the class may learn from the lecturer, will be doubled by what the lecturer, if he is wise, will learn from the class. . . .' For a whole decade,

> 'the coming of winter spelt a new life, or rather an old life revived after a summer's lapse. The leisurely hours of study between tea and dinner had to cease; instead, the stroke of five became an alarum to depart. It was now my lot to rise from the fire, collect great-coat and lecture-notes, and grope my way to the garage. An hour or more's driving through the chill hostility of a winter's night would bring me to hall or institute, where the frugality of the illumination and the uncompromising hardness of the chairs only heightened the impression of earnest endeavour which the audience contrived to convey. . . . It sounds, I daresay, a comfortless picture. Yet strangely those evenings of sober discourse – a parliament of half-hesitant, deeply thoughtful countrymen round a stove – were as stimulating as any in my remembrance. . . .'

In the little villages throughout an area hedged between Cotswold, Thames, Chiltern and Ouse, he lectured on a variety of subjects: English history and literature, biography, Shakespearian drama and, most popular of all, Local History.

'To arouse an interest in local history is not to be thought beneath the dignity of a teacher of adult students . . . it is not a study in which text-books, or any one book, can help much. So far as it is written, the history of a county or a village lies hidden in the corners of many books and, more often than not, in unpublished letters and MSS, buried obscurely in the muniment rooms of old houses. . . . The teacher, while studying every book which so much as mentions his stage, should frankly abandon all pretence that he is likely to know more about it than his class . . . he is to act primarily as a medium for drawing from its members their joint knowledge of their own past, to make them realise its importance. . . . He must never forget the immense significance of places to his listeners. What at first to him is only a meaningless hummock or cluster of trees is something intimate and all-absorbing to them . . . let him form his lecture round some spot and retrace its history with his class, whose contribution, if he conducts his lesson aright, will be more than his. . . . The charm of teaching history in a country place is without end.'[1]

During the summer, while reading for the Bar, he also undertook to do something in which he already had experience: the writing and production of pageants. In 1925, while he had still been Principal for Further Education in Cambridgeshire, he had been asked by the county's Federation of Women's Institutes to write a pageant which their members produced and acted in King's College meadow. A year later, after he had moved to East Claydon, the Oxfordshire Federation also asked him to write and subsequently produce a similar pageant in Worcester College garden. This led in 1929 to his being invited to return to Cambridgeshire to produce another pageant on a far more ambitious scale. This was the Fenland pageant for the town of Wisbech and its neighbourhood, in anticipation of which

'the yeoman farmers of the Fens – the hard core of my great cast

---

[1] *The Teaching of Local History*, by Arthur Bryant. Bewley House Papers, III, February 1930.

– used to assemble in the White Hart or the Rose and Crown to discuss the day's doings and the gathering plans for the pageantry of early September that was to make Wisbech seem in our eyes what, rightly considered by any true Fenman it always is, the centre of the world. Never did ale taste so good, or comradeship; those sun-drenched days in the fields and villages of the fruitful plain had warmed every heart and body to a tempo of perfect fitness. And the crown of that summer's enjoyment came at the end, for a pageant in which half North Cambridgeshire was a band of brothers, took place in a blaze of triumph and sunshine – and the sunshine, I thought, three-quarters of the triumph – on the loveliest English days I can remember. If I could live any two days of my life over again I think I should choose those two. . . .'

A.B. always referred to this interlude in his life rather wistfully. 'Wisbech,' he said, 'was rather like a little 18th century Dutch town. The icy weather of that February preceded a most glorious spring and summer. It was a wonderful wine year. I can remember the heat in the meadows and running about with a megaphone in my hand during rehearsals. At the end of the very first day of these, after we had been rehearsing in separate groups, I brought everyone together so that we could go through the whole thing. Some benefactor brought me a tankard of beer and I was so thirsty I drank it down at one gulp. I then started running about in my white flannels with renewed energy, only to slip up on a cow-pat.' Up till that moment his cast had apparently been somewhat suspicious of this dynamic stranger in their midst. 'But,' he continued, 'they loved that. Afterwards I could do anything with them!'

The production of pageants gave full scope to the often unused, active organising side of A.B.'s nature. His pageants were different in that

> 'instead of consisting of a succession of episodes in which local worthies represented in procession and set speech supposedly recognisable historical personages connected with the locality's past, they attempted by mass colour and sound, music and crowd movement, to recreate a single or perhaps two or three scenes from the history of the place that best lent themselves to out-of-door presentation. . . . Thus in the pageants in Cambridge and

74

Oxford in the 'twenties, I concentrated on the great medieval fairs of Stourbridge and St. Frideswide's and in the Fenland pageant a few years later on the visit of King John's army to Wisbech before its ill-fated crossing of the Wash. . . .'

'I always kept everyone on the move,' he said. 'I wanted the thing to be alive – no set speechifying – I wanted to make the audience feel confronted by, no, *involved* in, the *living* past. You could only do it by continuous movement.'

It was this participation and deep involvement in such a vast cross-section of national life, which had an effect on him hard to define. But having been brought up in a London where he had become aware of such clear-cut divisions between the classes, in the provinces he now began to sense something subtler: the complex variations which went to make a strong cohesive whole, and the necessity, as he felt, that within a certain framework men and women should be free to build and strive, instead of being compulsorily regulated into mediocre mass conformity. 'Civilisation,' he once said to me, 'has always depended on the existence of class, or what Shakespeare called "degree". You can't get away from it. It has been the emulation of all classes to attain and maintain high standards in infinite variety in a free and non-static society that has, by and large, made Great Britain great.'

'Individual freedom – freedom of imagination, freedom of incentive, freedom of action – is the mainspring of vitality. It is not enough by itself for there must be group purpose and discipline, too, to give such vitality continuity and the capacity for endurance, but freedom for the individual there must be if human nature is to achieve its optimum. It is not enough for freedom to be confined to a man's leisure hours . . . it must be innate in his work, too. . . . It is this lack of freedom for the working man in his work which as much as anything, I believe, lies at the root of the social malaise and discontent for mid-20th century industrial society. . . .

'Of all the ills that can befall human nature, stagnation is the most fatal. Man is like the Indian on the tight-rope: he must keep moving or die. . . . It is one of the rules of all life that man only functions by endeavour: he must live by the sweat of his brow, not only because such sweat can alone bring him his daily bread, but because soul and spirit will become dead within him if he does not. He must always be becoming and never be content with merely being. For man there is no such thing as static peace, save in the grave. Once a man gives up trying to evolve, he is spiritually dead.'

PART TWO

7

Interlude

'If a man is not given the opportunity
to create, he will, in his unconscious
frustration, destroy. If he cannot love,
he will hate; if he cannot lose himself
in the selflessness of creation, he will
perpetually bicker with his neighbour in
an anarchy of competitive selfishness.'

Illustrated London News,
29th August, 1964

After I had been working for A.B. for a few months he suddenly rang up early one morning and said, 'I've lost a shoe.'

Not being fully awake, I replied, rather sleepily, 'What sort of a shoe?'

'The one I had on last night,' he answered, in an aggrieved manner.

Although I knew his capacity for losing things was limitless, nevertheless I did not see how he could have managed to mislay a shoe during the few hours of the night when he was asleep.

'Where have you looked?' I asked him, trying to sound more efficient and business-like.

'Everywhere. Under the bed. In the bed. Under the cupboards. In the cupboards. In my chest of drawers. Under my chest of drawers. In my hold-alls. It isn't *anywhere*.'

He was obviously really upset now, and I tried to sound more sympathetic. Losing a shoe was a serious matter to him because he had trouble with his feet. They were very broad for their size and he hardly ever found a pair which fitted. Although he was always on the point of going to a shoe-shop with a view to buying new ones, or even having some made, somehow this seemingly vital expedition, as with so many similar ones such as to his dentist or oculist, was constantly postponed into an ever-receding moment in time. The shoe he had now lost evidently belonged to a pair of well-worn indoor ones, which he wore about the house and which constituted the only comfortable footwear he possessed. Priding myself on my ability to find most of the things which he invariably lost, I said gently, 'I'll have a thorough search as soon as I come.'

'Yes, but I want to go down to breakfast. I'm hungry. I can't go down with one shoe on.'

Although I could see in my mind's eye the vast miscellany of shoes of all descriptions that I had noticed lying in his cupboards, I knew better than to suggest he put a pair of them on until I arrived. He wanted the shoe he had lost and he was not going to give in lightly. We went back to discussing its possible whereabouts. 'The bathroom?' I suggested, brightly. There was a pause while he went off to look and came back to report defeat. 'Behind the cushion in your armchair?' I didn't feel this to be very likely, but I have known his best gold watch, which had originally been given to his father by King Edward VII, turn up disconcertingly in an old black evening sock. 'Underneath all your night-work on the table?' I ventured. 'I've already tried that,' came the reply. We were beginning to reach an impasse. 'No one could have *taken* it,' I said at length, rather desperately. 'They might,' he answered, 'someone could have come in and pinched it in the night.' 'But not *one* shoe,' I argued. 'Well, perhaps it was a one-legged thief.' It was no use. He usually had the last word. When I arrived an hour or so later the shoe had miraculously been discovered by Mrs Chalkley, the wife of his faithful maintenance man and caretaker as she emptied the waste-paper basket in the secretary's room, where it was lying firmly ensconced in a discarded copy of an old newspaper. Rather sheepishly, A.B. then admitted that during one of his habitual nocturnal prowls, as his own waste-paper basket was full, he had wandered into the secretary's room to dispose of certain impedimenta in a vain attempt at what he referred to as 'surface tidying'.

It would have been hard to find a man who spent so many hours of every night busily engaged in one sort of activity or another. Often when I left him in the evening, worried because I knew a certain article which he had scarcely yet thought about had to be in the post the following day, he would remark in a matter-of-fact tone of voice,

'I shall be doing that when I wake at five. I think I shall spend the first part of the night getting down to that awful pile of personal letters.' He seemed to regard the hours of the night, when everyone else was 'knitting up the ravelled sleeve of care', as a kind of bonus of which he made the utmost use.

Once, when I asked him if he could not possibly take things more easily, he replied, 'A lot of people have tried to make me. I remember when I was writing my short life of Macaulay,[1] I went to stay with his great-nephew, G. M. Trevelyan, at his Northumberland home. He came and sat on my bed one night and warned me about the dangers of overworking. His remonstrances didn't do much good, but I think you could say that work doesn't seem to have done me much harm.' Although I felt that perhaps it was not exactly helpful to his personal relationships, I had to admit that, physically, he was certainly a good advertisement for a nineteen-hour day, seven days a week.

One of the things which perhaps saved him – other than his extraordinary energy and persistence – was his capacity for rapidly switching his concentration from one task to another, even from one century to another, or occasionally, for a few moments, slipping his mind out of gear altogether. Although when in the throes of writing a book he could go 'all out' for hours on end, and any interruption was a source of justifiable irritation, the very nature of his particular kind of craft meant that he was often forced to pause while he got up and searched for a book or burrowed through the piles of papers which perpetually surrounded him. And he always maintained that he knew when to stop, even though his particular stopping-point was a long way past that of the average man.

In the decade before the outbreak of the Second World War, his life, though primarily that of a writer and historian, was taken up with

---

[1] 'He was, in my opinion, the greatest of all English historians, all the more so when one remembers how little of the material used for his vast, brilliant canvas (I mean the *History of England*, not the more superficial essays, good though these were) was in printed or calendared form when he wrote. And one has that marvellous sidelight in his diaries in that noble library beside the Cam – how I recall the joy of working in it during the summer of 1932, with a punt moored in that sunlit stream in which to eat my sandwiches in the intervals of labour! . . . Of course he was *morbid*! all historians are morbid, it is an occupational disease, as they helplessly contemplate the recurrence of human folly and stupidity being re-enacted before their eyes while they laboriously recount its earlier consequences.' *Letter from Arthur Bryant to Lord Trevelyan*, 10th March, 1972.

many other activities. It was as if it flowed in separate yet confluent channels, the deep main-stream devoted to the seventeenth century, the shallower edges concerned with the educational and political problems of this one. Although 'shallower' is not perhaps the right word. For the latter pursuits were at no time ephemeral or superficial. Whatever he undertook was done with intensity, deep sincerity, passion almost. And always the problems of the present were seen in the light of history. 'The key to a nation's future is in her past,' he wrote. 'A nation that loses it has no future. . . . We cannot recreate the past but we cannot escape it. It is in our blood and bone. To understand the temperament of a people, a statesman has first to know its history.'

In trying to understand him it was important to realise that it was history which had governed his life since he was a small boy. His father had read it to him. Later on he read it to himself in his father's library. He saw it all around him in the home where he was brought up, so closely linked to that larger palace home in which history was being made all the time. He inhaled it unconsciously, and thereafter it governed everything he did: the pageants he produced, the lectures he gave, the political views he held, the articles he wrote, even the old houses and antique furniture he acquired or inherited were all, to use a twentieth-century phrase: 'historically-orientated'. But his very versatility coupled with his secretiveness, his ability to conduct his life as if his right hand did not know what his left was doing, has meant that many people have always been unaware of this diversity of talents.

1929, however, marked a turning point in A.B.'s career. It was the year when history finally took precedence over four other occupations, any one of which he might have adopted as his main source of livelihood. He could, for instance, have taken up Law, for he had passed his Bar examinations and done a short spell in first-class commercial and insurance Chambers. He might have gone in for politics, having taken a post with the Conservative Educational Institute, then under the chairmanship of John Buchan. When this folded up in 1929, he had already published his first book,[1] *The Spirit of Conservatism*. He

---

[1] Two previous ones, a *Memoir* of his Harrow friend, Rupert Buxton, published by the C.U.P. in 1922 and a History of the *Harrow School Mission* in Notting Dale, 1921, were both privately produced.

might even have gone in for drama; his sense of history, love of colour, quick sensitivity to group atmosphere and ability in drawing the maximum response from his cast, suggested to more than one dramatic critic who had seen his pageants that he had the makings of an English Reinhardt. After his production of *Comus* at Ashridge in 1930 he was offered by Lilian Baylis the chance to produce a season of Shakespeare at the Old Vic, the opportunity going, after he regretfully felt forced to decline it, to Tyrone Guthrie. He might, on the other hand, have remained an educationalist, for now, besides keeping up his Extension lecturing, he had accepted a post offered him by Sir John Davidson, then Chairman of the Conservative Party, as part-time educational adviser to the new Bonar Law College which was about to open at Ashridge. Yet all these were to remain subsidiary to what was now nearest his heart: the writing of history.

On the floor beside me are records. They are only a fraction of the vast mass I know to be elsewhere in the house. The handwriting on them, though faded, is astonishingly neat. The edges of the paper, frayed by time, are clipped together by rusty brown paper-clips. But the pages themselves meticulously set out, live on as a silent yet telling witness to the days, over forty years ago, when A.B. dedicated the larger part of his working life to another century and to two men in particular who lived in it: Charles II and Samuel Pepys.

8

Charles II and Samuel Pepys

'Successful writing, like any
other human art or accomplishment,
is a matter of taking pains.'

Illustrated London News,
27th October, 1945

In 1929, an old school friend and reader to Longmans, the historical
and educational publishers, was so impressed by the industry and
enthusiasm which A.B., with whom he had been staying, was putting
into transcribing the seventeenth century Shakerley letters, that he
suggested his employers might consider asking him to write a new life
of Charles II, instead of reprinting Osmund Airy's standard biography
written thirty years before and now somewhat out of date. Intrigued
by the idea, A.B. offered to write a narrative account of Charles II's
dramatic escape from Worcester, so that Longmans could judge his
capacity. At that time he was fully occupied producing the Wisbech
Pageant, but immediately this was over he returned to East Claydon
and set to work, reading, analysing and making notes on every first-
hand account of Charles's flight, and then starting at great speed to
write a sample chapter.

In November he sent the completed typescript to Longmans and,
the moment the latter approved it, began two years' intensive work on
Charles's life and reign, supporting himself in the meantime by his
two part-time employments as educational adviser to Ashridge and,
during the winter evenings, as a University Extension lecturer. Into
those two years he crowded a vast mass of research which would
probably have taken the average scholastic historian – so much of
whose time has to be spent in teaching – two or three times as long.
He went through every volume of the Historical Manuscripts Commission Reports and every published private collection of letters,

diaries etc. covering the period of Charles's lifetime, as well as the normal official, calendared and other papers and documents, both printed and manuscript. This mastery of contemporary correspondence, already begun by his labour of love on the Shakerley MSS, gave his account of Charles's reign an unusual approach, one more in keeping with the attitude and ideas of ordinary seventeenth century Englishmen, than those of their twentieth century successors. This helped to give the book a sense of immediacy so that the reader felt he was actually living in Charles II's reign and experiencing the events of his life, instead of judging him and his people by the standards and beliefs of our own time.

All this research was embodied in thousands of folio sheets of closely written notes, arranged in chronological order, so that when in the late winter and spring of 1931 A.B. started to write, he was able to do so non-stop, drawing on an immense amount of first-hand contemporary material to illustrate his narrative. When it was finished he was faced with the fact that, because of the amount of information packed into it, it was, like most books, far too long. He then, for the first time, learned the invaluable lesson for any writer wishing to hold his readers' attention, of the need to cut out every unnecessary word. Going through it again and again, he reduced the book's length by a third without discarding anything essential to his central theme.

At this point J. E. (later Sir John) Neale, then Professor of Modern History at University College, London, who was then writing his life of Elizabeth and often stayed with A.B. at the White House, brought with him for a weekend there the Professor of English History at Yale, Wallace Notestein, the greatest living authority on the early seventeenth century in England. A.B. asked him if he would read his manuscript. After making various criticisms – which A.B. embodied – Notestein suddenly suggested cutting out the first nine chapters about Charles's life as a boy and starting the book with the Flight from Worcester, the original dramatic chapter he had written to show Longmans two years before. As this involved discarding nearly 40,000 words of closely researched and written narrative and the work of many months, the latter was understandably reluctant to do so. In the end, after Notestein had shown him how to work all that was really essential to Charles's early life into the existing narrative of the escape without breaking the continuity, he accepted his advice.

It proved the most valuable ever given him. For it was this dramatic start to the book which, two months later, caused the Book Society, to whom Longmans had submitted it, to adopt it as its October Choice. Up to this time, A.B. had never expected that this work of close scholarship could sell, at the outside, more than a few thousand copies or bring him in, as a result, more than a few hundred pounds to supplement his earnings as a lecturer and educational administrator. As it was, it made him, at the age of 32, a minor literary celebrity and opened the way to his earning his living by writing history which, though scholarly, was also sufficiently readable to cause the general public to buy whatever he chose to publish.

At that time a Book Society Choice and a scholarly history were hardly regarded as compatible, the latter being usually written by academics for academic prestige with little or no regard for general readability. As a result, the scholarship, research and factual accuracy of *Charles II* tended to be obscured by the fluency and charm of the writing. Yet despite its divergence from the generally accepted Whig view of the reign, with the latter's bias against a king who beat the parliamentary politicians at their own game, the book was also recognised by those best qualified to judge it as a work of real scholarship.

By the good fortune of a Book Society Choice, he now found himself in the position he would have been in ten years earlier if, instead of taking the Shortened Honours Course for ex-Servicemen, he had remained at Oxford for a second year and gained a First and a Fellowship. For in that case, supported like other historians by academic endowments, he could have devoted his life to the writing of history without the necessity of having to make his books sufficiently readable to be widely saleable. Yet though this latter necessity was to lay him open to charges of superficiality by those unable to recognise the depth and accuracy of the research behind his narrative prose, his work over the years, like that of his predecessor, master and friend, G. M. Trevelyan, did much to raise the standard of historical writing in the country, both by academics and non-academics.

In *Charles II*, he first applied the rules that he was to follow in all his subsequent major historical books. Doing his own research and copying, he read every book and calendared document, whether printed or manuscript, that could throw light on his subject, making notes as he did so, one copy of which he subsequently arranged in strict chronological order so that, whatever the order in which he did his reading, his completed notes provided him with a continuous sequence of ascertained fact. Only when his reading and note-taking were completed did he decide from the evidence now before him how to present his subject. He thus started on his work without preconceived ideas and only formed his ideas after he had completed his research. Instead of collecting material to support a thesis, he used the material he collected to suggest the thesis.

Having accumulated his material, he embarked on the second stage of his task, the rearrangement of the former in a form which alone could make writing from such a vast mass possible. For this he was to find that every book required a different method according to the nature of its subject. Biography, his task in the 'thirties, was much the easiest, allowing as it did for straightforward chronological treatment. For books of more general history the difficulty was to know in what order to treat things so as to give the reader a balanced and comprehensive picture. Historians, as a rule, knowing that whatever they say in a single sentence, paragraph or even chapter can never be the whole truth, are apt to qualify their statements. This does not make for easy writing and, therefore, easy reading. Writing as he was for the general educated public, A.B. knew that the secret of writing successful narrative history was never to let the narrative flag. Having erected his scaffolding of fact and reasoning to create his book, before giving the final product to the public, he had somehow to remove the scaffolding.

The last stage, that of the actual writing, proved the hardest of all. For writing history from a vast mass of garnered fact is necessarily an artificial process and, however experienced or talented a writer, it cannot be written straight 'off the cuff' like an essay or article. In a letter of A.B.'s which I found in his files, replying to a query from Northcote Parkinson, he enlarged on this.

'The truth is that it is only easy to read because after I have spent years on first collecting and re-arranging material – and how much there is no one who hasn't tried writing history can have any idea – I then re-write and re-write again and again until every unnecessary word has been eliminated and every sentence leads the reader naturally to the next and makes him want to find out what is in it. Most of my paragraphs have been re-written and re-typed at least a dozen, and some of them 20 or 30 times, before the writing reaches its final form. For, as you have had the perception to see in that article you wrote on my work in the *Fortnightly*, it is the making of accurate history readable that is such an immensely laborious and artificial process. To write a single paragraph I have probably 50 or 60 closely typed folio sheets of extracts from books and documents in front of me, and all one does in one's first writing of it is to transfer the great mass of facts from one sheet (or rather many sheets) of paper to another and the result when typed is utterly unreadable! It is usually only after many re-writings that a paragraph or chapter begins to appear like natural prose.'

As soon as he had completed *Charles II*, he wasted no time in applying his new-found ability to make a profession of writing history. Almost at once he embarked on a short biography, published in 1932, of Macaulay. For this, the latter's great-nephew, G. M. Trevelyan, allowed him the use of Macaulay's unpublished MSS diaries in Trinity College, Cambridge, library, so enabling him to embody a good deal of material which had not been used by Trevelyan's father, Sir Otto George Trevelyan, in his classic biography. G. M. Trevelyan recognised A.B.'s qualities as a historian from the start, but was obviously afraid that this talented young man would burn himself out. In September, 1932, he wrote to him: 'You must learn to say "NO", to have leisure and health to cultivate your great talents for writing history.' A year later, a further letter from him contained the words: 'You have two great gifts – the power of biography in the strict sense of the word – and the gift of telling social history the way men used to live.' A little later still, he wrote: 'I see in you the coming historian,' followed a month later by: 'You will hold an important place – you do already – as interpreter of the country's history to the new generation, probably more important than anyone else soon,' and then underlined, '*Do not kill yourself with work.*' That A.B. did not kill himself with overwork at a young age always seemed to me, as to many other people, little short of a miracle.

In 1932 the Cambridge University Press asked him to write the definitive life of Samuel Pepys. Because he felt that the scholarship and research which had gone into *Charles II* had been somewhat obscured by its popular success, he was glad to accept the invitation. The C.U.P. Syndics had taken over from Bell's – the publishers of the Diary – the papers of two deceased Pepysian scholars, both of whom had planned such a work, H. B. Wheatley and J. R. Tanner. Initially it had asked a distinguished late seventeenth century historian, Sir Keith Feiling, to undertake the book, but as the latter was already at work on a life of Warren Hastings, they accepted his suggestion that the work should be entrusted to the young author of *Charles II.*

Between 1932 and the outbreak of war in 1939, apart from a number of minor publications,[1] A.B.'s principal task was the preparation and writing of the three volumes of his life of *Pepys* which appeared in 1933, 1935 and 1938. About a third of the fourth and final volume on his subject's old age and retirement had been written when war broke out, temporarily dispersing the Pepys library and so obliging its author to turn to other work and another period of history.

The writing of Pepys's life not only took much longer than that of Charles II, but posed far more difficult technical problems. The papers bequeathed by Wheatley and Tanner, though considerable in bulk, proved to be little more than the material already used for the former's *Pepysiana* and the latter's monumental work of calendaring Pepys's naval papers and letters. Although for nine years of the latter's early manhood and official career he kept a diary providing a detailed record of his daily doings and private thoughts, for the rest of his long life the material was of such an entirely different kind that it was impossible to give unity and apply the same time-scale within the confines of a single volume. A.B. therefore decided to devote one volume to Pepys's early

---

[1] *The National Character*, 1934; *The England of Charles II*, 1934; *The Letters and Speeches of Charles II*, 1935; *George V*, 1937; *The American Ideal*, 1936; *Stanley Baldwin*, 1937; *Postman's Horn* (based on the Shakerley MSS), 1936; *Humanity in Politics,* 1937.

life and diary years and, initially, a second only to the remaining thirty-four. This first volume, *The Man in the Making*, which Desmond MacCarthy considered 'rivalled in interest the diary itself', added a new dimension to the latter by collating it with the massive record of official work and public duty contained in Pepys's naval papers, both printed and in manuscript.

After its publication in 1933, A.B. set to work on the second half of Pepys's life. Having made the first volume a best seller, he contrived to make the apparently far less human material of the second just as absorbing. In doing so he discovered so many hitherto unknown sources about this part of Pepys's life that a third volume became necessary. He made each of these later volumes a separate book in its own right, which could be read with equal enjoyment and under-standing whether a reader was acquainted with its predecessor or not. By beginning each with a vivid word picture, he placed his readers exactly where he wanted them to be at the start of a new self-contained story. In *The Man in the Making*, for instance, he took them to East Anglia, the geographical cradle of the Pepys family:

'North of Cambridge lie the Fens. The sea from which they arose laps at their northern boundaries, and north and east great rivers lazily wind across them, drawing black cattle to drink among the sedges at their brink. This land would be one of silence were it not for the innumerable company of larks, of bittern, coot and moorhen, of sedge warblers and reed sparrows, which ever provides it with a faint and not discordant music. In summer it is still, as the monk William of Huntingdon remembered it, a land of clouds and orchards and golden corn. Yet it is only so by right of battle waged ceaselessly by its inhabitants against the invading armies of water. Whenever civilisation has receded – when Roman legion fell back or monastery bell was silenced – the waters have taken back their own. Salt tides have swept in with winter gales through forsaken walls, and the rivers have flowed out, cold and remorseless, over the fields and houses of man.

'Winter mist and the horizons of summer have left their age-long impress on the fenman's mind. He is imaginative, quick to dream and quick to fear; on the confines of life for him hover ever the legions of the unknown – fiends and apparitions that arise out of the "hideous fen" and beckon him on through bramble and briar to the dark waters. Therefore he holds hard to life, dreading to lose even for a moment his grip on material things. Fog, damp, cold and ague have given him a fine zest for food and drink, and the hot summer's sun warming his fertile land inclines him to be amorous. Fighting against the slow and relentless ways of water, he is patient and untiring in labour; and from these things, for all his fears, his great heart is formed. For he holds the fruitful fields by right of work and courage.

'Out of this land came the Pepyses. . . .'

The beginning of the second volume, *The Years of Peril*, once again put the reader straight into the picture:

'On Wednesday, November 10th, 1669, Mrs Pepys lay dead in the comely house in Seething Lane which she and her husband had lived in and loved for nine crowded years. But, though half his heart lay buried for ever with the beautiful, jealous, foolish creature to whom he had given it, Samuel had little leisure to mourn her. Even before her body could be laid in earth beneath the stones of the church across the street and her virtues commemorated in his own flowing Latin on the wall facing the gallery where she had once sat so proudly beside him, he was writing as even he had never written. For almost on the day of his return he had been called upon to face the most serious attack he had known on his work and office. . . .'

During his work on this volume A.B. spent much time on Pepys's uncalendared manuscript papers at Oxford which had found their way after his death, unlike his carefully arranged papers left to the Pepys Library at Magdalene, into the great collection bequeathed to the Bodleian Library by the eighteenth century collector, Dr. Richard Rawlinson.

'Two or three days a week I would catch the train from my Buckinghamshire home and, gliding through the elmy, green north Oxfordshire countryside, journey to Oxford in a carriageful of farmers and chatting rustic housewives. There, burying myself in Duke Humphrey's library, I would spend long, intent, happy hours copying Pepys's unpublished letters. . . . The sunlight would slowly cross the lawn of Exeter College garden, and presently the dons of that institution would take tea under a tree, while I continued to sit at my wooden carvel scribbling as fast as my fingers could move until the clock warned me it was ten minutes to seven – the hour at which the library closed and my train left. Then, gathering my papers and bags, I would run like an absconding bookie through narrow, startled alleys and streets to the station. And all the way home in the train, amid the shopping-bags and stertorously-breathing graziers, I would gloat on the day's gathered treasures.'

A.B.'s industry resulted in him piecing together a thrilling and until then unknown detective story of how, by his astonishing industry and courage, Pepys turned the tables on his accusers and thereby saved his own life and that of his royal master, the Duke of York and future James II. This took up more than half his second volume, *The Years of Peril*, and, though based on meticulous scholarship and research, gave it a popular and even sensational appeal unusual in a historical work of this kind. He also found in its course two hitherto unknown minor Pepys diaries which attracted much attention in the Press at the time of their discovery.

The third volume, *The Saviour of the Navy*, which appeared three years later, told the story of Pepys's Tangier voyage, his second spell as Secretary of the Admiralty and head and spokesman in Parliament of the greatest spending Department of the Crown, and his re-building of the battle fleet – the 30 new ships of the line – which, after his retirement in 1689, became the foundation of Britain's 18th and 19th century naval supremacy. As in the first two volumes, the third opened with a scene portrayed by that extraordinary blending of poetry and fact which have always set A.B.'s works apart:

'As the fleet rounded Rame Head and the friendly slopes and roofs of Plymouth fell away into the August haze, Samuel Pepys, outward bound on the deck of Lord Dartmouth's flagship, passed from one life into another. Behind him were the tangled nightmares of four years of persecution and proscription – the angry Parliament men who had shouted him down, the Tower jailers with their chains clanging down stony corridors, the accusers who had perjured themselves under the rafters of Westminster Hall while the mob outside shouted for his blood.

John Scott, who had risen like some satanic spirit from the underworld to lie away his office, his honour and his life, was again a penniless fugitive in a far country humbly soliciting forgiveness; James the butler, who had betrayed him with false evidence, had died in anguished repentance; Shaftesbury, "the great little lord", was dead and defeated. Only the fine gentleman Harbord remained, clinging precariously to the fringes of a Court whose enigmatic King was either too good-humoured to harry a dishonoured traitor or too polite to remind a well-bred scoundrel of his villainy: no one could say which.

'Ahead, far to southward, was Tangier. . . .'

Although with the publication of his Diary Pepys became famous, until A.B.'s biography was published, the former's life outside those nine crowded years which he recorded with such detail, was little known except to scholars. By the general public Pepys was thought of merely as an amorous buffoon and gossip. 'To most people,' A.B. wrote in the Preface of *The Years of Peril*, 'his later career seemed as unreal as that of Sancho Panza or Figaro. Yet silently, Pepys clamoured to be heard. Between the unfingered covers of hundreds of volumes in the Bodleian and in his Library at Magdalene College were the materials which he had prepared to explain and justify his career. From the walls of the Admiralty, of the Royal Society, of his College at Cambridge, the stern old face of the great Secretary looked down as though angrily seeking a champion. . . .'

In Arthur Bryant, as in his predecessor, the great Cambridge and naval scholar, J. R. Tanner, he found one.

'Almost alone among the men of his century Pepys grasped what the sea might come to mean to his country. More than Raleigh before him or Halifax in his own day, though with only a tithe of their eloquence, he comprehended the future of England. The winds and tides that cradled her spoke to this landsman of her destiny. When most of his contemporaries were expending all their powers on contending for particular forms of government and worship, he was scanning the horizons which have since grown familiar. Beyond the island mists, yet within reach of a little people of five or six millions, could they but be made to realise it, lay the shadowy outlines of a wealth and power such as no race had ever before enjoyed in the history of the world. Bondsman of the pen and ledger as he was, comfortable materialist in peruke and fine linen, Samuel Pepys was yet sustained by vision. There was only one means by which that vision could be made a reality: the precepts he had spent his life in framing, and their observance by those who wrought the nation's destiny at sea.'

9

The Historian-Journalist

'Througout the whole of my own adult
working life I seldom seem to have been
without a pen or pencil in my hand.'

Illustrated London News,
15th November, 1969

Besides producing four best-selling, deeply-researched books on the
seventeenth century – as well as others of a less exacting kind – in under
ten years, A.B. still found time to formulate original, and what were
often to prove prophetic ideas concerning the century in which he was
living. Fate gave him two 'platforms' from which to expound them.
The first was to become a permanent one when, in 1936, he was asked
to succeed G. K. Chesterton as the weekly writer of 'Our Notebook'
in *The Illustrated London News*. The second, of a more transitory kind,
was granted in 1937, when he was asked to write J. L. Garvin's editorial
page for *The Observer* while the latter was taking a sabbatical year to
complete his life of Joseph Chamberlain. Both – especially the former –
gave A.B. a 'writing discipline', as he described it, and helped him
to make 'thinking a lifelong habit'.

To many academic historians, journalistic work of this kind might
have seemed a fatal deflection from their main purpose in life. To A.B.
it was an opportunity for applying his historical sense to his own age
as well as to the seventeenth century. Although he felt he may sometimes have made mistakes as a journalist, he also felt that his sense of the
past gave him a deeper understanding of the problems affecting the
public and political life of the present and of the issues which face
public men in all ages.

Of his role as Chesterton's successor, he wrote:

'Not being a professional journalist and having many well-
founded doubts of my ability to fill such a role, I should probably

have refused had it not been for the fact that I had already, by then, been writing the page for some weeks, and had grown accustomed to doing so, as a deputy for G. K. Chesterton, firstly in the sudden emergency caused by his illness and then immediately following his unexpected death. . . . Having an admiration for him both as a writer and a man, I had naturally felt very honoured by the proposal that I should temporarily deputise for him. . . . Gilbert Keith Chesterton had spent his whole life in teaching others how to live. To him the world was a strenuous field in which one went about doing battle with evil in order that good might endure. . . . He never penned a line or uttered a sentence that harboured a mean or ignoble thought. . . . It was the greatness of Chesterton's creed that the salvation he preached was the salvation not of the elect, but of the many.

'He had shown me much kindness during my visits to his home at Beaconsfield, where for several winters I had been giving University Extension lectures. Among those who attended them was Mrs. Chesterton, who often entertained me for supper, and her famous husband would sometimes sit, with touching humility, on a seat much too small for him – for the lectures were sometimes held in the village school – listening to my rather fumbling orations and taking part in the subsequent discussions as though his name had never been heard of outside that small community of neighbours. He and his wife, like another famous native of Beaconsfield, J. L. Garvin, used on such occasions to ask me back after the lecture. So I had additional reasons, of a very personal kind, for accepting the invitation to write his column for him until he was better. . . .

'The page itself has continued, in one form or another, for over a hundred years and is the oldest column in British or, so far as I know, global journalism, while the length of my own connection with it pales into insignificance beside that of the journal's wise and immensely experienced editor, Sir Bruce Ingram,[1] who took over its control in the last year of Queen Victoria's reign. . . .'

'I never met him,' A.B. recalled, 'until after I had been working for him regularly for fourteen years. Then we became great friends.' Mrs. Chesterton told him after her husband's death that the latter had never

---

[1] Sir Bruce Ingram died January 8th, 1963.

met the editor in all the time he had written 'Our Notebook'. It seems, however, that Chesterton was labouring under a misapprehension, for A.B. subsequently learned from Sir Bruce that sometimes G.K. would deliver his copy to the I.L.N. offices at the very last minute, handing it personally to his editor, although the former never realised it, because Ingram, the most considerate of men, did not wish to embarrass him by revealing his identity.

The very first morning I started to work for A.B. he was just finishing 'Our Notebook' under difficult circumstances caused simultaneously by my arrival, both his telephones ringing, and the desire to find the correct adjective in a certain sentence. He padded heavily and hastily about between a black telephone at one end of his library and a white one at the other, asking me *en route* for another word for 'ingenious'. Embarrassed at having arrived at such an inopportune moment, my mind went blank. But having dealt with both callers he seemed to have forgotten consulting me. Back at his desk I watched him frown, bite the end of his pencil, hastily scribble something, flick over the pages, cross out several words and then, without taking his eyes off the article, remark, 'There. That's that. I suppose I must have written about two million words over the years for this magazine. If anyone had ever told me in my schooldays that I should still be having to write a weekly essay during my seventies, I should probably have committed suicide!'

Later on, as I began working regularly for him, when the deadline for his weekly (soon to become monthly) copy drew near, I sometimes asked him what he was going to write about. 'No idea,' would come the cheerful reply. Secretly horrified, I would feel the minutes ticking by, praying that 'Our Notebook' would soon start to take shape. But I should have had more faith. When a man has performed the Herculean task of producing an article of between twelve to fifteen hundred words on the correct date week after week, year after year, since 1936, I should have known it would appear without fail, as it had always done; and that although I myself might be going home to sleep, A.B. would be sitting up in bed during the small hours, his writing-pad on his knees, his pencil in his mouth and the idea (hitherto unformed) forming in his mind. 'How many times,' he once wrote, 'have I written the words "Our Notebook" and my own name underneath it and stared blankly at the empty page trying to marry it to an equally empty mind. . . . Yet blank as my mind has so often proved during those awful last hours. . . . I cannot complain that the fates have not given me plenty to write about: the greatest global war in history, a major social revolution, the disintegration of the British Empire and its transformation into the Commonwealth and more economic crises than one can count. Produced in the interstices of historical work and often written in swaying trains and cars and sometimes during the war in aeroplanes or on upturned boxes on airfields or the platforms of crowded railway stations, these contributions – a contemporary if rambling commentary on our times – reflect the personal and political philosophy of an onlooker, holding no office or public responsibility except that of a purely voluntary kind, and speaking only for himself. . . . Yet. . . . I can honestly say that, whatever tedium I may have inflicted on my readers, I have enjoyed every word of it. I may have had little worth imparting to impart, but the mere fact of having to impart it has been a regular mental exercise which has done me, I feel, a great deal of good, rather like bicycling every morning round Battersea Park, as my father used to do in the 'nineties, or bathing like my Spartan younger brother before breakfast all the year round in Highgate pond or the Serpentine. . . . So I feel nothing but gratitude to the generous and patient editor who entrusted me with the task and to the readers . . . who have so tolerantly borne with my rambling reflections for so long. . . . If anyone wonders why my column in *The Illustrated London News* has any readers, I can only suggest the answer Charles II gave when asked to explain how a particularly stupid clergyman whom he had made a bishop, had converted his flock from dissent to orthodoxy: "I suppose his sort of nonsense suited their sort of nonsense!" '

*   *   *

A.B.'s articles in *The Observer* required an entirely different technique from those in *The Illustrated London News*. They were by no means, as he disarmingly put it, 'rambling reflections'. They were pertinent, provocative and highly political. Yet the message which came across from both these 'platforms' was that of a man desirous of peace, not peace at any price, but peace because its alternative, war, was something which struck at the very heart of all that he held most dear – not only England, but civilisation itself.

During the early 1930s when there was great political upheaval and mass unemployment, he sometimes regretted that he had not stood for Parliament. Inspiring, politically-conscious and a natural orator, he was twice asked to stand as a Conservative candidate, once for the Isle of Ely where he had become so popular through the Wisbech pageant, once for the Labour stronghold of Central Southwark. Curiously enough, had he accepted the second merely to gain political experience, in the great Labour rout and sweeping Conservative victory of 1931, he would, like many other young men, have found himself unexpectedly in Parliament, while had he, in the hope and expectation of getting there, been adopted for the Isle of Ely, he would never have done so, owing to a Conservative–Liberal pre-election pact not to oppose sitting members.

But he was always very conscious of one thing: that he had his living to earn. Without the private means which he knew to be necessary for a Conservative Member of Parliament, he felt unable to accept either offer, for

> 'in the Conservative Party, when I was a young man, member-
> ship of the House was a more expensive privilege than member-
> ship of a crack cavalry regiment. The candidate for a safe seat
> needed not only to be able to support himself while in Parliament
> and defray all the expenses of his position, but to contribute to a
> large part of the annual expenses of his constituency organisation
> and to defray the periodical cost – a very considerable one – of
> Parliamentary elections. Legislation was as expensive a luxury as
> polo. It was a vocation mainly for successful businessmen and
> industrialists and for the sons of landowners, bankers and
> capitalists. It could only be practised by the members of a well-
> endowed class. . . .'

Moreover, 'to achieve even the smallest success in practical politics,' he wrote, 'requires a man's entire time. . . . The only kind of profession compatible with a politician's is one that goes on automatically in his absence: "business" for instance, or the Law. But an author's profession never goes on automatically in absence: no man can devil for him, no assistant write his books. If he essays to be a politician, he must do so at the expense of his writing: if he wants to write, he must neglect his political objectives.'

Though he therefore never became a Member of Parliament, he nevertheless remained active behind the political scene, especially after his connection with Ashridge brought him into close contact with two Prime Ministers: Stanley Baldwin – 'the only P.M. who once ran my bath water for me!' – and later, Neville Chamberlain, whose speeches he was to edit.

The first time he met Baldwin was at a weekend conference of Conservative M.P.s, peers and candidates at Ashridge in 1930. Since becoming Educational Adviser in 1929, he went there regularly each week for a day, or sometimes two, in order to prepare programmes and deal with letters. It was through Ashridge at this time that he first met my father, having asked him if he would lecture there shortly after the latter had written *Farmer's Glory*.

In 1933, amongst other commitments, he wrote and produced a highly successful historical pageant for the Navy – comparable to the Army's Aldershot Tattoo – which took place at the Royal Naval College at Greenwich with a cast of three thousand performers. Running for ten consecutive nights, it was witnessed, in the King's illness, by the Queen, the Prince of Wales and, on one night, by the entire Cabinet, as well as several visiting royalties. The following winter he also gave a series of broadcast talks[1] on the National Character which were subsequently reprinted in book form under the same title. Baldwin gave the introductory address. 'I shall always remember,' A.B. said, 'how he told me what he proposed to say, talking for exactly half an hour with only one or two notes before him. When it came to the actual broadcast he gave almost the identical talk he had tried out on me. Afterwards I asked at Broadcasting House whether he

---

[1] A.B. was also asked at this time by Sir John Reith, Director General of the B.B.C., if he would join that organisation as a principal assistant and possible future successor. Though he refused, through his friendship with Reith he was instrumental in recommending to him one of the most famous of all broadcast announcers, Alvar Liddell.

had used a script, and was told they couldn't make him do so. It showed his capacity for concentration.'

A.B.'s growing respect for Stanley Baldwin, whom he described as a man who 'in his time, the first age of British militant socialism, performed the astonishing feat of taking the bitterness out of British political life', resulted in his writing a brief life of him as a tribute on his retirement. The original MS, written in pencil, is beside me as I type:

'One of the first times I ever talked with him he had just come from his victory over those who wished to dethrone him in 1930. He looked very tired, but the impression which most of my countrymen and I had formed of him by hearsay – of a sincere, honest but not very strong man – vanished in a moment. Honesty and sincerity was written all over his face, but there was more. This man was above all things a fighter. There was some spark of divine fire, some hard, indomitable grit about him. Here, at that moment, was not the leisured and literary pig breeder so dear to the illustrated press, but the hard old party "boss" with the light of battle in his eye, making mincemeat of the assailants who had so foolishly mistaken patience and forbearance for indolence and timidity. Once, on another occasion, I saw him stand in the gallery at Chequers with Cromwell's death mask in his hands, and gazing at those two faces I could not say which was the stronger. . . . It is in his strength that I have tried to draw him. . . . If I have added the warts too, it is because he wished me to.'

Yet, although in the decade prior to the Second World War A.B. was in touch with many of the political leaders and thinkers of the time, his attitude to affairs taking place on the other side of the Channel was, as always, that of a historian. His was the long-term view; for in politics as with everything else, he seemed to think in terms of centuries. He was therefore curiously and too much detached from some of the more immediate and disturbing events then taking place, especially in Germany. Far from being blind to the possibility of another war and always passionately insistent on the need for re-arming, it was the threat to civilisation itself which appalled and made him incredulous that any right-minded person on either side – especially one like Hitler who had fought in the trenches in the last war – should not do everything he could to prevent such a thing happening again: 'Peace,' he wrote in *The Observer*, in 1937, 'is dependent, not on rules, but on an attitude of mind. The only champion of peace whose professions are worth anything is the man who is ready to tolerate and try to understand his neighbour, even when he is shocked and dismayed by his standards and ways of life.

'It is right that we should prepare for war in order to remove the temptation of war. But it is not right that we should prepare for war in order to have war. And there is more than a tendency in Britain today to talk of our war-like preparations as though they were an inevitable and even rather exciting prelude to war itself. . . . The moment Britain becomes unduly sensitive, aggressive or oblivious to the feelings of others, the risk of universal war is immensely aggravated. It therefore behoves her people, as sensible folk who like to be accounted realists, to shun every idle word, written or spoken that might lead to war or increase the risk of its taking place. For, armed or dis-armed, no worse calamity could possibly befall them. The truth is that the whole interest of Britain is intimately bound up with the continued existence of civilisation. . . .

'Almost everything of value that civilised man possesses is the achievement and gift not of his own or any single generation, but of countless generations who have each in their turn added a little. . . . It is so easy to destroy, so difficult and painfully wearisome to build. A single generation can undo the patient accumulation of centuries. . . .'

Destructive force of any kind was abhorrent to A.B. Although, as a boy, he may have wanted to be a soldier, the crusading force which he came to believe in was of an entirely different kind. Writing about it many years later, he said,

'It was the philosophy of love as a creative force that established over a large part of the earth's surface the kind of life which we in this fortunate island know today and have long taken for granted. . . . If one wants to understand how Christian civilisation grew out of anarchy and barbaric tyranny one cannot do better than study the story of how in this country Roman monks and Celtic missionaries preached Christ's gospel of love to the heathen, that is, to ordinary primitive non-Christian men, and established germinative centres of example where that gospel could be put into practice.

'It was because, where the monks and missionaries made their settlements men lived together in amity, that they and their disciples were able to achieve advances in agriculture, the arts and ways of living that were impossible for societies torn by perpetual strife, fear and mutual destruction. Everything that was educative, creative and enduring in European society in the Middle Ages was the legacy of the Christian Church and its creed of creative love. And in the fulness of time the lessons taught by the Church were carried by European colonisers and traders into other continents beyond the oceans – the Americas, Southern Asia, Australasia and Africa.

'That they also carried with them, and displayed the faults and weaknesses inherent in all human nature does not alter the fact that the civilisation they planted beyond the oceans was of immense benefit to mankind. To destroy it, whether there or at home or in both, would be a suicidal folly. . . .'

It was with the thought of doing whatever he could to try to prevent such destruction that A.B., one Sunday summer's evening in 1939, flew from Croydon aerodrome on one of the strangest journeys of his life.

10

Forlorn Assignment

'Though the English act late, they also
act with astonishing resolution and
unanimity – and, therefore, with effect –
when at last they do act.'

Illustrated London News,
12th December, 1959

I came across the article one evening just before going home. In the centre of the page there was a picture of the Brigade of Guards trying out a new drill formation. The date at the top was August 5th, 1939, and A.B. had evidently just been on a trip to Germany. 'I had not flown over Germany,' I read, 'since 1918. One was not then a popular visitor and was apt to be greeted by white shell-bursts and angry barks and the stutter of machine-guns.'

Where had he been off to now? I wondered. A holiday resort? In Germany? In the summer of 1939? I read on:

'... From what I could see of it, this fabulous country of marching armies and no butter, of parades, pogroms and concentration camps, was as peaceful a place as England: a land of farms and homesteads and well-tilled fields and little ancient churches. Here at least were vestiges of a common civilisation: the neat ferry, glimpsed in the last slant of light, somehow recalled Bablock Hythe, and the thought of it as a prospective bombing target brought little pleasure to my curious English mind. As we sped on in the darkness, at intervals of every quarter of an hour, a little slip of paper would be passed back from the pilot's cockpit giving the name of some approaching gleam of light: Osnabrück and Minden where, two hundred years ago, hungry English troops with an English monarch at their head fought and conquered to gain their breakfast; and Hanover, which gave us our Royal Family and old Handel.

'Every now and then a great lighthouse would rise above the cloaked plain, like a beam of civilisation in a land where, for a quarter of a century, civilisation has not been the assured continuous background of life it has been in England, but a blessing often lost and always to be fought for, and in search of which men would fight and even suffer great crimes. And I recalled how, on my last visit to the land below me, sixteen years before, a dark, terrible poverty lay over all its idle towns, and then men and women in the streets bore the pallid stamp of hunger on their faces. Even before the marshalled lights of Berlin spun out of the darkness like a pageant, just four hours after leaving London, the consciousness was strong on me of how much, for all its superficial differences, our European civilisation is a unity. . . .'

The latter statement was intriguing, coming as it did from a man so strongly opposed, as he now was, to the Common Market. The article gave no clue as to the reason for his visit. When next the opportunity arose I asked him, in a lighthearted way, whether he was visiting Hitler.

'As a matter of fact,' came the astonishing reply, 'I was going to see one of his right-hand men, Herr Hewel.' He went on to say that he had been asked to do so in the possible, though forlorn, hope that a frank discussion might make some contribution, however small, to averting the holocaust which most people now thought inevitable. With the memory of the devastation at La Bassée which he had witnessed at the age of 19 still deeply impressed on his mind, the thought of that imminent holocaust seemed all the more terrible.

It appeared that his invitation to go to Germany had followed a visit earlier that summer of a party of German youth leaders to England. One of his friends, Francis Yeats-Brown, the author of *Bengal Lancer*, who had been entertaining them, brought them and their organiser over to tea at the White House. 'I remember them all singing round my eighteenth-century piano,' he recalled. 'They seemed the kind of young men who were the counterparts of the subalterns and company commanders who had fought for this country twenty years earlier in the First World War. None of them seemed to want another one. But I warned them that if Hitler ignored the British Prime Minister's guarantee to Poland and Rumania, Britain would certainly fight and go on fighting to the end.'

A.B. was uncertain what to do about the totally unexpected invitation which he received as a result of this visit. It was felt that, as a known supporter of the Prime Minister and a staunch patriot who had always sympathised with legitimate national aspirations, both British and German, and had never been afraid to express his opinions, however unpopular, his sober, straightforward warning to his young guests, if conveyed in time to the right quarter, might conceivably help to avert a fatal decision by the German Führer who, as yet, it was believed, had not finally decided on war. And though A.B. neither understood nor spoke German, it was therefore suggested that he should visit Berlin and Salzburg for an informal talk with Herr Hewel[1] who, having been a Ceylon tea-planter, spoke perfect English and, as one of Hitler's chief advisers on foreign affairs and a close personal friend, was in daily contact with him.

Apart from all other considerations, A.B. was not at all anxious to leave his work for such a seemingly hopeless assignment. He first consulted the Prime Minister, whose speeches, *Peace in Our Time*, he had just edited, and then, as Chamberlain thought he should go, he consulted Baldwin. As he, too, considered it his duty, he went.

It was a curious, secret lonely mission which he undertook when he left England on a Sunday evening in early July. During it

'I spoke very frankly with certain Germans, warning them of the inevitability of war with Britain if they persisted in their impatient and one-sided policy. I was treated with great kindness and consideration – the most so, it struck me, when I spoke most frankly. I saw too a Germany strangely different from the hysterical land of shadows depicted by the newspapers and even more different from that other Germany – sad, sullen and divided – which I had seen in the days of the Inflation sixteen years before. For it was a land which, for all the miseries of the minorities tucked out of sight and hearing, seemed at unity with itself and in which the common man felt himself part of a great nation moving, as he supposed, proudly and gladly towards a happier and assured goal. But, knowing what the plain German did not know of the blind resolve of his rulers and the unswerving and

---

[1] Herr Hewel was one of the very few who stayed to die with his Führer in the bunker in 1945.

inevitable answer to it of my countrymen, I could take little pleasure in the spectacle, for I then knew that the goal was the crucifixion of Europe.

'I returned to England, with a dying, desperate hope in my heart and none in my mind, seeing again in dreams two pictures. One was of a great lake close to the Austrian border where tens of thousands of children from the industrial cities of the north were rowing and swimming in the sunlight or camped beneath the pine trees, their faces gleaming with happiness and health and new-found knowledge of how to live. The other was of the stern face of the German with whom I pleaded long and earnestly for patience and understanding and who, carrying my words to his friend and ruler, could bring me back no other answer but that of a closed mind. The crowds of German sightseers flowed past the window as we spoke, as ceaselessly as the mountain river beyond, and, watching their faces, I knew that their minds were closed too....'

A few days after his return to this country he met Baldwin, as pre-arranged, during the Eton and Harrow match at Lord's. They sat in the Pavilion together and he told the latter all that had taken place. 'Baldwin looked grave,' he recalled. 'He kept nodding, though keeping his eye on the cricket all the while. I remember Harrow were doing rather badly at that moment. Once, when he started to say "The trouble is", I thought he was about to make some comment on my cheerless report, but he simply continued, "our bowlers just aren't good enough for them". Almost immediately, two Eton wickets fell and the matched moved forward again to a long-awaited Harrow victory.'

Although he had undertaken this mission with the blessing of both the then present and past Prime Minister, he was well aware that at the beginning of the Second World War he was regarded with disfavour in many circles, that he had been, to quote his own statement, both 'a passionate advocate of the then highly unpopular cause of rearmament – in which I was right – and of the by now even more unpopular cause of appeasement – in which I was wrong, not because it was wrong to try to avert the tragedy of a second German war, with the apparent waste of all the lives lost in the first, but because no appeasement of a rearmed and revengeful Germany was possible so long as Britain herself was inadequately armed.'

But of his feelings and regard for the Prime Minister's policy during that fateful summer, there was no doubt, as he wrote in retrospect thirty years later:

'. . . It can still hurt an aspirant to high office or the public ear that he was formerly a man of Munich, a supporter of Chamberlain's policy and government, a chap, say, who had once, in the far away days before the war, exchanged social pleasantries with Ribbentrop at Cliveden, or listened to the windy claptrap of Reichsmarshal Goering in his Prussian hunting lodge. More than one otherwise meticulously politic and blameless Conservative leader has suffered in his subsequent career for this sort of thing. Conservatives were, of course, particularly vulnerable to such criticism, having been in power at the time of Munich and during most of the decade that preceded the war. . . .

'When the skeletons in the cupboard of 1938 have been laid bare . . . what . . . do we find? That, had we gone to war in that much discussed September, we should not, in the view of Britain's then military advisers – men who, in the years of battle ahead were to prove their capacity for foresight and professional realism – have stood even the barest chance of victory; and that Neville Chamberlain, in his unavailing approach to Hitler, was making a personally courageous and, in the light of existing possibilities, rational and common sense attempt to avert the unspeakable slaughter, horror and destruction of a Second World War. He failed, yet in the light of what followed, who but a hater of the human race can blame him for having tried? Or his supporters for having supported him? . . .

'Had Britain's spokesman and leader been able to confront on equal terms that convinced believer in force, it is at least conceivable that the latter, who had some personal experience of British prowess in arms, would have hesitated before taking the fatal path that led to the ruin of Germany and his own ultimate suicide in the Berlin bunker. It may be argued that, as we were not strong enough to deter that evil man from the course of aggression, it would have been more dignified for Chamberlain to have stayed inert at home and never to have taken what he described in a letter to Lord Runciman, warning him of his proposed intentions, as "a sudden and dramatic step which might change the whole situation" – in other words his flight in his seventieth year to Berchtesgaden to beard the Nazi dictator in his den. But Chamberlain carried the responsibility for millions of human lives on his shoulders and he was right to try and save them. He was a good, brave and honourable man, and though we know – as we did not then – that war was inevitable, I am glad to think I was, in however humble a way, one of his supporters.'

During that fateful uneasy year before war broke out in September 1939, A.B. had been writing a book to explain why the German people, despite their defeat and subsequent sufferings, had placed themselves and their future in the hands of a fanatic political gang dedicated to avenging that defeat and those sufferings by violence. 'I did so,' he explained,

> 'with the full realisation that much that I had to relate ran counter to the prevailing and unthinking view held both in this country and Germany. I knew that many would blame me for reminding them of what they would prefer to forget. But I hoped, often against hope, that a historian's relation of what had happened . . . might conceivably help to direct opinion in Britain and Germany . . . towards a calmer and less reproachful atmosphere in which the problems of Europe could be first understood and then settled in peace. It was presumptuous hope and, as the upshot proved, an utterly vain one.
>
> 'For events outstripped me. I and those who thought like me were like men running downhill after a steam-roller hoping to stay its course by propping match-sticks against it. We foresaw the calamity for we recalled the causes from which it sprang, but we were unable to avert it. . . .'

The only copy I ever found of this extremely unpopular book, *Unfinished Victory*, was a tattered proof, for A.B., being exceedingly generous with his books, never seemed to possess any of his own first editions and this, unlike most of his works, only achieved one. Partly because it was the history of my own time and partly because of my interest in the character of the author, its reading captivated me. Here was the one-time would-be soldier and childhood admirer of Napoleon, making an impassioned, yet reasoned, plea for peace. Here was the justification for the beliefs he held, published, albeit too late but courageously, during the first winter of the war, with the staunch backing of its publisher, Harold Macmillan – a professed opponent of appeasement and supporter of Winston Churchill.

There are passages in this book, however unpopular, which seem to demand a second hearing:

'Last time as a result of vast efforts and sacrifices we won victory. But we did not win peace. We failed because we never took enough trouble to do so. . . .

'In our anxiety, or that of our allies, to delay the day of Germany's recovery as long as possible, we undid the whole worth of our lesson by teaching a contradictory one – that only by force and violence was she ever likely to free herself from the painful shackles in which we had bound her. For the moment it mattered little, since she was powerless. But we forgot that the will of our own people to keep her so would not last for ever, and, that presently, true to our traditions and forgetting the menace of the past, we should tire of sitting on an injured and revengeful Germany's head and let her rise. In the fulness of time, as was inevitable, we did so. If we repeat the mistake of 1919 we shall undoubtedly do so again. . . .

'The British people . . . knowing nothing of what the Germans had suffered since the war, failed to realise the causes and social implications of the Nazi revolution. . . . They disapproved intensely of a creed which appealed to force as a means of settling international disputes. Because of their long and insular absorption in their own affairs they were unconscious of the fact that no other means of settling such disputes had been offered to a disarmed Germany. They imagined these matters could be settled to everyone's satisfaction by the League of Nations. . . .

'As in every war we have waged we shall fight with absolute national unity. . . . If the worst should come, and we have done all we can to avert the calamity, let us resolve to face it. At least we shall have touched bottom, and ours will be the absolute strength of men who have nothing further to lose. And if we cannot save civilisation – and it may be that modern civilisation is not worth saving – we should at least have this to win, the recovery of our own souls. We have been fat and comfortable, and our enemies have mocked us because we have been. We shall be fat and comfortable no more, and we shall meet our enemies as equals, in the gate. . . .

'One thinks of the tough, eager-eyed, kindly people of this historic island – the rougher and the least educated of them most of all – and one knows that, faced by calamity, neither their toughness nor their eagerness nor their essential kindliness will desert them. If war comes, they may experience terrors and calamities such as never came to them in the last war. When the first shock is passed, they will set their teeth and smile the slow, humorous English smile, released once more after twenty years of bewilderment and the worship of false idols, and tackle the job in hand. We may go down fighting, or we may survive victorious, but we shall certainly not surrender. And though the whole structure of our civilisation may be utterly changed in the melting-pot, the faith of one Englishman at least – and he is aware that he is not alone – tells him the sweet, delicate and brave spirit of England will somehow live on, a beacon in a dark world guiding through storm to an unguessed at future.'

In the light of all that happened in the next six years, this passage, written by a professed appeaser on the eve of war and a year before Churchill's 1940 speeches, seems as moving as it was prophetic.

The Napoleonic Trilogy

'The days between May 29th and June 3rd, 1940,
were a turning point in the history of mankind.
. . . The Herrenvolk . . . contemptuously offered the
English peace. . . . Churchill and the British people
did not hear. . . . With all the terrible concentration
of their race, they were resuming a craft which
they thought they had abandoned for ever.'

> From *The Summer of Dunkirk*,
> first published in *The Daily Sketch*,
> June 3rd and 4th, 1943, later printed
> privately by Kemsley Newspapers in aid
> of *The Daily Sketch* War Relief Fund.

When *Unfinished Victory* was published in March 1940, A.B. was, to
use his own words, 'almost in disgrace'. It was now not only in his
public life, but also his private one, that he found himself in a lonely
and questionable position. For some time he and his wife had gone
their separate ways and shortly before the war their marriage was
finally dissolved. Eighteen months later, in February 1941, he married
Anne Brooke, a daughter of Bertram Brooke, the Tuan Muda of
Sarawak.

Until Hitler struck in the West in May, A.B. was still among the
small minority who had hoped that a military stalemate might have
brought the war to an end and so averted the destruction and tragedy
which the majority thought inevitable. But when the Germans broke
through the floodgates in the Ardennes and started to sweep across the
northern French and Belgian plain, he wrote in the middle of May an
article which appeared in *The Illustrated London News* on the 25th of that
fateful month:

> 'It is idle for men attacked by a tiger to dispute who raised him
> or helped to loose him. The only thing that matters for the

moment is to cage or destroy him. The only alternative to such a course is to be destroyed. In such an hour the worst mental suffering is suspense: the worst suffering idleness. Suspense must be borne by all, but it will be borne, as always in this country in its peril, with courage, constancy and humour. As for idleness, that cruel and corroding slavery should soon trouble no man. For there will be work and enough for every man to do until the danger we stand in is past: either the work of defeating the enemy or, for those whose lot it is to "stand and wait", the necessity to carry on short-handed the work of the nation. In complete absorption in the obligation of the hour will be found for all the blessing of inward peace. The coming of war was a tragedy: the coming of danger brings us release. Our business is clear, and common to every one of us: it is our proud lot to hold the English heart. In its keeping every English man and woman has a share. . . .

'Indecision, doubts, fears – for all who had them – are gone. There is only one choice for everyone: to grapple with the enemy and never let go till he releases his stranglehold. There can be no mistake now – it is him or us. . . . In the sad divided years behind us, many of us have, for one reason or another, doubted the wisdom of our country's official policy. There were those who said we should have made an earlier stand, including some whose prolonged advocacy of disarmament had helped to deprive us of the power of making such a stand. Others, like the writer of this page, while advocating rearmament, urged a timely revision of hasty and perhaps unwise treaties and vainly offered friendship to those who now are our life-and-death foes. Who of us was right and who wrong only history can say, and perhaps not history. But now there is nothing left for dispute. We are faced by a cruel and ruthless enemy who is resolved to destroy us and all that great heritage we have too much taken for granted and sometimes neglected. Now that it is threatened, it seems, as it should be, infinitely precious to us. . . .'

Shortly after *Unfinished Victory* came out, A.B. had published – in conjunction with Henry Drummond-Wolff, a former Conservative M.P. – a small book entitled *Britain Awake*. In it he had set down his beliefs on a subject to which both had given much time and thought during the previous winter: economic reconstruction, something which occupied the minds of many far-sighted people in those days who had faith enough in evil times to plan for a better world. It was a reasoned plea for closer trade and migration links with the British nations overseas and, by a modification of the Most Favoured Nation Clause in our international trading treaties, for making what was morally desirable and physically possible financially possible also, and so ending the divisive nightmare in peacetime of mass unemployment. 'How well I remember it all,' he said, 'and the educative, economic grindstone it involved for me under dear Henry's brilliant teaching.' 'It is sad,' he later wrote, 'to contrast our high hopes in those days with what . . . has come to pass.'

Now, so intense was A.B.'s desire that the mistakes following the last war should not be repeated, so aware was he that 'victory by itself was not enough', that during the summer of 1940 he set to work to incorporate those beliefs in a full-scale book which might reach a wider public. *English Saga*, which came out that December, was, as he wrote in the Preface, 'a record of a hundred years of crowded social evolution . . . written at a turning point in England's existence'. For, as he so often reiterated, 'the key to a nation's future is in her past. A nation that loses it has no future. . . .'

'I can remember the white-hot heat at which I worked on the book during the Battle of Britain and the blitz,' he said, 'sitting on the floor of the little room at the White House with all the proofs spread out around me, while various guests seeking a temporary refuge from London went to and fro.'

English Saga was an exceptionally powerful book, one which received instant acclaim and became another Book Society choice. It made a deep impression on many fighting men,[1] written, as H. V. Hodson described it, 'with fire and passion, love and anger':

> 'Nations like men must reap what they sow. The justice that is visited upon the children's children is an inescapable law of existence. Yet there is another eternal principle governing the

---

[1] Just before Alamein, when Lord Gort, then Governor of Malta, feared that unless relieved in time, he might be forced to capitulate to save the island's population from starvation, sooner than surrender himself with the island, he had valiantly and characteristically fitted out a felucca in which to sail for Egypt and had chosen two books to accompany him on his hazardous voyage: the *Bible* and *English Saga*.

world. It is that of redemption. Man may learn from his mistakes and, when he has made atonement, raise his stature by self-regeneration. Here, also, he learns and acts not as an isolated individual but as a member of a continuing society of which his own birth and death as an individual are but a seasonal part. A great nation is a society that learns from its prior follies and, in learning, recreates itself.

'England has always learnt her lessons from her past mistakes. That is why, in the last resort – on the Dunkirk beaches of her history – she is so great. She lost her first Empire by ignoring a great principle of human government. She kept her second by regarding it. She made war against the Boer burghers: she gave them freedom and self-dominion within ten years of their defeat. She denied nationhood to the Irish: she granted it ungrudgingly when the scales were lifted from her eyes. Her enemies have often recalled the crimes of England. Yet her true history is the record of how they were redeemed.

'England is now learning again that neither wealth nor power nor comfort, whether for class or individual, are ends in themselves: that the wealth of a nation consists in nothing but the virtue of her children and children's children. That no profits, education, law, custom or institution that does not contribute to their health and goodness is of any enduring value. That the proper test of all legislation, of every political programme and economic activity, is not "Does it pay?" or "Does it enrich this class or that?" but "Will it make better men and women?"

'An island fortress, England is fighting a war of redemption not only for Europe but for her own soul. Facing dangers greater than any in her history she has fallen back on the rock of her national character. Her future and that of the world depend not only on her victory but on her ability to re-state in a new form the ancient laws of her own moral purpose and unity. By doing so she may discover a common denominator for human reconstruction more glorious than anything in her long past.'

Among the many letters from complete strangers that the author received about the book was one from the former Socialist M.P. and broadcaster, W. J. Brown: 'Until a week ago,' he wrote, 'I had not read a line you had written, but I want to write to you about the Saga; . . . It is the noblest utterance of our day and generation. It must herald the English revival which – not Socialism or any other 'ism' – the heart of our people cries out for. It mirrors not only the history of a hundred years but the spiritual evolution of countless thousands of inarticulate souls. I am a slum product – father a plumber – and like masses of poor folk, I reacted against the injustices and stupidities of capitalism and embraced Socialism. Like thousands more, I have since reacted against that. . . . Your book comes like a light into my darkness and has given me a new vision. . . .'

The book brought a surprise from another quarter, as well as a future lifelong friend. General Paget, Commander-in-Chief Home Forces and the man who was expected to command our D-Day army, having read *English Saga* and been deeply moved by it, expressed a wish to meet its author. Early in 1942, it was arranged that the latter should dine at Paget's headquarters and subsequently lecture to his Staff at the Curzon Street cinema in Mayfair. Owing to the demand for Adult Education in the Forces, A.B., with his previous experience with the Oxford University Extension Delegacy, the Workers' Educational Association and, above all, Ashridge, was already lecturing to troops on several nights a week but only, as he put it, 'in a humble capacity, to searchlight batteries and so forth'. Now, for the first time, he found himself confronting, not just an ordinary unit of the Army, but one of its very top echelons. 'I was nervous,' he said, 'but it seemed to go down all right.'

Soon he was working the clock round. Not only did he carry on with his usual lecturing commitments, continue writing his weekly commentary in *The Illustrated London News* – then regarded by the authorities as our principal export journal – and embark on the research and writing of three consecutive books on a war whose strategic course so closely foreshadowed the existing one, but he was asked to travel by road, sea and air to places as far apart as Baghdad and Scapa Flow. On these occasions he lectured usually on History and Reconstruction but also, particularly at Army, Navy and Air Force Headquarters and the Staff Colleges of all three Services, on the course and strategy of the war itself.

116

'I was only a civilian. But in those years my work brought me into daily contact with those who were fighting our battles in the field, and I was privileged, as a result, to see something at all levels of the work of all three Services, as well as of civilian war-time England. It is a privilege I shall account of greater worth than almost any other I can remember; 1917 and 1918 were years of victory, but they were not, I feel, looking back, such great years as 1943 and 1944. For one thing we had not risen from so low a place; our victorious armies, battered and bled as they were almost beyond endurance, were not so superlatively trained, led and inspired as in those later years. From the day when Montgomery sent his men into battle at Alamein to the day, less than two-and-a-half years later when our armies in Germany and Italy broke the heart of the German Army on the Rhine and Po, the British people moved forward on a great tide of victory, impelled by their own high-hearted resolution and effort. It may not have been, in Wordsworth's phrase, bliss in those days to be alive: bliss was indeed the last word one could apply to those years of struggle and endurance. But there was pride: pride in one's heritage, one's kinship with the good and great, one's country. . . .'

It was this deep-rooted love of his country, and pride in its people's historic role of withstanding and containing a tyrant who had overrun Europe, which inspired the three books that followed *English Saga*. Begun in 1940 and covering the struggle against Revolutionary France up to the peace of Amiens, *The Years of Endurance* was published in 1942, a few weeks after the turn of the tide at Alamein and the North African landings. Its sequel, *Years of Victory*, published in 1944, told the story of the Trafalgar campaign and the Peninsular War; while the *Age of Elegance*, begun in the last year of the war, described the final two years of the war against Napoleon, including the Congress of Vienna and Waterloo. Written 'to enshrine the lessons' of that earlier struggle for national existence and European liberation, the trilogy covered a war which, although curiously unlike that of 1914–18, was, in its geographical strategy and problems, very similar to that now being waged a century and a half later.

'As in 1940,' he wrote in the Epilogue to *The Years of Endurance*,

'Britain was driven back to her last line of resistance, the sea. Her expeditionary force, deserted by its allies, was expelled from the Continent, the flanks of her trade routes exposed to attack and the ports of Western Europe closed to her ships. Her people suffered a food shortage as grave but far less equally borne than in the present war. Even her vaunted financial system came within a few hours of bankruptcy.

'But those who thought that Britain was defeated were proved wrong. In adversity her real strength becomes apparent. It lay not in her gossamer web of trade and usury and amorphous commercial empire – as the Jacobins, like their Nazi prototypes, supposed – but in the character of her people. Against that rock the waves of conquest broke in vain. In the hour of danger our ancestors closed their ranks. They made many mistakes but they never bowed under the consequences. They learnt from them and went on. . . .'

Published, like *English Saga*, at such a critical time in our history, by a publishing house, for whose chairman, the late Sir William Collins, A.B. had the greatest affection and admiration for his genius as a publisher and who now spared no effort to ensure these books the widest possible circulation, they reached every battle front, helping to sustain all who read them – including many prisoners of war – with a reasoned belief in our ultimate victory. 'I wrote *The Years of Endurance*,' the Preface to its successor ran, 'the story of how England survived a flood which overwhelmed Europe, when she was again alone, withstanding a worse and greater flood,

'I wrote it for the ordinary man who in this, as in other things, has been robbed of his heritage. The sequel tells how the British people – triumphing in turn over appeasement, attempted invasion, Napoleon's grand design to break their power at sea, the long enslavement of Europe and their own commercial isolation – put a ring of salt water round the tyrant's dominion, slowly tightened it, and then, greatly daring, sent in their armies to assail his inner fortress. The events of the past four years have made this story, too, strangely familiar. . . .

'Because we forgot our history we have had to re-live it. We, too, have stood where our ancestors stood in Napoleon's day. . . . I have made no attempt to minimise the horrors and

miseries of war. I am writing for a generation that knows its ugly
face too well. The road to Victory and the human future passes
. . . between the bodies of those who die to win it. But I have
tried, without underlining them, to draw war's lessons: the
unchanging truths of human character and geography, of success
and failure in battle, and of the underlying moral forces which
govern Man's nature in action. . . .

'. . . For in the last resort, tested by any moral touchstone, men
like Napoleon and Hitler are maniacs. And it was the British
people, with all their imperfections, who first afforded that
touchstone. . . . Pitt and Nelson, Moore and Wellington were
not weaker in courage and endurance than Napoleon. Nor were
their followers than his. Like their descendants today they derived their inspiration, not from the worship of Reason or Race
or from love of Glory and Conquest, but from an innate sense
of personal duty which was the unifying force of their freedom-
loving land. . . . To understand why England defeated Napoleon
one should study Wordsworth. In her hour of need she expected
every man to do his duty. It was not Napoleon alone who ship-
wrecked on that rock. It was seen again among the surging waters
of the world's turmoil in 1940. To the end of time Churchill's
signal will fly with Nelson's.'

When D-Day came and men set out across the Channel to reverse
Britain's role of four years earlier, A.B. described it in *The Illustrated
London News* as

'the most important thing that has happened in my lifetime or in
that, I think, of any reader of this page. The most important and
the most significant. It was not merely that it directly brought
about the downfall of Hitler and the Nazis and the liberation of
Europe. It did something more remarkable than that. It showed,
as nothing has done quite so well since Drake scoured Spain's
forbidden Pacific coastline in a cockle-shell and encircled the
world, that the spirit of man can triumph over the most tremendous obstacles, provided that that spirit is rightly founded
and directed. It is an illustration of the tremendous and heartening
truth that faith, and the human work which springs from faith,
can move mountains. . . . It was the testing point, the supreme
culmination, of everything that the men and women of our land,

and of many lands, had worked for through every aching hour of a long, weary, exacting war. It was the greatest day of our lives. . . .

'My own experiences in it were of the most trivial kind. Yet looking back, and at the time, they seemed invested with an extraordinary clarity and intensity: the whole nation, the whole world, it seemed, was that day at prayer. I remember so clearly how in the previous night I had left my work and stood on the lawn in a little Midland English village to watch, as I had so often watched during the past four years, the bombers passing overhead: not now the forlorn, doomed and gallant few of earlier days, but hundred after hundred of mighty planes, the throbbing of whose engines made the earth shake beneath my feet, whose lights were like the heavenly host on the march, the march of the avenging right and doom, like Great Birnam Wood marching to high Dunsinane Hill. The stars, it seemed that night, were moving, and they were all moving in one direction, to one appointed place. All night long they were passing, coming and going, shaking the windows of the old house in which I lay between sleep and wake. And while I, a gentleman in England, lay abed, unknown to me the men whom a short while before I had been with and lecturing to, were dropping from the skies or racing to their assigned tasks or tossing on the face of the dark, foam-flecked waters as the unseen outline of the French coast drew nearer and their rendezvous with destiny met them face to face.

'I had to leave for London early that morning. . . . It was not till evening that I was free to reflect in quiet on the full significance of the news that had been coming through on the wireless all day. I was due that night to give a lecture to British and American officers at the Churchill Club under the shadow of Westminster Abbey in one of the most beautiful houses ever built. . . . My theme, as on many occasions before, was the kind of world which the ordinary man hoped might arise after all this bitter fighting, loss and suffering: but it never seemed so apposite as on this night, and never had words seemed so utterly inadequate to express it. Yet there was little need to express much, for everyone in the audience was thinking the same thoughts. The whole English-speaking world was united in one great brotherhood that day. . . .

'A few weeks after D-Day I found myself lunching in the *Victory*, then the flagship of the Commander-in-Chief, Portsmouth; and from Nelson's cabin windows one looked out at that unbelievable scene of corporate activity that I had been witnessing all the morning on the quays and hards as the ships of all the world carried the men and armaments of Britain and America to the liberation of Europe. Nelson's ghost sat, as it were, on one side of me and the man responsible for that ceaseless flow of men and weapons across the water on the other: khaki and blue blended round that famous table; the present and the past. And there was one chair at the table – an invisible one – more famously tenanted than any; we were all, I think, conscious of its occupant who was the unspoken thought of millions, now battling and dying that humanity should triumph over the forces of evil. It was the spirit of the Future. . . .'

At the end of the war A.B. received honorary degrees at Edinburgh and St. Andrews with many of the war leaders. He was also awarded the C.B.E. In the citation recommending him for the latter, Field Marshal Montgomery, then C.I.G.S., acknowledged not only his war service to the country as a historian, but also his still greater service to the Army:

'. . . In the pages of his history . . . he has shown clearly how our national qualities and character as represented in the Army have enabled us time and again to stand up to adversity with the odds heavily against us.

'He has written for the ordinary man and has identified the achievements and ideals of the Army with the life of the Nation. No other writer has in this way and to this extent raised the prestige and status of the Army in the eyes of the people, and made it live as part of our national and imperial heritage. . . .'

At the beginning of the Second World War, A.B., as he himself admitted, had been 'in disgrace'. At the end of it he was honoured.

12

Losing the Peace

'To restore civilisation . . . will be,
perhaps, the biggest task of all.'

Illustrated London News,
21st October, 1944

Although, during the war, A.B. had continued to earn his living by his
books and articles, he had regarded himself, like those in arms, as a
servant of the State. The voluntary work he then did he treated as an
absolute priority, and all his writing had to be fitted in as best as possible. After the war he still continued to treat the calls of public service
as more important than his books, and this partly accounted for the
six year gap between the publication of *Years of Victory* in 1944 and
The Age of Elegance in 1950.

While working on the latter, he carried out an immense amount of
unpaid public work, almost, it would seem, as a personal crusade or
answer to the question which had been in the forefront of his mind for
so long: 'What is going to happen after the war? . . . We must not
neglect the war in order to win the peace. First things must come
first . . . but Victory and Peace that follows Victory are one and
indivisible. The victory, however complete, will be largely wasted
unless the peace is worthwhile. . . .'

During the early years of that peace he continued to lecture to the
Forces, while also serving on the Army Education Advisory Board
and the B.B.C. General Advisory Council. Towards the end of 1945
he accepted, too, the chairmanship of the St. John and Red Cross
Hospital Library Department and Committee, which provided and
distributed books and reading matter to all Service Hospitals at home
and abroad, as well as to half the civilian hospitals in the country. This
particular post was one to which he was still giving his time when, over
twenty-five years later, I started working for him.

In aiding these and other causes he used to the full his two great natural advantages: the written and spoken word, and his articles in *The Illustrated London News, Sunday Times* and other national newspapers gave him ample opportunity for making his ideas known. Because of the appeal of his Napoleonic War books, he was also constantly being asked to write appreciations of the wartime records of regiments, divisions and other Service units, requests which he did his best to meet; and during the last year of the war he had suddenly found himself in the difficult position of being invited almost simultaneously to prepare and write histories of a larger and even more time-consuming scale. The First Sea Lord, Admiral of the Fleet, Sir Andrew Cunningham, asked him if he would take on the official shorter Naval History of the War. A week later he was asked to write the shorter official War History of his old Service, the R.A.F. Having already accepted the first, he was obliged to refuse the second, although most reluctantly as he was urged to do so by someone whom, as in the first instance, he greatly admired, his friend, Lord Trenchard. But he made it a condition that, in carrying out the Admiralty's commission, his official staff and research assistants should contain a senior R.A.F. officer as well as the two proposed naval ones, for he was acutely aware that command of the sea during the war had been fought for as much over it as on it.

After spending a considerable part of the next seven years on this interminable project he was ultimately forced to relinquish it, partly because, as he had already feared and pointed out to the authorities, no definitive shorter history of the war at sea could be completed until all the relevant facts had been made available in the fuller and longer war history. He was also heavily delayed because, not being in full-time Government employment himself, he was not allowed under Civil Service security rules direct access to official 'secret' documents, all of which therefore had first to be copied for his perusal, at a heavy cost of time, by the regular officers employed to assist him.

Yet of all the public commitments, official or unofficial, the one nearest his heart was that inspired by the Services' wartime experiment in adult and civic education, which he and others who had shared in it were anxious to see incorporated into the peacetime life of the country. 'During the war,' he wrote, 'an attempt was made by those responsible for the training and morale of the Forces to provide forums of discussion in which the thousands of young men in uniform from factory, field and office could thresh out together the political and economic issues which concerned their future and that of the society to which they belonged and for whose survival they were fighting. Those who formed these groups had at first between them all the weaknesses of modern democratic society: prejudices formed from insufficient facts, refusal to listen to other views, angry and provocative abuse and denunciation. Yet, as the discussion groups developed and their members became accustomed to listening with attention and courtesy to the views of those who differed from them, they grew little by little into miniature parliaments of thoughtful individuals arguing things out for themselves with a respect for proved fact and toleration. . . .'

'Deep down,' he continued, 'for all their differences of opinion, those taking part believed in the same thing – they believed in justice.'

'By what method justice was to be achieved was a matter for dispute, yet what was accepted by all was the right of the individual to put his case to his fellows and receive from them, before judgement, fair play. One saw such men – comrades in a great venture – feeling their way towards that which the rest of the nation had still to discover, a common denominator for reconstruction. Unconsciously a meeting point was being sought and found between those who offered economic liberty without social security, and those who demanded what so many craved after the awful frustration of unemployment in the pre-war years –social security without economic liberty. And gradually one saw an, at first, almost imperceptible, but quickening movement towards the inevitable British answer for which we have been striving as a nation throughout our history – liberty in a framework of discipline or, in economic terms, social security *with* liberty.

'In the early days there was . . . on the whole, negative antagonism towards the frustration and complacent defeatism of our pre-war economic system – a feeling, however unjust, that our rulers had been guilty of a kind of universal *non possumus*, summed up in the words, "Can we afford it?" Could we afford, in terms of money, to clear the slums, to give decent education to the majority of our people, to redistribute our population between our overcrowded cities and the vast spaces of our underpopulated territories overseas, to find employment to make the things of which so many stood in need? . . . And those with whom one was discussing these things had come to see the inadequacy of that question – an inadequacy made obvious by the events of 1940. They had seen a nation which, in the face of deadly danger, had stopped saying "Can we afford, in terms of money, to do things which are necessary to save ourselves?" and had said instead, "Can we afford not to do them?" A nation which, out of sheer necessity had discovered that what was physically possible and morally desirable could be made financially possible, and had learned the lesson that wealth and money are not necessarily the same thing.

'There came to these discussion groups a realisation of something else. It was not a totalitarian society which had made either the machines or the men who won the battles of Britain and Alamein and stormed the D-Day beaches. For it was seen that there was no use in making guns, tanks and aeroplanes, in whatever abundance, if one did not also create the necessary virtues in the men who were going to use them, and that there was a vital difference between a strong State and a strong people. Germany was a very strong State in 1940, Britain a very weak one; yet it was the strong people, not the strong State which ultimately won. And the men to whom I was privileged to lecture were trying to make themselves masters of certain virtues; of physical and mental fitness, faith and competence, courage, endurance and discipline, of the capacity for self-reliance, initiative and self-sacrifice – virtues measured, it is true, for the narrow and wasteful purposes of the battlefield yet very real virtues for all that. And if it were true that, for the purpose of winning the war, human virtue was the highest form of wealth, the same must be true for the purposes of peace, and that the ultimate aim of society, and the test by which all institutions, political, legal, economic, should be judged, was the simple one, "Does it tend to create decent men and women?" For if it did not, however much it might pay in terms of money or serve the aims of some particular ideology, it would break down on the human factor in the long run.'

In these discussions which A.B. held with these citizens of the future about the kind of society which they wished to found and live in after the war, he used to suggest that there were six basic human needs, without whose satisfaction man could not rise to the full height of his potential.

'He needs enough to eat, not only in quantity but quality; food, as our medieval ancestors used to say, that is "good and wholesome for man's body". He needs security of tenure and regularity of employment, not only to earn a living but because his nature prompts him to take pride and pleasure in his achievements and security in his home, which includes decent conditions and education for his children. He needs security from war, the bubonic plague of our age. Yet the satisfaction of these material needs is not enough. Man needs something more if he is to be at peace with himself and his environment. He needs self-respect and status. He needs liberty and freedom of choice, freedom from irritating control and cramping interference. . . . On the satisfaction of this need so much which gives life zest depends: love, adventure, even danger; the free choice of one's mate, freedom to dare and take risks, the gleam of the unexpected.'

And there was still something else, he held, transcending all other needs: the need for faith and an ideal, and a common cause for which to live and even, if need be, to die.

It was this falling away after the war of a sense of national unity and purpose which so concerned A.B. at this time, and why he was anxious that the discussion groups should continue under a new form. For four unforgettable years the Forces had taught the Serviceman to take an interest in the political and social issues of the day. Lectures, brain-trusts, debates, discussions, A.B.C.A.s,[1] news rooms had all been fostering a taste for active citizenship, not only in a small intellectual minority but in the average man. In the latter stages of the war the discussion groups had taken on an increasingly physical form, especially in the R.A.F. where in its airfields more static conditions prevailed than in the Army.

'Here the News Room, first established in a few pioneer stations in 1942, had become by the end of the War almost

[1] Army Bureau of Current Affairs.

universal throughout the Service and had grown into something more ambitious, a Community Centre where, in its library, clubroom, handicrafts room, games room and canteen, decorated by serving artists and craftsmen, miniature parliaments of Servicemen and women were creating the potential of a new national institution.'

In a little book on Community Centres by Air Vice-Marshal Thorold and Squadron Leader Farrow, published in 1945, to which A.B. wrote a preface, he described 'the gaily and imaginatively painted inn signs outside the News Room, the bright curtains and decorative panels within, the books, pamphlets and magazines so invitingly strewn about the tables or neatly arranged in subjects round the walls'. 'Repeated with infinite variations,' he wrote,

'it bore witness to an educational and cultural ideal based on an understanding of human nature. The object of this kind of education was first to attract, then to direct the mind to useful study. The News Room or Community Centre was first a club, then a society for mutual discovery. Drawn imperceptibly by its good cheer and pleasant atmosphere, the airman began almost unconsciously to discover a new world both inside and outside himself – the world of the mind and the imagination and the world of organised society. . . . Listening to the discussions of the groups within – shrewd, objective, idealistic and practical, one could hear the voice of a new Britain.

'The Minister for Education has recognised the need for Community Centres . . . and has accepted responsibility for their provision. It has been laid down that their management must be local and democratic. The widespread desire to commemorate our war effort in some form that they may assist the returning soldier as well as honour the dead suggests a way in which Community Centres could spring out of the armistice. All over the country, houses exist for which under new conditions it will be difficult to find a use and whose preservation will be demanded by all who value our national heritage. A nation-wide association might be founded to acquire homes for Community Centres and at the same time provide an outlet for the educational and social aspirations of the returning Servicemen. . . .

'If democracy is not to founder, on the shifting quicksands of apathy, ignorance, suspicion, exploitation, impotence, anarchy and Party despotism, a meeting-place must be found where citizens of all classes and opinions, not merely on the highest level but on that of the ordinary man, can study and debate the problems they have to decide. To say that we cannot afford it is beside the point; if we are to remain a democracy and gather the fruits of victory we cannot afford to do without it.'

Because he felt this to be all-important for the future of the country, he pursued every means for building, on the foundations laid by the Services, voluntary institutions through which he envisaged a real grass-roots democracy might one day operate. He kept in close contact with others who were thinking along the same lines, like his tragically short-lived contemporary Sir William Goodenough, the chairman of Barclay's Bank and the Nuffield Trust for the Forces, and with such promising experiments as Citizenship House. His chief hope, however, lay in the re-opening of Ashridge, of which he was still a governor but which, during the war, had been requisitioned as an emergency hospital.

Throughout 1946 he and Viscount Davidson (who had succeeded Baldwin as chairman of the Governing Body) were in negotiation with the Conservative Party Organisation with which, as the Bonar Law Memorial College, it had been partly linked. They wanted to free it from any Party affiliation and see it re-open as an entirely non-partisan adult educational residential college. For, as A.B. was well aware and was able to make plain, it would be impossible to fill the college and support its enormous overheads without drawing students from all three Parties and, even more important, no Party at all.

As a private Act of Parliament would have been needed to change its constitution, the educational control and direction of Ashridge was therefore vested in a completely independent Educational Council composed of eminent educationalists and industrialists. A.B., as its chairman, Lord Davidson and two other governors provided a link with the Governing Body which, under the college's original foundation, retained control of its finances. Ashridge re-opened in January, 1947, at the start of the bitterest winter of the century, with A.B. giving the opening address. 'One of the most helpful places in England,' he called it, in an article written after two years under its new auspices, where

> 'a succession of men and women of every calling, class and opinion, drawn from all parts of the country, come together for the study and discussion of public affairs and find, often to their surprise, that they are not alone in their aspirations. The essence of Ashridge – the spirit that informs the place – is brotherhood: the spirit which alone can redeem mankind from the suicidal envy and frustration of class conflict and ideological war. . . . Ashridge is open to followers of all parties, but its philosophical basis is that, in peace as in war, only a wider and more generous conception of national and human unity can enable democracy to offer a constructive remedy for our riven civilisation, and so ensure its triumph over authoritarianism.
>
> 'For Ashridge's objective might be described as the Common Denominator. Its students are encouraged to do two things: to base their studies and their conclusions on ascertained fact, and to listen patiently and courteously and with an open mind to all views, whether they agree with them or not. Only by doing so, it is held, can democracy be made to function efficiently and so prove that it is a more enduring and satisfactory form of government than its totalitarian and despotic rival. In this Ashridge is pursuing a parallel line to that of the great experiment in political education made during the war in the Armed Forces.'

A.B.'s chief service to the new post-war Ashridge was to procure as its first Principal the pioneer and great champion of Service education, General Sir Bernard Paget, who, as Commander-in-Chief Middle East Forces, had been his host at Cairo during his lecture-tour of the Middle East in the last winter of the war. On the categorical understanding given by both the Educational Council and Governing Body that the work of the college would be conducted on strictly non-Party lines, General Paget retired from the Army, where he had served as a Commander-in-Chief since 1941, and took up his new and humbler post. Of his work there A.B. wrote,

> 'no one who visited Ashridge during General Paget's term as Principal and saw the amazing transformation wrought in the minds of those who attended its courses – and they were often

embittered minds – by the attitude of that great and understanding teacher of men towards the social and political divisions of our time, can fail to have been impressed by a growing sense of the needlessness of those divisions. The effect that the house, gardens and atmosphere of a great house like Ashridge made on the growing numbers of industrial workers who visited it under General Paget's regime was revealing. It can be summed up, as a very discerning man who started work in boyhood in a Lancashire cotton-mill summed it up, by saying that the typical attitude on the day of arrival was that the place was a social crime, on the second day that it was a beautiful place, on the third that it was a national heritage and ought to be preserved at all costs. Few of those who expressed such views were, politically speaking, Conservatives. But they had suddenly become aware of the need for conservation. They had done so for two reasons: that they were made personally acquainted with something worth preserving, and that its value was made clear to them by someone with imagination and fair-mindedness to enter fully into their own point of view. It had become to them, as so many of them put it, "our Ashridge".'

Unfortunately, Bernard Paget's breadth of vision and insistence on toleration and understanding of conflicting views did not always go down with those who had been used before the war to thinking along Party lines. Lord Davidson, the Chairman of the Governors, though himself a man of very considerable vision, had been chairman of the Conservative Party before the war. He and his wife, who had succeeded him as the highly popular Conservative Member for the constituency in which Ashridge stood, lived, when not in London, in a house at one end of the college.

Almost from the start misunderstandings arose between the hundred per cent politician and the hundred per cent soldier, and the relationship between them became increasingly strained. Neither was it helped by what A.B. referred to as 'those dear, retired elderly ladies', enthusiastic past supporters of both Ashridge and the Conservative Party who had been longing for the day when they would be able to revisit the college and find everything as before. It was rumoured after the first Course that two of them had confidingly asked General Paget whether he did not agree with them that 'Mr. Attlee ought to be boiled in oil'. They couldn't understand it at all when the Principal drew himself up, fixed them with a stony stare and admonished them 'not to talk like that at Ashridge!' Off they went, spreading the word – which inevitably reached the Chairman of the Governors – that the new Principal was a Communist!

This increasingly difficult and tragic situation became all the more so for A.B., because he was personally devoted to both Paget and the Davidsons. It bedevilled all the hopes he had cherished that Ashridge would become the first of a chain of country houses, supported by both sides of industry, where men and women of all Parties and classes could gather to discuss and resolve their differences in an atmosphere of peace and beauty. It led to clashes of opinion on the Governing body, where A.B. had to defend views and policies which, like its Principal, had the unanimous support of the entire Educational Council. Eventually, at the end of its third highly successful year, just when General Paget and his many friends and backers in industry seemed on the point of securing massive financial support for a great extension of Ashridge's activities, the Chairman of the Governors, without informing the Educational Council or Principal, arranged to incorporate into the college another residential educational establishment: a political and social finishing school for young ladies of a more or less uniform class and background. However admirable an institution in itself, it was incompatible with everything the new Ashridge stood for.

The inevitable result was the immediate resignation of General Paget, together with his fine tutorial staff – which included the young Ludovic Kennedy – and of the entire Educational Council, led by A.B. There was no other honourable alternative for them. But their regret at having to do so was shared by countless supporters and well-wishers throughout the country who had seen Ashridge as the embodiment of a great ideal, an ideal to which A.B. remained loyal all his life.

For though, in his younger days, he had worked for the Conservative Party, had written a book about Conservatism and at one time aspired to being a Conservative Member of Parliament, he was never an orthodox Conservative. He was far too individualistic and too much a 'law unto himself' to toe a Party line. 'I am no Communist; I am not even a Socialist – my instincts are fundamentally conservative,' he wrote, 'but by far and away the most important thing to conserve in this country is the character of its people.' This attitude, shared by many thousands with whom he had worked during and after the war, was set out in a letter which he had written in August 1945 – eighteen months before the re-opening of Ashridge and shortly after Labour's sweeping electoral victory – to Colonel George Fillingham, at that time Principal of No. 5 Formation College at Luton Hoo where, among so many similar Service establishments, A.B. had lectured and taken study groups.

'I think you are a little too hard on the Tories. Their real trouble was not so much lack of guts (many of them had fine last-war records) as lack of brains; they failed, as did nearly everyone else, to see the fatal flaw in the working of our economic system, and from that, every inexplicable failure to do the necessary and obvious, followed. They really thought they couldn't afford to do what was physically possible and morally desirable, and so didn't! As I was, in a humble capacity, among them, I can't comment! And the Labour Government in 1931 made exactly the same mistake.

'As for the Election result . . . the thing needed at the present time is national unity; the task ahead is quite as formidable as in 1940. We can't return, even if we wanted to, to the social and economic framework of 1939, for it no longer exists, and the task of our rulers now is to create a new framework without causing social chaos in the meantime or saddling us with a totalitarian system. Without holding any exaggerated belief in the wisdom of Socialists, I believe the latter are more capable at the moment of doing this than the Conservatives who are under the dominance not only of vested interests but of something a great deal worse – vested ideas! And unlike the Conservatives the Socialists do understand the discomfort and inhuman conditions under which so many people are today living and working. Apart from all this, I feel that the Election will have two good results; it will still further strengthen the growing sense of responsibility among Labour (it would have been tragic if this had been lost in a further sojourn in the wilderness) and it may re-educate the Conservative Party and make them think and send them back to their true but forgotten national principles. I said before the Election, in which – hating abuse and disunion – I refused to take any part or stand, that, if the Conservatives won, I should join the Labour Party and that if Labour won, I should become a Conservative again. But before I implement the latter resolve – if I do – I shall take good care to wait and see if the present Tories show any sign of learning from their defeat. After twenty years of disillusionment I am too old to crusade any more for Tory ideals only to find that one is being a smoke screen for stupidity, inertia and greed. . . .

'Yes, it's sad about Winston – it seems so ungrateful and ungracious. Yet from his own point of view, how that defeat secures his place in history! It is as though he'd been assassinated like Lincoln in the hour of victory; "Now he belongs to the ages". Yet he still remains alive on the earth he loves so well to enjoy good brandy, good company, . . . and a few years of his own immortality. He is also left to us in cases of emergency; I don't feel European peace is yet very safe. . . .

'If the Socialists can really lead a great national crusade – comparable with that other crusade which Winston led from Dunkirk to Lüneburg – to make England nearer the English dream than England is (and God knows it needs to be) it will be the greatest adventure of our time or almost any time; and I, for one, will follow them gladly. And if they can't (and they'll have to shed a lot of their urban, bureaucratic theories before they can) their victory should at least lay the foundations of a constructive future on which others may build, break the long deadlock of finance-locked minds, and restore the balance of British politics by proving that an alternative Government is not a national disaster as too many Tories and "haves" have arrogantly and unpatriotically assumed.'

* * *

A.B.'s concern over the post-war problems confronting the country, his preoccupation with and subsequent battle over Ashridge which, pounced on by the Press, grew for a few idle weeks into one of the major issues of the day, had taken up time from writing which he could ill afford. Dedicated as he had been to this cause and persuasive orator as he still was, it marked the final end of his hopes of ever being able to do anything for his country save by his pen.

But though grieved by his failure and defeat, he did not allow it to embitter him. Putting it firmly out of his mind, he returned to his solitary task of writing history. As long as Bernard Paget, by then Governor of the Royal Hospital, Chelsea, lived, he ceased, out of his deep respect and affection for him, to communicate with John David-son, except for an annual interchange of Christmas cards with his much-loved wife. But after the General's death in 1961, feeling that there was no longer any reason to remain estranged from such old and loved friends, he resumed his former friendship with them as though the quarrel over Ashridge had never taken place.

Although his writing now came first, A.B. by no means retired from public life. Voluntary commitments or responsibilities still continued to take up much of his time. He was a member of the King George Jubilee Trust, had been president of the English Association in 1946, and in 1949 became chairman of the Management Committee of the Authors' Society, a post which he held for the next three years. When, long afterwards, I came to work for him, he was serving on the Advisory Architectural Panel for Westminster Abbey, was a trustee of the Historic Churches Preservation Trust and the English Folk Music Fund and a Vice President of the Royal Literary Fund, and, in recognition of the many services he had given to various causes, was an Honorary Liveryman of the Leathersellers' Company, a holder of the Gold Medal of the Royal Institution of Chartered Surveyors, an Honorary Member of the Southampton Chamber of Commerce and a Knight of Grace of St. John of Jerusalem. Yet, while he fulfilled many public obligations, none of them ever compared with Ashridge, out of which he had hoped to see grow something which, in the fulness of time, might have served to strengthen the social unity of the future. 'I cared so much about it,' he once said to me. 'As a chairman I cared too much. I was probably a far better chairman of the St. John and Red Cross Hospital Library Committee, where they endured me for a quarter of a century, because I was more impartial, altogether more detached.'

And despite the mounting regard and approbation which now came his way, detached he remained. Though outwardly social and an amusing and delightful companion, there was also something inherently solitary about him. He was liked by many, dearly loved by some. But happiness and contentment so often seemed to elude him. While he appreciated quiet domesticity, I knew how quickly he could become restless, easily bored. 'I've often wondered what it is that makes people tick,' he said on another occasion, 'what it is they most want and what they fall back on when they don't get it.' His overriding passion had always been to do something for the country of his birth. He was unashamedly patriotic. When he wrote of that most important of human needs, a cause, it was in his case, quite simply: England. He often intimated how, in the late 'twenties and early 'thirties he would have liked to serve this particular cause through politics. When this was not to be, he used other ways of working for the same objective. Always he worked. It was his stabiliser. It accompanied him like some kind of inescapable attachment. On the shortest of railway journeys, out would come his brief-case. As time went by work grew to be an obsession. He had tremendous charm when he cared to exercise it but he was not an easy man; neither was he easy to work for. He expected a lot and sometimes his life seemed little short of 'blood, sweat, toil and tears'.

One day, when the amount of commitments with which he was faced appeared overwhelming, I asked him how it was that he had never broken down under the strain; for I knew there was hardly a letter in his files from personal friends which did not contain a passage exhorting him to take life more easily. In some of my rare moments of free time I made a list of these, which I showed him in the hopes that perhaps such cumulative and significant evidence from varying sources over such a long period of time might have a more salutary effect than any single remonstrance of mine. It began with an affectionate warning from the man to whose war diaries, long before I knew A.B., he had devoted five years of his working life, and then went back to cover three decades of much the same sort of advice.

> 'I was aghast to hear of the way you had been treating yourself,
> . . . sitting up working all night, then working feverishly till
> 4 p.m., shaving, packing and rushing off without having eaten
> your lunch! It was not as if you were going to rest, for I am

convinced Monty[1] kept you hard at it! I feel I am now old enough a friend of yours to appeal to you from the bottom of my heart not to treat yourself in this way. You are something *far* too precious to this country and to the whole literary world to take such risks with your health! Should you be prevented from continuing to produce your wonderful works through ill health, it would be an irreparable calamity.'

> *Field Marshal Lord Alanbrooke*, December 27th, 1956

'My very dear friend, . . . I fear you are overworking and ought to rest. . . . You are an amazing man! How you go on producing work of such quality together with all your outside work and your running to and fro, I cannot begin to understand. . . .'

> *Stanley Baldwin*, November 14th, 1938

'I note with sympathy that you are having trouble with your nasal organ but I also note that it is fairly permanently to the grindstone. . . . All work and no play, but then you could never be dull!'

> *Leslie Henson*, March 3rd, 1952

'Do somehow try to do less.'

> *General Sir Richard O'Connor*, June 9th, 1952

'How you compete with all you have on hand with *no* break and such endless hours I cannot imagine, but I do trust that daylight and a little rest is in sight. . . .'

> *Lady Mountbatten*, September 7th, 1956

'I just don't know how you keep up your production to your own standard. . . .'

> *Lord Woolton*, October 27th, 1957

'I hope you are giving yourself a breather. You so deserve it. How you keep it up at your age I don't know. You seem to work as hard as you did 30 years ago, if not harder.'

> *Herbert Van Thal*, December 8th, 1969

A.B. studied the list and seemed quite interested in it. As a historian, he always enjoyed documentary 'evidence', especially when this was put before him neatly in easily assimilable form. But from the point of view of making any difference to his way of life, I could see I

---

[1] For many years, A.B. had usually stayed a night or two with Montgomery at his Hampshire home, Isington Mill, whenever the Field Marshal was finishing a book of reminiscences or speeches, and wished him to cast a friendly expert eye over it.

had been wasting my time and was powerless to stop something which had become second nature to him. This was the way he had lived and worked for years, and I felt that, however much he protested to the contrary, this was probably the way he wanted it to be, that he worked better under pressure when forced to produce something on a certain date and, in fact, if he were not occasionally up against an unalterable time-limit he would never conform to life at all. But not being so constituted myself, it dismayed me to find I was making mistakes through hurrying: typing badly, writing illegibly, packing parcels insecurely, resulting in the inevitable dash down the stairs with extra bits of string and sticky tape to catch A.B. as he went off, hot foot to his favourite letter-box because none other (and no other person) could really be trusted with his *magnum opus*. Often I longed to shout, 'Stop the Press, I want to get off!'

I once asked him whether he ever felt the need of a holiday and he was silent for a while. Then he said, 'I don't object to holidays. I've survived and enjoyed many a one in my younger days. But I wish people wouldn't think they're all that matters. Nowadays everyone seems so intent on making money but not real wealth. In the past most people enjoyed their *work*, took a pride in it, *created* something and were therefore satisfied. Now all they want to do is as little as they can for as much as they can and hop on a plane to the Costa Brava. When things get a bit too much,' he continued quite cheerfully and philosophically, 'I just let them flow over me. After all, you can't put a quart of water into a pint pot. . . . Now, would you write a nice, polite letter to this lady who wants to name her dogs after Charles II's mistresses and tell her I really haven't got time to look up the various ladies' names now. . . .'

13

Years of Achievement

'When a man, paid or unpaid, labours not
for remuneration, or even honour, but
because he has discovered satisfaction in
doing his work, whatever it may be, as
well as it admits of being done, he has
found the recipe for forgetting trouble.'

Illustrated London News,
29th August, 1964

At one of Christina Foyle's early Luncheons at the time when the
Nazis had just seized power, H. G. Wells made a speech which my
father, who was also speaking on that occasion, was always to remember. For Wells, having made especial reference to Germany and the
'clumsy lout's' rebellion taking place all over the world against liberal
civilisation, against thought, sanity and against books, ended with these
words:

'But . . . in the long run the judgement of books will win, and the
clumsy lout will be brought to heel. . . . In the long run the
judgement of books will settle with the braying and bawling
heroics of these insurgent louts. . . . Books are a refuge and a
reservoir of power. . . . Men may suffer and men may die, but
human thought embodied in science and literature goes marching
on. So I will make an end of speaking. Let us get back to enduring
things. Let us get back to our books.'

After the failure of Ashridge, A.B. went back to his books. Having
had his hopes dashed of being able to help build that better world about
which fighting men had dreamed during the war, in the fifteen years
between the late forties and 1963, he wrote his three most ambitious
histories, although of these years, five – between 1954 and 1959 – were
given up to two other books of a very different kind. *The Turn of the
Tide* and *Triumph in the West.*

The first of these major historical books was *The Age of Elegance*. Its early chapters on the end of the Peninsular War, completing the Revolutionary and Napoleonic War trilogy, had mostly been written before 1946. Only the account of Waterloo, for which all the material had long been prepared, and which, being quite apart from the rest of the book, he had left until last, was written in a single week in the spring of 1950 at the kind of concentrated all-out pace which, scarcely pausing to eat or sleep, had left him, he recalled, as exhausted as if he had been through the battle himself.

When portraying the post-war England of the Regency, A.B. had been engaged on a different, longer and far more difficult task: a comprehensive picture of an entire nation and people in time – their political history, social life, religion and thought, agriculture, trade and industry, architecture, art, literature and customs, not in isolated chapters but, as in life itself, a continuous living whole. His theme was a victorious country embarking on a long period of peace, a very different period from the impoverished and post-war one in which he was then writing.

'Britain's strength and prosperity was the wonder of mankind. She had annihilated the fleets of an enemy who, when war began, had nearly three times her population, defeated all attempts to keep her troops from the Continent, and, forcing Napoleon to expend half a million men in Spain, had roused and united Europe against him. In the closing months of the war she had subsidised the entire Grand Alliance . . . and in the process grown rich – richer than ever before. The twenty-two years' struggle had doubled her export trade and trebled her revenue. The carrying trade of the world was in her hands. . . .

'Cohesion without coercion, wealth without slavery, empire without militarism, such was the spectacle Britain presented. . . . Was the reality behind the splendid façade, the nation behind those proud white cliffs as strong and healthful as it seemed?'

This was the question which A.B. set himself to answer. 'Living,' he wrote in the Preface,

'in a post-war and revolutionary age, I have tried to describe . . . the impact of the bewildering economic, social and ideological phenomena of the time on a victorious Britain, which, without realising what was happening, was undergoing a major revolution, one which had been hastened, but concealed, by her long struggle and splendid victory. . . . What I have attempted is to show the synthesis between the Industrial Revolution and its aftermath and the society it both supported and undermined: to depict on a single canvas the nation's wealth and splendour, its tough, racy, independent rustic and sporting life, its underlying poverty and degradation, and the clash between its ancient faith and polity and its newer needs and aspirations.'

Much of *The Age of Elegance* is taken up with descriptions of that England in all its dazzling variety: its wealth, its brilliant metropolis, the beauty of its countryside, its arts and literature, elegance, class distinction and snobbery, sports and pastimes, injustices and social strains, the dark reverse of its brilliance and virility, its slums, Alsatias and grinding poverty. 'About nearly everything English,' he wrote,

'there seemed an air of what, to a foreigner, was almost an insulting opulence. The verminous tatters of the continental peasantry had no part in this tidy countryside; such distress as existed was tucked away out of sight. . . . One saw that illimitable wealth as one travelled the country; no class had ever enjoyed such riches as the landed gentry of England. . . . One saw it displayed in the west end of the capital, with its mile after mile of splendid mansions, wonderful clothes and horses, liveried servants and glittering barouches and landaus; in the new Edinburgh – a paradise, it seemed to contemporaries, of order, light and neatness – which had arisen from the crooked closes and stench of Auld Reekie; in the country towns with their crescents and railed squares aping London's West End, their exquisitely windowed shops and classical assembly rooms. . . .

'Almost everything the English rich did served the ends of style. . . . It filled London and Brighton, Cheltenham, Leamington and St. Leonards and the new suburbs of every ancient city with tree-lined avenues and Grecian and Pompeian crescents and terraces of white stucco and railed and green-painted *jalousies*. . . . It spread itself across the countryside, adorning it with park walls, crested gates and castellated lodges, with Ionic arches and obelisks and Corinthian pillars, with metalled turnpike roads traversed by beautiful equipages harnessed in all pride of the lorimer's art, with silver trappings and coloured housings and outriders in yellow and scarlet jackets.'

While A.B. was always in favour of a society where all were free to attain and aspire to ever higher standards, so long as it was within a framework of justice and order, in Regency England, he wrote,

'the rich had become almost too rich for reason. . . . The little set who under the dictatorship of the vulgar, haughty, indefatigable beauty, Lady Jersey, managed the dances at Almack's had introduced something new into English life: a rigid narrow pride as stupid as it was inhuman and uncharitable. . . . Stendhal, who visited London in 1821, found society divided like the rings of a bamboo, every class aping the manners and habits and striving to emulate the expenditure of the class above. . . . Under the influence of this restless competitiveness class feeling was turning into a religion. . . . It was here that the nemesis of the contemporary passion for elegance lay: so admirable when, as in the eighteenth century, it had arisen spontaneously from a widespread love and craving for beauty, so dangerous when it became an obsession, driving men of all classes to a heartless competitive extravagance. . . . Across the elegant surface of the national wealth ran a yellow streak. The cad – showy, heartless, deceptive, and bouncing – was a special product of the Regency; the Regent himself was one.'

In writing of that other side of Regency England, the Industrial North and Midlands, where the 'creation of wealth and the perpetuation of poverty went hand-in-hand', and where labour-saving machinery had effected a social revolution, 'it was a tragedy,' he continued, that

'the prevailing economic philosophy should have been so fanatically opposed to any protective regulation of conditions of employment. For here . . . was revolution more permanent . . . more terrifying than any wrought by mob or guillotine. A whole society was being transformed by the impact of whirling wheels and grinding machines, while the nation's traditional leaders, far removed from the wild moors, mosses and lonely valleys where the revolution was being enacted, stood aside and let it take its course. . . . In the industrial districts the whole appearance of the countryside was changing . . . the landscape was growing black, the villages turning into towns, the towns running each other. . . . The trout streams were being poisoned by dye-vats and the valleys studded with smoke-stacks; the willows and hazels of the Irk blackened and laid waste, the groves of birch, wild rose, and rowan and the green hills with the classical names and haunting rustic deities – Babylon Brow and Stony Knows – desecrated by money-grinders. . . .

'And every year machines exerted a greater tyranny over men's lives, forcing them to work yoked to automata which neither wearied nor rested. For the overall effect of machinery, though immeasurably multiplying and cheapening consumer goods, was disastrous for man considered as a producer. No longer was his work adapted in long-proved ways to his nature – his physical needs, pride, skill, affections. Instead he was forced into the unnatural mould of forms of work dictated by the capacity of machines and the figures of machine-made accountancy. He was deprived alike of liberty, the control of his tools, and of his familiar home, of access to the fields and the fresh fruits of the earth. Herded into factories like prisons and fever-haunted squatter towns like pig-styes, he saw his children grow up to a life utterly unlike that in which he and his forebears had lived. The old mould from which "God's Englishman" had been made was broken.'

The Age of Elegance, another Book Society Choice, won the *Sunday Times* £1,000 prize and Gold Medal for Literature and, in completing the Napoleonic trilogy, was instrumental in its author receiving, a few years later, a further gold medal from the Royal United Services Institution which awarded him its Cheney Gold Medal for a major contribution to Military History, a rarely-conferred honour which he shared alone with Winston Churchill in that decade. It was described in a review by his fellow historian, A. L. Rowse, as his 'most brilliant book', carrying the reader forward with 'a sweep across the bare landscape of Spain, the fields of France and Belgium, the smiling countryside of Regency England – England at the peak of its beauty. . . .' 'What,' Rowse continued, 'are his qualities as a historian? He has an extraordinary gift for historical landscape, so that his scenes live intensely in the mind; then there is the love of every sort of humanity, particularly the fighting man. . . . Suffusing the whole book, is the poetry, the poignant sense of the past, the feeling: how can one be a historian without these? He loves the past – a better recipe for understanding it than the superciliousness of the uncreative. . . . He is not a dry philosophical historian – though his reflections are often as much to the point as theirs: he is a descriptive narrative writer, with something of Dickens and again of Rowlandson in him – the humanity, the humour and the poetry.'

*　　*　　*

With the publication of *The Age of Elegance*, A.B. had completed ten years' work on the Revolutionary and Napoleonic Wars and their aftermath. Although he seldom took a holiday, he sometimes took a 'busman's' one by switching from one period of history to another. Before attempting a fourth and final volume covering, as he had intended, the years 1822 – 1840 and so linking his trilogy with *English Saga*, he decided to devote the next year or two to writing a boys' history of England.

The reason for this, however, was not entirely to get away from the early 19th century. He felt he might still be doing some practical service to his country, despite the failure of his hopes of being able to translate the great experiment of wartime Service education into the peacetime life of post-war Britain. The tragic end of General Paget's Ashridge achievement which, had it continued, might have pioneered a whole chain of similar country-house residential Community Centres and helped to bridge the fatal economic and political gap between the two sides of industry and the conflicting social classes they represented, was something he felt deeply. While continuing to devote himself to the writing of history, this time he intended to do so for the growing generation.

Yet when he set himself to his task, he quickly found that, outside the specialist knowledge of his ten years' pre-war work on the latter 17th century and his subsequent ten years' work on the early 19th century, he knew comparatively little about the history of Britain apart from what he had learned at school and university. Before long, in attempting to find answers to all the questions he needed to know, he found himself researching and writing, not so much a boys' history of England in one volume but, as he put it, 'an old boys' history in many'. As with his previous undertaking, once the research had begun, the material itself had 'taken over'.

In essaying this far greater project he retained, so far as the style and simplicity of the writing was concerned, his original design of a book that could be understood and read with pleasure by the young. It was this which made the first of his two volumes of *The Story of England: Makers of the Realm*, such an unusual and original book. The other quality which distinguished it and its successor, *The Age of Chivalry*, is that, while telling chronologically, and with illuminating first-hand detail, the political, constitutional and military history of the nation, it dealt, with an equal wealth of detail, with the more enduring achievements fo our medieval forebears – something often omitted from general political histories – in particular, the building and rebuilding of our cathedrals, abbeys and parish churches.

Yet of the difficulties which he had set himself, A.B. was only too well aware:

'In these days of specialised and cumulative scholarship, for one man to try to survey a nation's history in all its aspects is an act of great presumption. It involves problems of arrangement and writing so baffling that it is seldom attempted, and with reason, since, through compression and generalization on the one hand and the selection of misleading detail on the other, it can so easily lead to over-simplification and misrepresentation. I am very conscious of the imperfections of a work which seeks to cover a field of knowledge so much wider and deeper than any single mind can master. Yet, if my work has any virtue, it is that it attempts, however imperfectly, just this. For if the ordinary reader is to understand his country's past, someone must essay the task or the truth will go by default. . . .

'I have written for both young and old, for those who know a little of England's past and for those who know scarcely anything at all. My aim has been to set down in a small compass the essential things a man or boy should know who wants to understand his country's past. I have taken as little for granted as possible, but have told the story, so far as my scale admits, as it unfolded itself to the men and women of the time. Throughout I have tried to picture the outward form of their lives; to show how they lived and what our country looked like: to recall the warmth and actuality of an existence once as real as ours. Private lives have been as much grist to my mill as public, and the hearth as the throne. Chaucer's Canterbury pilgrims and Christian setting out with his burden have been seen as part of the same pilgrimage as Drake circumnavigating the globe or Gladstone touring Midlothian. . . .

'My history contains fewer names, battles, political events and Acts of Parliament, but dwells longer on certain deeds and words that stirred the hearts of Englishmen and awoke their imagination. For history, as a living poet has written,

> "is a pattern
> of timeless moments."

Paulinus and Aidan preaching to the Northumbrians; the Saxon thanes dying to the last man at Maldon and the house-carls in the stricken ring at Senlac; Becket towering above his murderers in the darkened cathedral, and the jingling Canterbury pilgrims riding through the Kentish fields "the holy blissful martyr for to seek"; Robin Hood in the greenwood, and the "grey goose feather" falling like hail at Crecy and Agincourt; the staplers with their wool-packs, and the church towers among the limestone woods and dales; such were the stuff out of which England's banner in time was woven. . . .'

In pursuit of his aim, now such a much more ambitious one than originally planned, A.B. found himself engaged on an intensive study of a period of history regarded as the specialist preserve of medievalists and in which he was handicapped by the lack of the personal floodlight thrown on the past in later periods by contemporary letters and diaries, and of which he had been able to make such use in his books on the 17th and 19th centuries. After he had spent two years on his first volume of *The Story of England*, he was immensely helped by the publication of the first volume of *English Historical Documents* with its wide and balanced selection of translated original sources for the early history of the country. Stimulated and informed by this first-hand insight into the medieval mind, he spent a further year completely re-writing and transforming it. As a result, to his surprise and pleasure – for he had always stood outside and, therefore, for all his meticulous scholarship, had found himself a little suspect as a populariser by the general academic world – its publication was hailed as something of a *tour de force* by the country's leading medieval scholars, traditionally jealous of the intrusion by historians of other periods into their own highly specialised field. Reviewing it, the Professor of Medieval History at Liverpool, Geoffrey Barraclough, wrote that, 'the familiar criticism of "popular" history, that it lags a generation behind scholarship, would misfire if levelled against this book, which takes its stand fair and square on the results of modern research,' while Professor David Douglas, the leading authority on the Norman period, predicted that 'If the remaining instalments sustain the high quality of this volume, we shall have the best popular history of the country.' The most valued tribute of all came in a letter from the doyen of English medievalists, Vivian Galbraith, then Regius Professor of History at Oxford, 'No brother historian will but envy the beauty and simplicity of the writing. You have achieved your avowed purpose more completely than any other book of its kind that I can remember.'

*   *   *

A year after the publication of the first volume of *The Story of England*, a book which brought its author a knighthood, he felt obliged to lay aside the work he was doing on its successor for a very different and even more exacting task. Some years before, he had been approached by the Royal Regiment of Artillery with a request to write the life, after his death, of the man regarded as its greatest living son, the Master Gunner, Field Marshal Lord Alanbrooke. During the last year of the war when Sir Alan Brooke, as he then was, had been Chief of the Imperial General Staff and, as Chairman of the Chiefs of Staff Committee, Churchill's and the Government's chief strategic adviser, A.B. had had to seek an interview with him on a minor though complicated and confidential matter. Realising that he could scarcely expect the great man to spare him much time, he had carefully prepared what he was going to say. But he became aware, almost as soon as he began to speak, that Alanbrooke had already grasped the reason for his visit. He had, he said, the quickest mind he had ever encountered.

Knowing what he did of Alanbrooke's war services, A.B. felt it was impossible for him to refuse to write his life, provided at the time of his death he was free enough of other commitments to do so. In the meantime it was agreed that the Royal Regiment should employ a research student, who had served on the Chief of Staff's secretariat during the war, to collect material about the Field Marshal's early life and his association with his wartime colleagues.

Four years later, in the autumn of 1954 A.B. was asked by the Royal Regiment if he would look at the material by then collected to see whether it was worth collecting any more. Valuable though it proved to be – for the research student had done her work well – by far the most important part proved to be a transcription by Alanbrooke himself of the private diaries which he had kept throughout the war, initially for the purpose of having what he called 'an evening talk on paper' with his much loved but absent wife, and relieving the well-nigh intolerable tensions of his lonely position. Having, since his retirement, deliberately put the war out of his mind and devoted himself to his beloved family and hobby of bird photography, he had refused all requests to write his wartime memoirs or to have his life written, until he learnt that A.B. was prepared to write it after his death. He had then unlocked his diaries and started to copy out for his biographer such passages as he felt would be helpful for him or proper to be published. So absorbed did he become in his task that he copied the diaries in their entirety, adding further recollections or 'autobiographical notes' which, remembered as they were in tranquillity, made his diary entries even more fascinating than before.

It was a copy of these remarkable diaries and additional notes which confronted A.B. on his return to London that autumn after three months' peaceful but concentrated work in the country on the faraway reign of Edward I. Its implications were enormous. It was obvious that these manifestly truthful diary entries made night after night and at the time, by this unambitious, yet brilliant and far-seeing soldier, contained the real story of how the vital decisions had been made which, in 1942, turned the tide of defeat into victory and wrested the initiative from, till then, a seemingly all-powerful and irresistible enemy. They showed that now, more than a decade later, the true history of how British strategic genius had decided the course of the greatest war of all time, was being obscured. A false, but almost universally-believed legend of how victory had been won was growing up which, in a few years' time, when public interest in the war would have faded, would be impossible to combat.

A.B.'s duty, as he saw it, was plain. However reluctant he was to lay aside his history of England, here was something essential to that history to which he felt he alone, at the moment, could contribute. His work for the Forces and his historical and military writings had brought him into contact with most of the Service chiefs who had directed wartime operations, and he knew from them how great Alanbrooke's contribution to victory had been. On November 30th, 1954, after a preliminary discussion with his trusted publisher, he accordingly wrote to the Field Marshal:

'I have re-read your very remarkable Notes most carefully and have thought a great deal about them. What they contain seems so important to this country that, if only a small part of it can now be made available in a form which will neither hurt nor create division and ill-feeling, I feel that there is much to be said for making the attempt. It is nearly ten years since the War ended and thirteen since you set in motion the train of events which led – after 1942 as I see it almost inevitably – to victory. Through that wonderful and very moving partnership between you and the Prime Minister this country contributed in that year something greater than its stand in 1940: the implementation of Churchill's brave definition in May 1940 of our war aim: "Victory in spite of all terror". I have always felt that Alamein was, strategically speaking, almost the most dramatic victory in our history – the only parallel is the battle of the Nile (so similar in many of its circumstances). And your Notes and narrative put it in its true setting and make it seem even more moving than before.

'The truth about it which they reveal – one which, if presented rightly and with discretion, could reflect nothing but credit on those concerned and, most of all, on this country – ought to be told while people, here and in America, are still sufficiently interested in the War to be receptive. If it is not told now, it may be too late. In that case, as with Haig and the British Army's achievement in 1916–18, a false legend will have been established which it may take a century or more to shake. And that legend will rob this country, as it has already partly done, of the credit of a magnificent achievement.

'Because of their complete truth and frankness, and partly because of their very brilliance the diary and Notes obviously cannot be published in full for many years. Even the full-length biography that the Royal Regiment wants written cannot be published within any foreseeable period, for, if it is to be regarded as definitive, it should not be published or even written in your lifetime – and even a Field Marshal can scarcely be expected to commit suicide in order that a false legend should be combatted before it is too late! Yet I feel that there is room, if you agree, for something to be done now – a work based on your diary and Notes – to make people realise how Britain in 1941–42 laid the foundations for victory.

'I should like to suggest the publication of a short book, to be called, say, "The Turn of the Tide", telling the story of what happened between the fall of France and Alamein and, in particular, of what happened in your first decisive year as C.I.G.S. If you decided it should be written, I should like to write that book, and I regard it as so important that I would be prepared to lay aside what I am doing now in order to write it. After studying your Notes very carefully I think it could be done in such a way as to cause no controversy or offence, and yet, by quoting from them wherever practicable, to present the story with something of the same vividness as you tell it. It would not, I admit, be easy, but I think I could do it.

'The object of the book as I see it, would be to tell the story of (a) how Britain held the ring of sea-power round Germany and Italy in Europe, first alone, and then with a desperately stricken Russia and a still unarmed America by her side, and so prevented them from breaking out to form with their Japanese ally a solid Axis block from the Pacific to the Atlantic; (b) how, while struggling for survival, she prepared the way for the counter-attack which began with Alamein, "Torch", and Stalingrad. That story would be the setting, as it were, of the jewel which I should extract from your Diaries and Notes. . . . It would make no attempt to deal with the details of operations (the business of the official war histories) but would, from the time you became C.I.G.S., focus the light solely on that little pinnacle of high decision on which you and the Prime Minister, the C.O.S. Committee, and the British and, later, American war leaders lived.

'The presentation of the story should, I suggest, be completely objective. I should make no comments and pass no judgements, even by implication, but let the story tell itself, as you and the P.M. wrestled with events, and slowly and in the face of so many difficulties wrested the initiative from the enemy. The principle that I think should be followed is that as much of the truth as can be told now should be told, and in as vivid a way as possible (that is, wherever practicable, by quoting from your diary and Notes) subject to the proviso that nothing should be said or used that could hurt or give offence to those who were your colleagues and companions. And, though this might somewhat modify the prevailing conception of the P.M.'s omniscient part in directing and dictating the entire course of the War – one which if left uncorrected will almost certainly be followed by a violent and damaging reaction after his death – it would not, I feel, diminish his stature, but, in the long run, enhance it. For the effect of your Notes has been to make me see him as, not a lesser, but a greater man – because so much more real and human than the rather boring and infallible image which a stupid propaganda is creating. Your pages, for all the natural and transient irritations of the hour, reveal better than anything I have ever read his courage, wonderful vitality and, above all, underlying mag-nanimity. I don't know which of the two I am left admiring more at the end – he for never overriding you when you stood firm despite all his passionate attempts to convince you against your will, or you, not only for your unerring strategic sense, but for both standing firm and staying put, when any other man would have lost his balance under the strain and thrown in his hand. You must often have almost hated one another, yet you finished the journey together. There seems something very fitting, after that companionship, that you should both be today Knights of the Garter.[1]

'For the rest, the book would give me the chance to do what I had hoped to do, had I been given the chance – in the unfinished official War history on sea-power 1939-45, on which I worked in my spare time for seven years for the Admiralty and Air Ministry – to present, free from all the cluttering mass of detail of official War history, the broad perspective of the War which you, and you alone I think, always saw clearly. In one of my chapters in *The Age of Elegance*, I called Wellington "Neptune's General" – and the title might apply as aptly to you. Had Hitler seen the strategic truth as you, I don't see how we could have held and turned the tide in that year of decision, 1942.'

For the next five years, therefore, A.B. put away academic history and entered into the much rougher and more troubled arena of contemporary military history. He had originally intended only to cover the eighteen months between Alanbrooke's assumption, on the eve of the fall of Singapore, of the chairmanship of the Chiefs of Staffs Committee and the landing in Italy in September 1943 which marked our return to the Continent and the culmination and triumph of all Alanbrooke's plans. But the public interest aroused by the diaries caused him after the publication of *The Turn of the Tide* in 1957 to continue, in close co-operation with Alanbrooke, to work on them for another two years until the publication in 1959 of *Triumph in the West* completed the story of Allied victory.

A.B.'s job as author of these two books was the researching and writing of the strategic narrative of a world-wide war to provide the background to Alanbrooke's laconic diary entries. It was the only way to make clear to the reader the nature of the problems and decisions which continuously faced the Chiefs of Staff Committee over which 'Brookie', as his friends called him, presided, and which 'an expert precision-instrument for directing a vast war-machine', became under his incisive chairmanship, that 'rarest of all military weapons – a Council of War operating with the consistency and speed of a single

---

[1] Earlier that year, through Alanbrooke's kindness, A.B. had witnessed Churchill's installation in the Garter Service in Windsor Castle Chapel.

will'. It was a task of immense complexity, taxing all A.B.'s powers as a military historian.

Only a few people like Attlee who, in Churchill's absences, had presided over the War Cabinet, Sir James Grigg, the wartime Secretary of State for War, and Lieutenant-General Sir Archibald Nye who had been the Vice Chief of Staff, appreciated the full nature of what A.B. accomplished. The public excitement and furore which attended the publication of the books was naturally concentrated almost entirely on the sensational and, so many of them being necessarily personal, ephemeral nature of the diary entries themselves. For here were the innermost thoughts of a man who, to most of his associates at the time, had presented a completely different image, someone who had seemed totally without nerves, aloof and imperturbable in the face of every danger and disaster. Yet the diaries revealed just what that 'front' had cost an intensely sensitive and imaginative man in terms of inner torment. 'We are bound to have some desperately anxious moments,' he wrote, while waiting for news of Alamein during that fateful October of 1942, 'there are great possibilities and great dangers. It may be the turning point of the war leading to further success combined with the North African attacks, or it may mean nothing. If it fails I don't quite know how I shall bear it.' Later, he wrote, 'I remember that evening as if it were yesterday . . . sitting at my writing-table in my Westminster Gardens flat, finishing those last lines and remaining seated staring into space.' 'Watching a battle from a distance,' he wrote to Montgomery, 'is far worse than being mixed up in the middle of it and absorbed by running it. . . . Since our return from Cairo I had been inwardly eaten up with anxiety as to the results of this attack. The very fact that these feelings had to be kept entirely to myself made them all the harder to bear.'

Although *The Turn of the Tide* and *Triumph in the West* were hailed as 'military classics and the most important publications on the Second World War that have appeared', their reception was also a stormy one. For although Alanbrooke, who had been at Churchill's side day in and day out for three and a half years, described the Prime Minister in his Foreword to *The Turn of the Tide* as 'the most wonderful man I have ever met; it is a source of never-ending interest studying him and getting to realise that occasionally such human beings make their appearance on this earth – human beings who stand out head and shoulders above all others'; and although A.B. had written of Churchill 'without him there would have been neither turn of the tide nor triumph in the west', there were many, especially in Churchill's immediate circle, who felt that the diaries denigrated him and by revealing his human side, lowered his stature.[1] Churchill at that time was a hero, a god. To the more reverent of his devotees there seemed something almost sacrilegious in Alanbrooke's affectionate but amused description of him in the Moorish bed at Marrakesh, dressed 'in his green, red and gold dragon dressing-gown, his hair, or what there was of it, standing on end, the religious lights shining on his cheeks and a large cigar in his face'; or again in his account of their flying the Atlantic for urgent consultation with Washington, Churchill, just before take-off, looking 'like Pooh Bear', humming 'We are here because we're here!' and both leaders, 'somewhat doubtful why we were going, whether we should get there, what we should achieve while we were there, and whether we should ever get back.'[2]

The Beaverbrook Press, in particular, came out with sharp criticism of *The Turn of the Tide*, Robert Pitman in the *Express* writing an extremely denunciatory article falsely implying that the authors had not submitted what they had written to the Secretary to the Cabinet and the War Office before publication, as they were officially bound to do. As this was both completely untrue and professionally highly damaging to A.B. as a responsible historian, the paper was forced publicly to apologise. Yet he was never a man who bore resentment for long. Some years later, when he met the brilliant young journalist who had written the article – the latter having been sent to interview him – the

---

[1] G. M. Trevelyan wrote to A.B. of *The Turn of the Tide*: 'So far from lowering my estimation of Winston, the book, to me, has raised it. Napoleon fell because he would never take counsel; his marshals were only his servants, whereas Winston treated his generals as his advisers. This habit of taking counsel, combined with his own personal qualities, is what won the war.'

[2] *The Turn of the Tide*, p. 399–400. 'We were facing a journey of twenty-seven hours in the air. . . . On our arrival in the flying-boat he' (Churchill) 'sent for the steward and said to him, "The clock is going to do some funny things while we are in the air; it is either going to go backwards or forwards, but that is of little consequence, my stomach is my clock and I eat every four hours".'

two became firm friends, so much so that A.B. dedicated *The Lion and the Unicorn* to the memory of 'Bob Pitman, who was both Great Heart and Valiant for Truth'. For although he was often bitterly upset and indignant at what he felt to be injustice, I knew from experience that it was always quickly over and that his inherent tolerance would reassert itself. 'After all,' he recalled, 'Pitman was only doing his job. For Beaverbrook[1] was such a staunch supporter of Churchill that any criticism of him, however mild, was taboo. It was Churchill who once paid Beaverbrook the finest of compliments one man can pay another. He called him a foul-weather friend.'

What mattered to A.B. far more than the criticism and controversy over the books, was the effect on his reputation as a serious academic historian of the sensational publicity accorded to them. The sales of both books in America and Britain were enormous, even greater than those which had attended the publication of his earlier histories; though owing to the incidence of taxation on higher levels of income, this benefited him but little. But there was one factor which made up for much. With great difficulty he had persuaded Alanbrooke to agree to share in his profits on a fifty-fifty basis and had advised him how, in the creation of a trust for his family, he could escape, as a first-time and non-professional author, tax on his share. It gave A.B. great satisfaction to think that this larger amount now went to Alanbrooke, and that he had thus been instrumental in redressing a gross injustice done to the former by the post-war Labour Government's decision to refuse him the parliamentary grant traditionally voted after victory to the country's principal war leaders. This had been promised by Churchill but, instead, Alanbrooke had merely received for his supreme war services a gratuity of £311. He had had, as a result, to sell his home and his cherished illustrated bird books in order to make ends meet.

Whatever knocks A.B. had taken over the publication of the Alanbrooke diaries, he was rewarded by the fact that he had done what he had set out to do. He had succeeded in ensuring the story of Britain's

---

[1] Whatever differences there may have been at the time were forgotten by Beaverbrook himself who, on meeting A.B. some years later, not only tried to persuade him to write for his papers, but wrote on the title pages of two of his own books which he presented to him: 'For Sir Arthur Bryant, the Master', and 'For Sir Arthur Bryant, with admiration and humility, Beaverbrook'.

achievement in the Second World War would not be 'transmitted to posterity without the figure of her greatest soldier'. 'When you started,' Alanbrooke wrote to him on the eve of the completion of *The Turn of the Tide*,

> 'I had no idea that you would be able to produce anything like this. You have seen so clearly what my strategy was and looked at the War through the self-same spectacles as I did, and, as a result, have handled my diaries and notes as no one else could possibly have done. I cannot find words to express my deep gratitude for what you have done . . . and for having so well understood what I aimed at during the War and my reasons for doing so. It has always been a source of some sadness to me that so far so very few have realised this. I do feel that your book will assist others to understand what my strategy was and why I stuck to it so fast.'

Three years later, after the publication of the sequel, *Triumph in the West*, Alanbrooke wrote again,

> 'When I look back at the stupendous task it was, I wonder how you ever had the courage to undertake it and the heart to carry it through.'

*   *   *

In 1960, A.B. returned once again to his real business in life: the writing of readable but scholarly history. 'It was a relief,' he said, 'to be getting back to people who had been safely dead for seven centuries!' Owing to his work on his own time, *The Age of Chivalry*, the second volume of his *Story of England* and probably his greatest historical work,[1] was not published until 1963; had it not been for the interruption of those five years, there might by now have been a third or even fourth volume. It proved a far more difficult task for its author than its

---

[1] The *New York Times* wrote, 'The sureness with which he moves through his material, the skill with which he chooses the detail, his ability to marshal the facts into a suspenseful narrative, all proclaim the top-drawer historian,' and the Swedish *Svenska Dagbladet*, 'Perhaps all that he has written before should be regarded as a long preparation for this masterpiece, the hallmarks of which are deep insight, thorough learning, and a brilliant art of presentation. Sir Arthur is a very convincing, a very great writer.'

predecessor. For, with the growing complexity of a nation's development, there was so much more to describe and explain than in the earlier volume. 'With little more than a century to cover in over 500 pages,' wrote the great medieval scholar, David Knowles, then Regius Professor at Cambridge, of his achievement, 'we are moving scarcely faster than the authors of the *Oxford History of England*, and to cover on that scale a period of such complexity and controversy is to expose oneself to perils of every kind, the more so as critical readers will carry fresh in their memories the volumes of Sir Maurice Powicke and Professor May McKisick. Without attempting to compare the incommensurable, it is fair to say that Sir Arthur achieves his end as well as they achieve theirs, and that not only the general reader, but even the historian of another period, would receive from these pages a clearer and more easily assimilated image of the age than he would from either of the volumes just mentioned, excellent and in the case of Powicke uniquely rich, as they are.'

Although *The Age of Chivalry* dealt with the comparatively brief period of the high Middle Age, it included the first evolution of Parliament, the beginnings of the legal profession, the legislative reforms of Edward I – 'the English Justinian' – the conquest of Wales and the Scottish Wars of Independence, the Hundred Years' War, the Black Death, the Peasant's Revolt, the building of the Decorated and early Perpendicular cathedrals and churches, the emergence of English as the national speech, the poetry of Langland, the genesis of the Inns of Court and the Oxford and Cambridge colleges:

> 'To anyone who has not thought deeply about it, it must seem utterly remote from our age, and utterly irrelevant. Yet without it, as I now see very clearly, the world we live in would not exist, not, that is, in the form we know it. For it was in what has sometimes been called the high Middle Age that England became, not a democracy as she is today, but what in a different form she still is and without being which she could never have become a democracy: a parliamentary monarchy – a society in which a strong central government was tempered and restrained, yet not nullified, by the existence of a consultative national assembly with the inalienable power to criticise and oppose that government and, in the last resort, to deprive of their power those who

misused it. It is this that makes a comparatively brief period in our past so immensely significant and so worth studying. . . .

'Before Plantagenet England can be understood its background must be realised. England was part, though an isolated part, of western Europe, and her king and nobles were of the same stock and spoke the same language as the French on the other side of the channel. She has to be seen in the context of that wider world. . . . This world of medieval Europe was far more harsh and cruel than ours, though some cruelties and strains familiar to us were unknown to it. . . . Yet on the borders of that violent world were the marches of Heaven and Hell; it was this that made it for its people exciting and significant. Most of the things they created and lived by have been destroyed. Yet some remain, a towering testimony to the strength and permanence of the greatest of their beliefs: their intense and abiding sense of the grandeur and immutability of God. To this day their vast cathedrals, made with puny tools and child's machinery, tower above the cities of modern Britain; there is nothing in Salisbury which compares with the tower and spire that Richard of Farleigh built in the time of the Black Death or with the choir and nave that his predecessors raised a century before. There was just as much folly, credulity, greed and vain glory in the age of faith as in any other; the sons of men do not change. It was a good time to live in for the fortunate so long as their fortunes lasted, and a bad time for those whom fortune passed by. Yet, when all is said that can be charged against them, there was something that the Middle Ages had that we have not. Stand beneath the west front of Wells or Lincoln or under the tower of Ely and think. And then look at the piled boxes of concrete, glass and girder erected today with one object and one alone, and that the most transient of objects, and think again. . . .'

PART THREE

14

At Rutland Gate

'There are only two things that matter
in this world. They are love and courage.'

Illustrated London News,
8th November, 1969

In 1969, six years after *The Age of Chivalry* came out, a short biography I had written about my late father was published, with a Foreword by Arthur Bryant. To my great joy, this book achieved an unexpected success, much of which I felt to be due to the kindness of the man I had yet to meet. The Foreword was based on a very moving tribute which he had written in *The Illustrated London News* nearly three years previously at the time of my father's death, and which had been especially appreciated by my mother and myself.

On May 6th, the same day as A.B. flew back to this country after one of his all-too-rare holidays abroad, he came to a dinner party to mark the publication of *My Father, A. G. Street*. Despite a tiring journey, the mountain of post which greeted him and what must have been an overwhelming desire to stay at home, he nevertheless came out to dinner in order not to disappoint someone whom he knew by correspondence only. I remember him well that evening as he came into the room, somehow larger than I had been expecting, shyer than I imagined and apologetic for being, as he put it mildly, still 'a little bemused by my flight'.

After this, just under two years went by before I actually began to do any work for him. During that period we met only occasionally on one or two social occasions, when I stood slightly in awe of such a distinguished historian. Yet in some respects, despite the overwhelming disparity in our respective knowledge, we shared a certain way of looking at things which made working for him, when the time came, that much easier.

Even so, it was by no means simple. My training as a secretary was nil; I had merely taught myself to type in my youth and my shorthand was non-existent. On my first morning at Rutland Gate – his London home for the past quarter of a century – when he passed me a pencil and notepad suggesting that I 'take a letter' in my fast but indecipherable longhand, the pencil promptly broke and the pad slipped to the floor. It was not a particularly encouraging beginning. I began to think I should never measure up to what was expected of me, and for some time felt that my sole qualifications for the job were that I was not afraid of work and was prepared to do it at all hours, as and when he required.

As the weeks went by I realised that this was something which meant more to my employer than any secretary, however efficient, who came and went at a certain time. Sometimes, when he had spent most of the night reading or studying his notes and therefore had not actually written anything at all, he confessed that he started worrying about what he was going to give his secretary to do when she arrived. He was then apt to present her with a whole mass of copy-typing from reference books – which was often never required – merely in order, I suspected, to get her safely ensconced in her little aerie out of harm's way on the third floor, leaving him on the first to get on with whatever he was doing in peace.

Although I felt that there was always more than enough checking, sorting and tidying to be attended to with which several secretaries could occupy themselves *ad infinitum*, without doing any typing at all, A.B. usually seemed either too absorbed or too loath to hand over even the filing to anyone else. Moreover, as it was a rule that nothing was ever discarded without his sanction, and as he was invariably far too occupied to give this sanction, it was inevitable that a stranger, faced with a tray of miscellaneous letters of varying dates from 1932 onwards, together with a suitcase full of press-cuttings and half a dozen cardboard boxes containing a collection of unaccountable articles of doubtful shape and antiquity, often felt defeated before starting.

On the other hand, as the day wore on and he had perhaps been writing non-stop, it was all any secretary could do to get his manuscript typed fast enough, especially with the forty-one stairs to compete with and the possibility of a couple of dozen letters suddenly and un-expectedly thrown into the affray about 4 p.m., many of which were required to catch the 5.30 post.

The daily drama surrounding the post at Rutland Gate was some-thing which needed to be thoroughly experienced to appreciate its *modus operandi*. Except to his nearest and dearest, to whom he was a prolific correspondent, A.B. loathed having to write or dictate letters, although when he did so he took infinite trouble and his personal ones were always little masterpieces, often illustrated by unusual spidery drawings of people or animals described in the text of the letter. But his method of dealing with his correspondence caused me, until I came to accept its capriciousness, acute anxiety and was, indeed, something about which we never saw eye to eye.

Although some factors never varied: that of keeping a Post Book in which all letters both received and sent were noted down, a rule that no stamp must ever be licked in case it was contaminated with germs, and that the Lancelot Place posting box was the only one which could ever really 'be trusted', I was never quite certain which letters A.B. might decide to answer or which he might 'sit on'. Rather like a squirrel, in and around his desk he appeared to have a labyrinth of little nests and cubby-holes in which he distributed his correspondence according to some deep-laid plot, the secret of which was impossible to fathom. Often a letter which I felt demanded an immediate reply would be relegated to a non-urgent compartment; occasionally one which I felt could conceivably wait had to be answered at once. Sometimes, a letter which was typed and ready for signature was, for some unaccountable reason, held back in a state of suspense, while A.B. presumably cogitated on whether to send it or not, or simply forgot about it altogether.

To my annoyance, if such a neglected missive (often looking the worse for wear) managed to surface and inadvertently caught his attention, he might happily post it off still dated a month or so pre-viously. Or, equally to my annoyance, he would decide to re-write. 'I owe you a most contrite apology,' he would dictate, 'for not having answered your letter before, but I have been working the clock round to finish my book on Wellington. . . .' 'But,' I might venture, 'you're replying to someone who wrote to you over a year ago. Isn't it one of those occasions when you consider the time lag means the letter has answered itself?' 'Not at all,' might come the cryptic reply, 'this time I've merely delayed. It's quite understandable. I've been working, as you know only too well, all out on *The Great Duke*. You have to put first things first. Think how delighted Mrs. H—— will be when she receives a reply just when she's given up hope. Now, where was I?' 'A most contrite apology for . . .' I would begin, faintly, and off we would go again.

That this refusal to deal regularly with his day to day correspondence maddened many of his associates was inevitable. As his secretary, I felt it was extremely naughty of him and my sympathy went to his correspondents. Having been strictly brought up to answer every letter by return, it took me a long time to get used to this completely different attitude to the daily post. And as the spring of 1971 gave way to summer and A.B. went 'all out' on finishing his current book, *The Great Duke*, a study of Wellington as soldier and commander, it seemed as if I was left to plough my way uncertainly along between a growing mountain of mail on one side and Wellington marching through India and the Peninsula on the other.

It was the great duke, of course, who mattered. Often I felt A.B. was no longer sitting in the library at Rutland Gate. He was out there taking the army across the Kaitna before the battle of Assaye or holding the Lines of Torres Vedras. Even now, on his daily sortie into Hyde Park – of necessity somewhat temporarily curtailed – he seemed to be striding along, deep in thought, deciding whether to order Uxbridge to launch the Household Cavalry or wondering whether Blücher would come up in time on the field of Waterloo. Rather like an actor who 'lives' the part he is playing, A.B., when writing about Wellington, *was* Wellington; when writing about the early invaders of this country, he *was* an early invader, rocking precariously about in some little coracle as he navigated the English Channel.

This intense, chameleon-like quality for entering into the past and conveying it to the reader with such lucidity was, at times, almost uncanny. After *The Great Duke* was published, among the myriad of letters he received, were two which expressed this particularly well.

164

'It is really a *tour de force*,' wrote Harold Macmillan, 'and brings to the inexpert reader a sense of drama of a military campaign which is unrivalled in any similar book.' The other letter came from Macaulay's great nephew, Lord Trevelyan, and read: 'It is really a great book . . . so vivid that it does not seem to be history but has an immediate quality, making one feel that one is present at events happening now . . . the final impression left by the account of Waterloo is overwhelming. . . .'

It was hardly surprising, therefore, that when he was engaged in producing such a work, and suddenly the present day broke into his train of thought in the form of an unimportant telephone call at a point where he was just beginning to get the better of Napoleon, the unfortunate caller was apt to be treated as his arch enemy. It could, of course, be perfectly reasonably suggested that A.B.'s secretary was not doing her duty in allowing him to be so interrupted. But the curious answer to this would be that he had an obsession about answering the telephone himself, unless absolute pressure of work, such as the final all-out race-against-time to finish a book, precluded it. He was a 'telephoner' *par excellence*. He had two numbers – both ex-directory – at Rutland Gate. One belonged to a cherished private instrument which he carried about in a hold-all (once absent-mindedly packing it in his luggage, where it turned up with him eighty miles away) but which was customarily plugged into a socket in his library or beside his bed, thus avoiding the possibility of anyone listening-in to his conversations. The other number related to a slightly more 'public' instrument with ordinary extensions all over the house. Yet even when this rang, however annoyed at being disturbed, it seemed as if he had some inner compulsion to 'see who it was' himself, and it was quite a while before I was entrusted to handle any such calls at all. When I was at last allowed to do so, if A.B. happened to come into the room and overhear what I was saying, he would invariably admonish me – sometimes most disconcertingly while the call was actually taking place – to be 'a great deal firmer' and not to sound 'so apologetic'.

Occasionally, I would arrive for work to find him pacing up and down his library fuming with rage because, through some fault on the telephone exchange, he was being plagued by calls from people asking for tickets for a concert at the Albert Hall. The next hour or so would then be spent in mock warfare. A.B. would sit on his private line asking for the *Chief* Supervisor (no lesser a personage would do) who, if found to be only momentarily out of her office, would simply add to his indignation, and though not actually accused of 'stuffing herself with quails at the Dorchester', was almost certainly, according to him, 'drinking herself to a standstill on coffee at the canteen'. While hostilities were being waged on his private line at one end of the library, I was asked to man the guilty instrument at the other, with strict instructions to ascertain where each of the provoking calls was coming from. During the brief periods of respite when neither of us was actually engaged in speaking, I was further instructed to 'take a letter' protesting to the Postmaster General, *The Times* or *The Telegraph*. Eventually, when the Chief Supervisor had at last been run to earth and had referred him to the Chief Engineer (whose important identity was meticulously noted down for future attack), A.B. would put down the receiver and rumble on: 'I suppose the powers that be are all saying, "There's that man again." ' On occasions, he had an endearing way of being able to laugh at himself.

Another thing which both irritated yet amused him was when he was congratulated, as he so often was, on being able to write so easily, as if it poured out of him like ectoplasm and that all he had to do was pick up paper and pencil and the rest was 'money for jam'. Even for such a hard-working and best-selling author as Arthur Bryant, most of the 'jam' was scraped away by the tax man, and the sheer mental and physical effort involved in the writing of history such as his, where every fact down to the last little footnote had to be checked and re-checked, often left even his robust constitution drained of all vitality. His books were not novels where he could push his characters around at will. His people were real. What they did actually happened. Wellington was the one who did the pushing; it was up to A.B. to ascertain exactly how, when and where he pushed and present this to his readers in the most accurate, yet attractive, form possible.

'Sometimes,' he would say to me mournfully, after I had arrived to find he had been plagued by a series of time-wasting telephone calls or pestering letters, 'I believe people seem to think I'm some kind of public benefactor. And look at this,' he expostulated one day, riffling through his post, 'Does this dear lady whose name might be Badger or Bodger or even Dodger, *really* think I've got the time or the inclination – even if I could read her signature – to delve into her dubious ancestry and work out whether she is a descendant of Mary Queen of Scots on her mother's side? Just write a firm, polite note saying . . .'

Although every day he received countless, genuinely sincere, appreciative and often very moving letters about his writing, which were forwarded via his publishers or *The Illustrated London News*, he was often beset by these other kind of letters, the senders of which seemed to take it for granted that he would automatically comply with their requests. 'Dear Sir Arthur,' they would begin, 'I am sorry to bother you but I have written a book about my great-uncle in Tasmania (or my aunt in Tahiti, as the case might be) which I feel sure you would be interested to read and would be glad of your advice as to how to get it published.' Often the writers failed to soften the blow by any kind of apologetic preamble, merely launching into an attack based on some misinformed assumption such as, 'Dear Sir Arthur, Although I did not see you myself, I have been told by the sister of a friend that last night you appeared on television leading a demo together with Miss Bernadette Devlin, and I shall never read another word you write unless you can assure me that it was not you. . . .' There seemed no end to the variety of queries and demands with which he was faced. They fell through his letter-box like insidious snow-flakes: 'Dear Sir Arthur, Can you come and light a bonfire, restore a church, give a lecture, make a speech, fly to Newcastle, lend your name, send your autograph, chair a meeting, become a President, write a Foreword, give an interview, do a broadcast, write to the Prime Minister, ring up the Queen. . . .'

Often he would acquiesce if he felt the cause or the person justified it. The example of duty and *noblesse oblige*, instilled into him in youth, made it difficult for him to refuse calls on his time which he could so ill afford. What one felt he should have been doing was getting on with the important work which he alone could do: write history. Yet he somehow felt it incumbent on him to take on a variety of charitable duties which only increased the consternation as to whether a particular historical work would be published on the appointed date, and which certainly gave rise to a further kind of fan letter: 'Dear Sir Arthur, How much longer do we have to wait for the fourth volume of Pepys?' or 'Dear Sir Arthur, Where is the third volume of *The Story of England*?'

With *The Great Duke* scheduled to be out in time for Christmas 1971, it seemed as if the summer of that year at Rutland Gate passed in a state of almost wartime emergency. It was hot, very hot. A.B., dressed in his oldest clothes and with a curious straw hat perched on top of his head, would often write out of doors, sitting on the little balcony at the back of the house, surrounded by papers, books, 'Bear', his writing-pad and a bag of stale bread for an army of hungry, inquisitive pigeons.

One day, I arrived to find him there looking very worried. 'Something serious has happened,' he said. I thought maybe he had lost a chapter or I had omitted a sentence in the previous evening's typing (a heinous crime about which he was most censorious). But no: 'It's the pidgies,' he continued. 'I've just been told by an ornithologist friend that bread is very bad for them. Blows them up. Ruins their livers. What must I have done to the poor things?' I looked at the bevy of healthy well-fed birds around him, strutting about without a care in the world. Even the fat, sleek, silly one whom I called the 'Company Director' was sitting on the fence looking particularly pleased with himself. I laughed. 'It's all very well for you to laugh,' said A.B., seriously. 'Bread must be off their menu from now on. I want you to go out and buy a packet of bird seed. My ornithologist friend says you can get special stuff for wild birds.' I said I would go as soon as I had typed Wellington over the Pyrenees. 'But I want you to go *now*,' replied A.B. 'The pidgies want their lunch. How can I sit here and let them watch me eat mine? It wouldn't be fair.' I picked up my bag and started down the stairs, marvelling that, for once, pigeons had taken precedence over the great duke. As I opened the front door A.B. called out over the banisters, 'Better buy at least two dozen packets. . . . It looks as if there might be a strike.' The possibility of any kind of strike caused a certain amount of consternation in his mind lest it should interrupt his work, and resulted in the necessity for 'taking precautions'.

Of all the mental pictures I have of A.B., I think the one I retain most vividly is of him sitting on the balcony at Rutland Gate feeding his pigeons; that, and perhaps the times when he became a host. He looked much more happy on those occasions, more relaxed. He obviously enjoyed entertaining and giving others a meal, whether it was pigeons or people, and the latter was something he did with generosity and to perfection. He never had more than four guests to dinner, usually just one or two; but he took infinite trouble over the preparations, turning himself into amateur butler, seeing to the wine and getting out the silver.

Sometimes I was asked to assist on these occasions. I felt them to be evenings not altogether of the present day; they seemed to belong to another era, Edwardian perhaps. The conversation, the candlelight and the courtesy of the host as he poured the wine, seemed to set them apart. Even the house itself appeared different. It came alive and gave the impression that this was what it was intended for. Nearly all the other houses in Rutland Gate had been turned into flats or embassies, but Number 18 remained what it had always been: a residence. One forgot about the inconvenience of the stairs, that all the electric light switches were in the wrong places, that the kitchen sink was too low and the stove almost obsolete. The flowers, the portraits, the furniture and the way that the host had specially re-arranged it all for the evening, gave the place an elegance and a dignity which delighted all who came there. Perhaps this was never more aptly described than by John Betjeman who, after dining at Rutland Gate one late spring evening in 1972, wrote afterwards: 'The memory of that burgundy lingers yet, so deeply satisfying in the mysterious half-light of your stately Victorian mansion. I enjoyed every moment of it. . . .'

15

The Country Lover

'I have now settled down to advanced middle
age and all its unromantic limitations. I
still have pipe-dreams, but they are of a
more reasonable kind. I want to excel at
my profession and to make things grow.'

Illustrated London News,
17th July, 1950

When I first started working for A.B. in 1971 I was disconcerted to
find calving lists appearing amongst his manuscripts. I was also dis-
tressed to discover how much time he spent studying them. Moreover,
despite being a countrywoman myself, I was more than a little annoyed
to be asked to study these lists also and check Duchess's or Bluebelle's
'due date'. For I was painfully aware how concerned his publishers
were about another kind of date: the delivery of his next book. I
remember regarding his cows as a tremendous nuisance. To me A.B.
was a historian, a famous historian who lived in London, a place
where he had grown up and in which he had always had some kind of
home or *pied à terre*. But I really knew so little about him, and that
which I did know – especially as he was always desperately busy and
tantalisingly elusive about everything except his work – had to be
'picked up' as I went along. Whenever a formal engagement forced
him to change out of his ancient and disreputable clothes (admittedly
more suitable for the West Country than the West End), he seemed the
complete 'man about town'.

It was true that he disappeared every so often for fleeting visits to a
country house in Buckinghamshire and a somewhat – at least, to me –
mysterious farm twenty miles away from it. It was also true that I had
read with great interest and delight some nostalgic accounts of his
various country homes and farming pursuits in *The Lion and The*

Unicorn, published in 1969, about which I should like to have learned more. The book consisted of some seventy of the seventeen hundred weekly articles which he had by then written for *The Illustrated London News*, together with a few longer pieces such as *The Summer of Dunkirk*, first published in 1943. In its Prelude he described it as partly autobiographical and reminiscent, partly a commentary on the times and partly a profession of faith. Although such an uncommunicative man about anything personal, the book nevertheless did reveal two things quite clearly: his love for the English countryside and his belief in Christianity. Its Epilogue in particular, where he wrote with great simplicity and conviction about the latter, was constantly bringing him appreciative letters long after publication, and to which I sometimes helped him reply.

He had sent me a charmingly-inscribed copy of *The Lion and The Unicorn* some months after I first met him but a year or so before I came to work at Rutland Gate. Yet when I did so, possibly because all his compulsive energy was then concentrated on another of his books and I was caught up in this vortex, I failed to appreciate just how much the 'country habit had him by the heart', and had done so ever since, as a child, he had fallen in love with Wincombe – and, through it, England – 'in that little corner of earth where Wiltshire joins Dorset and the infant Nadder rises'. He had been born in the country – in Norfolk. It was here, he wrote, 'I first breathed the air and woke to consciousness. . . . And whatever chance brings me to that coastline, the years drop away and I am back where I began, a spirit of air and earth and water before the heavy, indigestible weight of flesh and experience made me what I am.'

> 'It is a land of little, wide-open, wind-swept harbours, where tiny yachts and sharpies tack up and down between sandbanks and mud-flats; of fast-moving grey seas flecked with white; of air like the finest vintage champagne, crisp and invigorating yet light as thistle-down. . . .'
>
> 'Here, the Anglo-Saxons, who are the dominant strain in our long, mixed ancestry, landed and became seized of the land which bears their name. The wild duck, straining in a trembling V across the moving waste of waters . . . are the prototypes of that

remote sea-folk out of whose loins we spring. They came fiercely facing and bringing death, but creating, even as they slew and fell, life which was to endure and far transcend their own simple beginnings: the free, courageous life of England that has gone out into every corner of the world and infused on both shores of the Atlantic the love and institutions of freedom.'

For though most of his early years had been spent in London, the poet's nature inherited from his mother had made him, even as a child, unusually sensitive to the beauty of his native land. 'It is difficult to believe,' he wrote in an article shortly before I came to work for him, 'that there can ever have existed on earth a countryside lovelier than that of this island sixty or seventy years ago. . . . For all the horrors of the grim utilitarian drabness of South Lancashire and the smoking minefields and South Welsh valleys and the nightmare East End of London, the England on which I opened my eyes at the turn of the century was transcendently beautiful.'

I came to realise that this intense love of the countryside and the beauty of its landscape was something which ran through all A.B.'s books, recurring again and again, possibly most of all in *The Age of Elegance*, when England was its loveliest and 'man had everywhere civilised nature without over-exploiting and spoiling it'.

'The first thing that struck every visitor to England was her beauty. It derived from her exquisite turf and foliage and soft, aqueous atmosphere; what Leigh Hunt, pining among the Appenines for the buttercup meadows and elms of the vale of Hampstead, called the grassy balm of his native fields. Everywhere was the sense of peace, wealth and security: the avenues of huge elms, the leafy Middlesex landscape, the great trees on Hampstead's airy height, the blue horizons, the farmhouses of beautifully fashioned brick and stone, the pastoral Thames still set, as Horace Walpole had pictured it, amid enamelled meadows and filigree hedges, with brightly painted barges, solemn as exchequer barons, moving slowly up to Richmond or down to Syon, the sculptured, classical bridges, the wayside alehouses with placid drinkers under their spreading oaks and chestnuts, the old grey churches and barns, the ghostly trees in the evening twilight, the drinking cattle and homing rooks, the mystery and the mist.'

Through his study of the past A.B. was very conscious that it was the larger hereditary landowners, forever planting, building and improving who had first taken the lead in this civilising and beautifying process, transforming the old medieval England of forest, heath and open field into 'the landscape immortalised by Constable and the great English water-colourists'.

'The countryside was dotted with their lovely palaces and noble avenues, the fields and woods of the whole kingdom were open to their horses and hounds, the genius of man, past and present, was brought to decorate their houses and gardens, to fill their libraries with masterpieces of the classical and modern mind in bindings worthy of them, to cover their walls with paintings and tapestries, and adorn their tables with exquisite silver and porcelain. Theirs was an ample and splendid design for living. . . .'

And English country houses, as he wrote, ranged

'from palaces like Blenheim, Petworth and Castle Howard to unassuming residences of pilastered stone, brick or white stucco little bigger than the houses of the professional classes in the county towns, but set amid the common denominator of park, lawn and drive. They were, above everything else, the distinguishing ornament of the landscape. A gentleman stranded on the road could be sure of shelter under the roof of one of his own kind, where he would find, though with infinite variations, the same classical or Gothic architecture, the same fine furniture of mahogany, walnut and rosewood, the same oriental carpets and china and their English counterparts, the same ancestral worthies in gilded frames flanked by masterpieces or pseudo-masterpieces from Italy and Holland, the same libraries of leather-bound books containing the solid culture of three centuries. And outside would be the cedars, the close-mown lawns, the flower-beds, conservatories and ice-houses, the vistas cunningly blending the artificial with the natural, lawns, park, water merging into the landscape which they commanded and to which they belonged.'

Sometimes I would come across A.B. poring over photographs in *Country Life* of the stately homes which he felt had contributed so much to the past life of England, and I could not help wondering whether, in his mind's eye, he was picturing himself living in one or another of them. A quarter of a century earlier, immediately after the war – as I later learned – when so many country houses were empty and when few, in that time of shortages and controls, were prepared to cope with the daunting problems of restoring and living in them, A.B., needing a house large enough for his ever-growing accumulation of books, papers and manuscripts, had entered into negotiations with the owners of several smaller, temporarily abandoned historic houses, with a view to renting and restoring one of them. That the kitchen quarters would need completely renovating and the plumbing brought up to date were problems which, although of necessity he devoted a good deal of time and thought to them, entered far less into his considerations than the potential beauty of their deplorably dilapidated rooms and overgrown gardens. Of one such house, a former medieval monastery, where the kitchen was over twenty feet high, he had optimistically brushed aside the objections of the long-suffering distaff side of his household by pointing out that the flies on the ceiling would be far too far away to bother them! He was, as a mutual friend remarked to me, 'naughty' about kitchens.

Yet there was no doubt he was extremely 'good' about furniture; his 'passion for many years', as he described it to me.

'Though I have never been able to afford "collectors' pieces", I have enjoyed an immense amount of happiness first in buying – mostly at sales – and then in using and constantly observing beautiful household objects. Most of them have been old relics of the seventeenth, eighteenth and early nineteenth centuries – partly because so few beautiful pieces of domestic furniture have been made since; partly because, being a social historian, I am naturally interested in the evidences of past modes of life. The pleasure I have had in them has nothing to do with the price I have paid for them (except so far as good fortune in this respect has enabled me to enjoy what I could not otherwise have hoped to enjoy), still less with the price I might have got for them had I wanted to sell them. It has been, in other words, an aesthetic pleasure, not a commercial; a human one, not a synthetic. I can't think of anything, except my work, which has given me such continuous, unbroken satisfaction as the sight and daily use of these beautiful things. . . .

'Every week, during the summer and winter seasons, for as many years as I can remember, there has flowed through the great West End salerooms of London a never-ceasing stream of beautiful objects. . . . It has been my practice . . . whenever in London, to take an afternoon walk once a week to Bond Street or St. James's, to look at them, to learn from them, to admire and sometimes, I fear – for human nature is greedy for beauty – to covet some of them; and always to marvel at the genius and ingenuity of man and the glory of great craftsmanship. And they have made me realise, better perhaps than anything else visible and tangible, the greatness of my country's past and of its tradition. For the vast majority of those lovely treasures, issuing from the homes and country houses of England in an apparently inexhaustible procession, were made by Englishmen, many of them very humble Englishmen. They were called into existence by the demands of a society that valued beauty of design and craftsmanship far more highly than we value it today and which, as a result of that demand, enabled large numbers of men to devote their lives to the making of beautiful things. Nothing can make me believe that the lives of such men were poorer than those of their present-day descendants who, with a higher standard of living and a greater measure of social security, are doomed by the society for which they labour to spend their working lives manufacturing objects in whose creation there is little pleasure and pride for themselves and in whose possession little aesthetic enjoyment for others.'

This highly developed feeling for all things beautiful, be it old houses, antique furniture, the English countryside, pictures, music, poetry or pretty women, permeated all A.B.'s more prosaic undertakings, adding, to a surprising degree, a sense of romance and extravaganza to his daily life. His talent for re-creating the ambience of days gone by in his own homes paralleled that which he displayed in his books. Even his disregard for modern labour-saving devices only tended to exemplify the way he unconsciously 'adopted' another century. But if something did not quite come up to his artistic standards, if the arrangement of a room or the hanging of a picture failed to please, he behaved in exactly the same, and often maddening, way as he did with his writing. He kept changing it all round until it did. In the creation of both books and houses – and it was sometimes hard to say which mattered more – he wanted perfection.

*　　*　　*

Before the war, for more than twenty years his home had been at East Claydon in Buckinghamshire. At the end of the war, finding his beloved White House no longer practicable in the changed conditions of the time, he had reluctantly migrated to a little Gloucestershire William and Mary manor house called Rapsgate which, though of the same modest size as the White House, possessed what the other lacked: separate accommodation for a married couple. Set among the Cotswold sheep-walks above Colesborne and the deep combes that slope southwards from Elkstone, its new tenant recalled Rapsgate as 'standing like some enchanted fairy-tale hunting lodge among its sentinel yews'.

Yet for all its beauty, this new home never took the place of the White House in Buckinghamshire, where his heart had been so deeply rooted and where he had written *Charles II*, the three volumes on *Pepys, English Saga, The Years of Endurance* and *Years of Victory*, as well as a number of lesser books, including *Postman's Horn* – an anthology of 17th century letters partly based on his transcription of the Shakerley manuscripts, and *The American Ideal*, the published version of the *Watson Chair* lectures on American history and biography which he delivered at University College, London in the winter of 1935–6.

During the two years after A.B.'s move to Rapsgate in 1945, he had continued to look for a permanent country home to take the place of the White House. He sought it first in the familiar elm and clay lands of North Buckinghamshire and its neighbouring counties and, when this failed, in the Dorset he had so loved during childhood holidays. Here, he had negotiated in turn for the lease of three beautiful and then empty 18th century houses: Chettle, Cranborne Lodge and Steepleton. Yet none had offered what he wanted, a chance to farm, a desire which, when he told me about it, seemed in some curious way to tie up with the work on which he had been in those distant days engaged: depicting the pastoral England of the Regency.

This ambition had obviously been forming in his mind for some time, as I discovered on coming across among his papers, a symposium, *Return to Husbandry*, to which, in 1943, he had contributed the opening essay, stressing the need to 'replace a mechanistic conception of society by an organic, and man as a mere consumer and middleman by man as a producer and craftsman'. It showed that among his unceasing activities during the war he had somehow found time to attend discussions and become a member of a small group interested in organic farming called the Kinship of Husbandry. Through it he had become friends with several pioneer farmers and leading soil-conservationists, including Lord Lymington – then soon to become the Earl of Portsmouth – Rolf Gardiner, Sir George Stapledon, Lord Northbourne and H. J. Massingham. The experience had made him feel that, if he were still to have a country home after the war, he ought to take some active part in the productive work of the countryside.

It was this which had caused him, early in 1948, to accept the offer of 80 acres of a derelict wartime gunnery range which the Army was about to de-requisition on the Dorset coast and, with it, the ancient and romantic Purbeck manor house of Smedmore, on whose interior and gardens – a shambles after long military occupation – he was to spend the next eight years restoring to their former beauty, while simultaneously writing *The Age of Elegance* and *Makers of the Realm*. Until the land was de-requisitioned, he market-gardened, and then, as soon as he was able, started to farm, explaining to me, with a certain amount of dry humour, that one of his first operations had been the ploughing up of a live shell.[1] 'I had a lot to learn,' he continued. And so, apparently, had the succession of equally inexperienced young ex-servicemen with an enthusiasm for organic farming whom he enlisted to help him in his bold enterprise. Yet the experience, the knowledge which gradually came with it and the actual work on the land itself proved reward enough for him, something he was never to forget or regret.

---

[1] At Southern Command Headquarters where, owing to his close association with the Army, he was no stranger, the day on which this fortunately harmless incident occurred was long known as 'black Monday'!

'All afternoon and evening we worked in the cornfield, stooking the crop which was to feed our little stock, and so, indirectly, man, during the coming year. The machines for cutting and binding arrived late, and several days of a week of sunshine had been lost waiting for them; the air was translucent and the distant horizon of cliffs and sea so beautiful that the thought of rain was never far away. We therefore worked urgently, following close in the sweeping tracks of the binder, moving slowly in from the wide circumference towards the narrowing heart of shimmering corn. None of us, save the men on the machines, was very experienced in the art but, knowing what depended on it, we worked with a will and with that steady unceasing compulsion which all work with living nature seems to necessitate. The goal in our minds was not the hour at which labour ceased, but the completion of the work, the last stook stacked, the field clear and garnered.

'Even the beauty of the scene was incidental. Only occasionally did we raise our eyes from that high, slanting field, sparkling and rustling in sun and wind, to take in the wonderful panorama below: the old grey house, with its William and Mary red brick chimneys rising out of the trees, the green clay pastures stretching to the margin of the sea, and the tawny downs, the jagged cliffs of shale, limestone and chalk spread in fantastic panorama from Broad Bench to Ringstead, the blue of Weymouth Bay and Portland lying like a distant giant floating on the bosom of the Channel, the high, white clouds driving like solitary galleons out of the west. No more beautiful setting to the husbandman's business can have ever existed, and, as the shadows lengthened and the rooks began to wheel home, its loveliness and peace surpassed the human power of description. Our throats and lips were parched, our feet battered by the iron, uneven ground, our bodies pierced with innumerable spear-points of oats and barley, but, as the corn vanished and the stooks rose, in sunlight, twilight and, last of all, in moonlight, a feeling of aching triumph and satisfaction overcame weariness. We had been all-day participants in a battle and it was nearly over. The enemy, next winter's want, on our little piece of the farming front – all that we could see and experience – was in retreat. A victory had been won.'

That first harvest was essential. Only licensed farms were then allowed to purchase animal feeding-stuffs, and there had been no farm at Smedmore before the war. With food for pigs and poultry and, later, beef-stores, it proved possible to make a start. But success only came after an advertisement for an assistant to the current farm manager brought a reply from a North Country farmer's son who had been invalided out of the Army and, after an apprenticeship in racing stables at Newmarket, had graduated to a Midland Jersey farm. He turned out to be a genius at breeding, just as Smedmore, with its mild Channel Island climate turned out to be an ideal habitat for Jerseys. Buying old pedigree cows at knock-down prices, he bred from them a young herd of distinction which placed Smedmore at the top of the National Milk Records averages for small and, presently, large Jersey herds in Dorset.

Then nemesis struck. Early in 1955, when the herd was thriving, the right staff had at last been found after much trial and error for both farm and house, and the latter had been transformed from a near ruin into a comfortable home of great beauty, the whole of its vast stone roof, which the landlord had undertaken to make good in return for the restoration of the interior and gardens, was found to be in danger of imminent collapse. For more than a year, A.B. sought every way to avert the inevitable, but as, once the roof was off, his domestic staff would be without anywhere to live for an indefinite period, he finally secured what compensation he could from his landlord and prepared to move to his boyhood's other home, Wincombe, thirty-five miles away on the Wiltshire–Dorset border. This, to his embarrassment – for his hands at that time had been more than full turning Smedmore into what he had hoped would be his home for the rest of his life – had been unexpectedly offered him by its then owner three years earlier. After long hesitation, in order to save its threatened beechwoods he had managed with great difficulty to borrow enough capital to buy what remained of the estate, including the house and 140 acres of woodland. His intention had then been to continue living and farming at Smedmore until the end of his existing 21 year lease, using the 40 acres of park in hand at Wincombe for feeding young stock and dry cows and recovering, as it became possible, the rest of the land from his two farm tenants before gradually converting it to good leys and pasture to supplement, and one day take the place of, the 80 acres which was all he had at Smedmore to feed his growing milking-herd. In the meantime his 78-year-old widowed mother, in order to help him look after Wincombe, gallantly volunteered to move from her nearby home into the empty house.

Its possession thus proved a lifeline in an otherwise hopeless position. In the autumn of 1956 he moved there, crowding his household furniture, pictures and books into the part of the modest Regency house – a much smaller one than Smedmore – not occupied by his mother. The herd followed a year later as soon as he was able to buy out from his two sitting farm tenants enough land to feed it. Yet for him it was a tragic decision, for he and his wife lost the two Canadian sisters who had kept house at Smedmore but, now having to leave it, preferred to return to their native land, and, worse still, the brilliant herdsman, John Lancaster, who had since become his farm manager and who, like them, loved Purbeck so much that, sooner than migrate to the harsher climate and soil of Wincombe, regretfully took a post on another south Dorset farm. And all the work that had been done at Smedmore in re-seeding worn-out pastures, creating new leys and putting up modern farm buildings, had to be done all over again at Wincombe, while the milking-herd after the move inevitably suffered a heavy fall in yield.

Nor, for lack of a domestic staff, could he any longer entertain in a country home where he could combine farming with the writing of history as at Smedmore, for which its sheltered garden and mild winter climate had made it an ideal medium. For the next seven years, from 1956 to 1963, in the intervals of his work on the *Alanbrooke Diaries* and *The Age of Chivalry*, which now of necessity had to be done mainly in London, he continued to farm and replant the 360 acres of the Wincombe estate, contriving somehow to get down there for whatever weekends he could spare from writing and crowding into them all the supervision and accountancy demanded by the farm. For he had no longer, as at Smedmore, a farm manager who, for all his skill and experience as a herdsman, was qualified to cope with paper work. The burden of the latter now fell almost entirely on himself. Only the woodlands which he had known and loved since childhood and of which, by his purchase of Wincombe, he had become the temporary guardian, afforded him any real pleasure and escape.

'I am merely, in part and temporarily, a person responsible for them. I am so because I love them and have made some sacrifices to be allowed to share in their guardianship. I merely, with the help of others, bought them when they were in imminent danger of destruction. . . . Yet as I very well knew, I let myself in for a packet of trouble and a great deal of hard work to pay for that trouble when I assumed my transient trusteeship of these few beloved acres. . . .

'My place is on the lowest and humblest rung of the forestry ladder, but it is an entirely satisfying one and I would not change it for any other in the world. In a minute I am out of view of the house and far out of sound of telephone or questing voice. The great trees surround and close round me like the walls of the tunnel down which Alice fell into Wonderland and I am back where I walked and dreamed as a boy fifty years ago.

'Presently I come to the clearing in the woods which is my secret destination, throw my tools across and climb the wire fence that shuts it in. Below me and the path I have been following lies a steep southern slope thick with bracken, laurels and brambles, and, rising among them, thousands of larches and little beeches whose weeding I have reserved for myself and whose future is my particular charge. The lives of the other trees I plant each winter are only mine to order and care for by proxy and process of accountancy, but these few thousand plants on this remote slope are as much mine to tend and care for as though I were their mother. Whether they live or not and whether some of them will one day become giants of the forest, like the great trees around them, depends on unpredictable factors, both human and divine, far beyond my control. For the moment their future is in my hands. A false slip of the hand, a glancing blow with sickle or swinger, the failure to remove some encroaching bush or bramble, may mean death to an arboreal infant which might otherwise outlive me by a couple of centuries and give shade, solace and timber to generations unborn.

'Much of the work has to be done on one's knees, pausing to prop up the earth under the shallow roots of trees which had been pressed down the slope by bracken, deer or weather. And here, until dusk falls and I can no longer see the tiny trees I am tending, I continue, aching in leg and back and with blistered hands, but happy and released from all thought or care but that of the delicious life of the woods.'

During all this period of his life, from 1948 when he took on the lease of Smedmore until 1963 when, in his 65th year, the growing inroads on his time and resources forced him to sell Wincombe, he was simultaneously writing his three greatest historical works as well as *The Turn of the Tide* and *Triumph in the West* and – before his large professional income had been eroded and diminished more than fivefold in purchasing-power by inflation – was maintaining and improving successively and, for some years, simultaneously, two farms entirely out of earnings and royalties. It was not quite as great a folly as it seemed, for most of the cost of doing so would otherwise have been absorbed by taxation. And as Wincombe, unlike Smedmore, was his own, the money he had borrowed on mortgage to buy it and the expenditure on the farm he created there, meant that, largely through the tremendous rise in land values during his twelve years of ownership, the capital value of the estate had automatically multiplied by almost the same amount as the purchasing-power of his income decreased.

Yet the fact remains that this was something which he neither intended nor wanted, and the loss of both places gave rise, in each case, to something little short of heartbreak. In a nostalgic essay in *The Lion and The Unicorn* entitled 'Lord of Many Acres', reprinted from two *Illustrated London News* articles, written at a time when he still owned Wincombe but had lost Smedmore, he described how, lying in bed in London during an attack of influenza trying to work 'amid urban sights and sounds and unfinished manuscripts and chewed pencils and elusive pieces of india-rubber', he consoled himself with the memory of the many lovely places he had known in his life and was free in imagination to revisit 'at any hour of the day or night'.

'Suspended as my home is on the very borders of Wiltshire and Dorset, so that I am domiciled on the beechy slopes of the one, yet look on to the tree tops and downs of the other, I belong in heart to both. Forced by my calling and obligations to spend much of my time in London, I find myself, as I grow older, repeatedly day-dreaming· of those two dear counties, each so different yet so entangled with my life and memories.

'Journeying frequently from town to country, from metropolitan scurry and uproar to woodland quiet and solitude, I realise I have many compensations. It never fails to make my heart leap to see, each time with the thrill of surprise at its perfection and beauty, the spire of Salisbury Cathedral rising from the cup of the downs as the winding London road descends from the Plain into the valley of the Avon; to glimpse, from a distant hillside, the woods of my deep western combe and the silhouette of barns filled with hay borne home on summer evenings, to hear the rooks cawing in the beeches as I stop to open the gate before entering the descending tunnel of trees at whose far end lies home – the low white Regency house with its painted verandah and rambling grey stone walls and chimneys, the lawn poised above space, the enormous multiple rhododendron which for three weeks in the year flowers in half-a-dozen brightly contrasted colours, and between whose shade and that of the little rough-fenced paddock, where the young heifers snuffle and graze in the darkness when I go out after putting down my work at night, my old dog, Jimmy, lies in his casket of ashes.

'It was here that he always ran, wild with excitement, on being released from the car to lift his leg before, amid triumphant barks and unavailing cries from his human guardians, he disappeared in the direction of the rabbit warrens in the valley below. And following him in imagination, I enter the woods, stopping at each familiar beech and chestnut, whose ancient trunks and vast spreading branches I have known for more than half a century. All around me is the other world of beasts and birds, to whom the woods also are a sanctuary; at night from my window I can hear their cries and movements as they go about their nocturnal business, seeking their food and mates. I love to think, amid the sound of the London traffic, that this life of theirs and of the living vegetable woods around them is going on at this very moment and will continue to do so though I am far away, just as it did before I was born and will continue to do after I am dead.

'I have other country resorts to which my heart repairs when my body is imprisoned in London. There is the beautiful house by the southern sea with which I struggled, trying to restore its war-ravaged beauty and order, for eight seemingly wasted years until the whole of its vast stone roof had to be taken down to renew its death-watch-beetle ridden timbers. Yet the sight of its mellowed mauve stone and of that peaceful garden, first a wilderness full of snakes and rabbits, strange weeds and discarded army junk and later a measured pleasance of trim lawns, bright flowers and formal trees, is something which neither time nor absence can take from me: that and those incredible cliffs, amid whose scenery the house and its quiet gardens and surrounding pastures were set. Here, too, my dog was – and is – always with me; nosing for rats' nests and snakes in the, for him, ecstatic days of the garden before it had been made tame and dog-dull, or racing wildly on the down edge high above the house, scattering rabbits in every direction and inhaling the wild sea wind.'

Jimmy, a rough-haired terrier had been the pivot round which A.B.'s life and that of his wife had revolved for fourteen years since, as a half-starved stray, he had joined them on the Cornish cliffs during a brief wartime holiday in 1942. He died in London just before the move to Wincombe where his ashes were buried. In 1960, at the request of Sir Bruce Ingram, the editor of *The Illustrated London News*, in whose pages the little dog had often figured, A.B. commemorated him in a book, *Jimmy, The Dog in My Life*, in the final paragraph of which he wrote,

'That inseparable friend of so many years lies now beneath the turf of a West Country lawn looking down a valley where Dorset and Wiltshire meet and in whose woods he had often hunted rabbit, fox and badger. Gone are the last sad memories of vet and injection and the growing pain and infirmity of those last years – so bravely and patiently borne. There only remains the recollection of an unquenchable vitality and capacity for life, above all for love and loyalty, and of something which for want of a better word I can only call nobility. True to his nature as a dog – fierce, independent, proud and predatory – he displayed towards the humans who had befriended him a trust, a selfless tenderness and devotion that nothing could alter and which, as much as any experience of life, has convinced me that, in some mysterious way beyond our understanding, love is eternal.'

There was, I believe, much of the mystic about A.B. as, indeed, he himself had felt about his mother. He seemed fey, altogether too impractical and not down-to-earth enough for the business side of his multifarious, highly ambitious and sometimes quixotic ventures. Yet many of them, in a strange, disorganised way – a little like his filing system – appeared to 'work', often through his uncanny capacity for choosing and inspiring a certain kind of individual to become inescapably involved with whatever he had taken on. That the Chalkleys, the gardener and maintenance man who, together with his wife, had first come to him as an under-gardener in the early days of Smedmore, were to remain, despite all vicissitudes, devotedly in his service for nearly thirty years, was but an instance of this.

At the end of the same year as *The Age of Chivalry* came out, 1963, A.B. went back to Buckinghamshire. Having negotiated a year's standover for the farm in which to wind up and sell his herd, he sold the Wincombe estate to a neighbour, a keen forester who he knew would look after his beloved woodlands. With the proceeds of the sale, he bought the South Pavilion, Wotton Underwood, a Queen Anne house not far from his old Claydon haunts. Having now farmed for fifteen years, he had no intention of continuing to do so, but in the following spring an unexpected offer of the home farm at Wotton, coupled with his reluctance to leave his present farm manager without a home and job caused him – unfortunately as it turned out – to change his mind. Owing to an eleventh-hour decision by the sitting tenant not to move, the promise of the home farm could not be fulfilled and he was offered instead a farm at Crafton, twenty-two miles away on the Bedfordshire border, which possessed an attractive 16th-century farmhouse in addition to a modern manager's house. It so happened that two old friends, a retired business man and his wife, who were looking for a home in Buckinghamshire, offered in return for the farmhouse to help manage the farm; it was this which alone made it possible for him to accept the second offer. But a year elapsed before they could move into the house and give, as they did, their devoted care to the farm, whose soil was clay, too heavy, wet and uninviting, as he found, for his gentle, friendly Jerseys who had had their origins in altogether softer and much more suitable surroundings. In this interim period a disaster occurred which ruined the whole new undertaking from the start. Possibly as a result of infection during the move, the Smedmore herd was found to have contracted that bane of all dairy farmers: brucellosis – the eradication of which, partly through the skill of two splendid herdswomen, took the next six years and involved him in heavy loss.

In some curious way it seemed as if it was now almost impossible for A.B. not to find himself beset by work and worries. He often wrily remarked that he appeared to amass the former in much the same way as other men might amass money. He became like a man in a treadmill and, possibly because of this, for several years wrote no major books,[1] apart from his comprehensive, early social history of England, *The Medieval Foundation*, published in 1967, which earned the tribute from Dr. John Foster, Professor of Ecclesiastical History at Glasgow: 'Some men are great historians, some are great writers, just a few, like Gibbon, are both. And of the few is Sir Arthur.' Though he continued to assemble a vast amount of material for his third volume of *The Story of England*, the writing was laid aside. He was, of course, getting older. 'Always remember I'm one year older than the year we're in,' he used to say.

But later on, witnessing, as I did, the tempo of his life in his seventies, it was hard to connect him with age at all. He seemed ageless, timeless. There was a hob-goblin quality about him, moments when he seemed centuries old, at others, a naughty child. When he was sixty-eight he was made a Companion of Honour. *The Daily Telegraph*, dated June 10th, 1967, lying beside me as I write, shows a photograph of him in the centre of the page. It is a curious face, contradictory in many ways: curly mouth, aquiline nose, hooded eyes. I knew how quickly its expression could change. In the space of seconds it could take on the look of a lion, the guise or disguise of the unicorn.

---

[1] *The Fire and the Rose*, 1966, and *Protestant Island*, 1968, were compiled partly from the corpus of his previous works.

16

Open Options

'If we were to join the Common Market and
accept its bureaucratic and rigidly legalistic
constitution, we should lose the ultimate control
over our rulers which Englishmen have enjoyed for
centuries, and still enjoy, through the libertarian
formula of the sovereignty of the Crown in
Parliament. Though it has operated during our
history through many changing forms, that sovereignty
ensures that, while there is no limit to what the
elected Parliament of the hour can do in giving
effect to the popular will, it cannot bind any
succeeding Parliament.'

The Lion and The Unicorn

In the same year as *The Great Duke* was published, 1971, although A.B.
still retained the South Pavilion at Wotton Underwood, he gave up
farming. It was for him a very sad decision and it was, perhaps, fortunate that on the actual day when the sale of his Jersey herd took
place, October 11th, he himself was laid up in bed at Rutland Gate
recovering from an injury to his back brought about by his insistence
on rearranging all the books in his library himself.

His one-time manager, who had done so much to build up the Herd
in its early days, came up from Dorset to help organise the sale and,
once it was over and all farming operations ceased, there was no doubt
that A.B. felt a great relief. For although he was so strangely averse to
committing himself to any decision, once something was a *fait accompli*
he never wasted time on useless regrets. 'I try to look to the bow wave,'
he sometimes said, 'not the stern. It's a principle my old friend,
Bernard Paget, always advocated.'

Nevertheless, the agitation generally pervading prior to a final
decision was invariably fraught with last minute provisos and alter-

ations. Unless pinned down to a certain date or time such as a dinner engagement, a lecture or the departure of a train (and even then I often felt he would have liked to telephone British Rail for a temporary adjustment to its timetable), he did his best to give himself the maximum amount of licence in order that he might be able to change his mind at the last minute. In other words, he liked to 'leave his options open'. This was so important and so much part of him, that if those around him found his sudden change of plan disconcerting and even disappointing, that was something they had to learn to accept.

They also had to learn that quite often – in fact, more often than not – his plans might not be communicated to them at all. On one occasion he was expecting the Chinese Chargé d'Affaires and a party of twenty Chinese to tea without having mentioned the fact to anyone. That the situation was saved by a half-hidden packet of China tea miraculously discovered at the back of a store cupboard when they were practically on the door-step, did little to ease the tense atmosphere pervading throughout the household after their departure. Likewise, sometimes A.B.'s lunch, such as it was, would be brought up on a tray by the faithful Mr. Chalkley (his employer considered it highly discourteous to refer to any of his employees by their surnames only), merely to discover the person for whom it had been prepared had gone out for the day. That this seemingly appalling lack of consideration created domestic chaos was inevitable. Often I wondered whether I had stepped into Alice's Wonderland. But such was the force of A.B.'s personality that there could be no half measures for those involved with him and the world in which he lived. One could do only two things: take it or leave it. And many was the time when, temporarily, I took the latter course.

For instance, I felt there could be few houses where such an unusually strict security system was enforced. It was true that Rutland Gate was large, rambling, particularly vulnerable from the back and, but for the faithful, ever-present Chalkleys in the basement, sometimes empty. It had already suffered two burglaries, squatters were rife, and the insurance company had intimated the necessity for burglar alarms if more stringent alternative security arrangements were not put into operation. All internal doors had therefore been fitted with special locks, both at the top and bottom. These were to be kept locked *at all times*. But it proved especially irritating and inconvenient – to say nothing of time-consuming – when it happened to be the door of a lavatory and one was in a hurry, the more so if, on having grappled with unlocking the door to get in, locking it up once inside, and re-locking it from the outside when leaving, one then found one had left something inside, which necessitated the repetition of the whole process. Moreover, although admittedly, it did not happen very often, there were times when A.B., evidently dismayed and not a little annoyed at thinking his orders had been disobeyed because he found a certain door left open, would immediately lock it up without taking proper care to ascertain whether anyone was actually inside. This was all right if the prisoner happened to be in a room with a telephone, but not otherwise. Yet although such requirements seemed to make life unreasonably hard for those around him, one always had the definite impression that A.B. himself would have been genuinely grieved and horrified to think he was upsetting or inconveniencing anyone. In short, he had an almost naïve belief that everything, in the most charming and inexplicable way, would come right in the end.

Sometimes I would arrive at Rutland Gate to find him cogitating on what were to be the priorities for the next few hours. 'We must send the Lord Mayor' – on one of whose committees he was then sitting – 'that copy of *Jimmy* I promised him,' he might begin. This would be quickly followed by the enumeration of a variety of other matters which were momentarily uppermost in his mind, such as: 'Would you get through to Glasgow and find out about those proofs?' – 'I must get that letter off about the Petition against the Common Market' – 'My article for *The Illustrated London News* ought to be in the 5.30 post unless we can get them to send down for it in the morning' – 'I must draft a letter to *The Times* about the proposed demolition of those beautiful houses at the top of the square' – 'My hair needs cutting' – 'I said I would finish that Foreword for that man who rings up every other day whose name I can never remember' – 'Did you send my dinner-jacket to the cleaners and tell them it was onion soup on the lapel when I was jogged at an unfortunate moment?' – 'I've lost that letter from Vic Feather' – 'Would you slip out to Harrods and buy me that new book on dieting that was advertised in the *Sunday Telegraph?* – 'You've forgotten to sharpen my pencils' – 'Where is the bird seed for those poor dear pidgies on the balcony?' – 'I think we ought to have a few more tins of sardines in the house in case there's a strike' – 'Would you write a nice, polite letter to this lady who wants me to lecture in Surbiton and tell her that my present commitments are so over-whelming that. . . .' And then would come the final and most important salvo of all: '*When do you think everyone will leave me alone so I can get on with my book . . . ?*'

I often felt, because of the incredible pace at which A.B. always seemed to have lived, that by all common-sense standards he should have been a candidate for a coronary long ago, or at any rate one or another kind of stress disease. But although he was blessed with the strongest constitution I have ever come across, and although he virtually abused this good fortune to the extent that he drove himself far beyond the limits of the most hard-working man, there was one extraneous factor that may have contributed to his good health which, for a long time, I ignored. A.B. had great faith in a doctor who used homeopathic treatment, which involved collecting remedies from a homeopathic chemist on the other side of Hyde Park.

Often, because he felt it to be good for his liver, he would hurry across the Park to collect his prescribed pills himself just before the chemist's closing time, having asked me to ascertain by telephone whether they were ready. For some reason, one day there appeared to have been a hitch in the smooth-running arrangements carried out regularly between doctor, chemist and patient, and his pills had not yet been made up. 'Not ready?' roared A.B. He was already half way across the library. 'Just let me speak to them. . . .'

But his bark was always worse than his bite. Underneath what some-times seemed a remote, uncaring exterior, he meant well, especially to his nearest and dearest, although it often appeared as if he came closer mentally to those from whom he was physically parted. He was, perhaps, the copybook example of the two old adages: 'Absence makes the heart grow fonder' and 'Familiarity breeds contempt'. With his intense love for, and preoccupation with, the past, he felt a deep sense of both moral and financial obligation to all those people

190

with whom he had been particularly associated or who had helped him during his life. To his old school he showed gratitude and affection in many ways. While for someone whose character and work he admired, from whatever walk of life they came, he would go to no end of trouble. He became an extremely active champion of 'Camberley Kate', the elderly retired Yorkshire cook, who kept open house for stray dogs:

'Of those who have shown by their deeds their awareness of the value of canine affection and trust, there can be few who have surpassed the record of an old lady now living in the little Surrey town of Camberley. Anyone passing in the middle of the day along its crowded high-street . . . may catch a glimpse, if he is lucky, of an astonishing spectacle. Preceded by a certain hubbub, he will see an elderly woman making her way along the pavement surrounded by dogs of every kind and species, pushing before her a small wooden go-cart made of box planks over the edge of which peer the proud and happy faces of three or four privileged members of her canine flock while the remainder, tethered to the cart, wave their sterns in enjoyment and appreciation of their two hours' regular walk. . . . Their benefactress is a poor working woman . . . living alone on an old age pension, who for over twenty years has kept open house for unwanted and ill-treated dogs and who devotes her whole life and her all to their maintenance. Obeying Christ's precept to "take no thought for the morrow, what ye shall eat or what ye shall drink," this valiant and tender-hearted woman, because she loves, understands and pities these gentle and affectionate beasts betrayed and abandoned by man, shares with them her home and food, refusing none that are brought to her door, keeping them till she can find them homes and, in the meantime, trusting that somehow Heaven will provide for them. Some years ago, moved by the sight of that valiant little figure as she manoeuvred her pack along the pavement and guessing what her self-imposed mission of love and service to those lowly creatures must involve in labour and sacrifice, I wrote to her out of the blue and begged her to accept from a fellow dog-lover a small Christmas present for her dogs' Christmas dinner. She replied: "When people like you see them and understand what I am trying to do, it helps wonderful. . . . I have known to be so up against it as to kneel down and ask at 2 a.m. and it's come. . . . I can only do a tiny bit, but I will spend my last years in taking, caring and loving them." And that, when one comes to consider it rightly, is the spirit that made this country great.'

After this article was published in *The Illustrated London News* in 1964, A.B. found himself the recipient of an overwhelming flood of enquiries and donations – even one from behind the Iron Curtain – which necessitated the setting up of a Trust Fund on Kate Ward's behalf. The work which he undertook in connection with this would have been excellent, perhaps, for someone not already committed to other affairs; for A.B. it was another 'extra', but one which, sharing the same views as Kate, he shouldered with willing equanimity. Whenever I accompanied this inveterate dog-lover across Hyde Park, the entire outing was punctuated by little tête-à-têtes with strange dog-owners. Although, at that time, for domestic reasons, he himself felt unable to keep a dog of his own, the sight of anyone else exercising his or her dog gave him immense delight, especially if it happened to be a terrier. Owners, becoming aware of his obvious interest, would smile and stop; the dog's name would be ascertained; it would then be patted, praised and finally admirer and admired would regretfully go their respective ways until someone else's pet appeared on the scene to attract his immediate attention.

At the time I was working for him, he was also championing two other causes, both of these, however, on a national level. One was that of preventing Cublington in Buckinghamshire from becoming the site of the third London Airport. As a founder and President of the Friends of the Vale of Aylesbury, he was partly responsible for the success of this contest. The other was a battle in which he had been engaged for many years: that of his campaign against Britain joining the Common Market. As President of the Common Market Safeguards Campaign, he was deeply opposed to this and had expressed his views clearly and forcibly in a small pamphlet, *A Choice for Destiny*, published as long ago as 1962, being a collection of various articles which he had already written from time to time in *The Illustrated London News*. Britain, he maintained, was not simply some off-shore islands of Europe. She was the creator and centre of a worldwide community of British people, linked by sea, living under and wedded to free forms of government that had evolved not on the continent but in Britain herself.

Because, as a professional historian, he never ceased to view almost all the problems of the present in the light of the past, 'for at least six or seven hundred years,' he wrote,

> 'under whatever species of government or social order, this country has conducted its affairs on the basis that the Government of the day should be completely free to adopt whatever policy seems to it most beneficial for our people, with the inevitable corollary that every subsequent Government should enjoy the same freedom and be at liberty to change or reverse its predecessor's policy. It has been this legal entrustment throughout our history of absolute and unqualified sovereignty to the Parliament of the day that, more than any other single cause, had distinguished England from other nations, their policies and history. It has been responsible for both the elasticity and adaptability we have shown in every kind of crisis and emergency during our·long history. . . .
> ' "We must be free or die who speak the tongue that Shakespeare spake" is something more than a fine phrase of poetry; it is a matter of fact and, I think, unanswerable expression of an unchanging and unchallengeable national truth. . . .'

To be free or die. Just as A.B. wanted to be free to live his life in his own way and to change his mind if he so wished – 'to keep his options open' – he wanted his country to remain as she had been throughout her history: free to adapt her policies to the changing needs and circumstances of the hour. To him it was anathema that she should be bound by the dead hand of the past and the rigid terms of the Treaty of Rome. On one point he was adamant. His love for his native country transcended all others. He stood, wrote and spoke for England and for the unchanging spirit which, throughout her history, he felt England had embodied.

Perhaps the lines of an American critic reviewing one of his books put this best: 'Sir Arthur's hero is not any individual or group of individuals, neither a class, nor a people, nor a system but quite simply

England itself. His love for England is Churchillian and it gleams through his writing with a Churchillian radiance. As the whole is greater than the sum of its parts, England, to this author, is something greater than the men, the events, the systems, and the sufferings he chronicles. It is a splendid Ideal. He is not blind to the blemishes which disfigure the image he creates: but over and above all the flaws he recognises and salutes as basic and essential the greatness of the human spirit it embodies.'

17

Unicorn at Large

'Almost every Englishman, it is said, belongs
to some club.'

The Lion and The Unicorn

'All along either side of Pall Mall, up St. James's Street and scattered
about the northern escarpment of Piccadilly,' A.B. wrote in one of his
then weekly *Illustrated London News* articles in the days of shortages and
egalitarian rationing just after the War, 'are the historic clubs of
London. They are among the last strongholds of dignity and spacious
comfort surviving in England, and there are still tens of thousands of
Englishmen who, having grown accustomed to dignity and this kind
of comfort in their happier youth and middle age, cling to what
vestiges of it remain.

'Whenever they can, they slip away from the crowded prison
and the tumbril, and, momentarily forgetting the revolution
through which they have passed, glide through the great glass
and mahogany portals and disappear into the quiet, nostalgic
fragrance within. No inspector or tax-gatherer follows them; no
wireless blares or politician bawls; the sounds of the outer world
are respectfully deadened, and the sights of it, glimpsed through
the huge, aloof, plate-glass windows, are telescoped into a kind
of remote distance. . . . They have been the sheltered abodes of
men of polished dignity and assurance for so long that it is almost
impossible for anyone entering them to behave in a manner
inappropriate to them. . . . They command instantaneous and
instinctive obedience to their unspoken conventions and give out,
as automatically, the strength and assurance which derive from
an unalterable and ordered fellowship. I know of nowhere, not
even the officers' mess of a great regiment, where the secret power
of England is so clearly revealed. Hitler, who never entered one of
these ancient temples, had already – though he knew it not - met his

doom in them before he crossed his Polish Rubicon. The English, in their aggregate and silent disapproval, are a dangerous lot. . . .

'A few years ago these great rooms rocked and trembled to the crashing of bombs and the staccato fury of guns. I remember taking lunch in one of them – a military and naval establishment – during the flying-bomb summer, when nearly everyone responsible for directing Britain's war effort, except those already in Normandy, seemed to be eating at the same moment in the room. No one took the slightest notice of the chugging and whistling overhead or of the periodic crashes; the enduring atmosphere of normality within was far more powerful than the temporary atmosphere without.'

'It is these clubs, monumental designs for a certain kind of living,' A.B. concluded his article of thirty years ago, 'that inspire my muse to-night. . . . They may be escapist, they may be snobbish, they may be an anachronism, they may be an affront to an egalitarian age, but whatever they are in current ideology, I wish them well and admire their strong capacity for survival. May they continue for ever, or at any rate, until the first atom bomb!'

Nearly a quarter of a century later, both they and he were still showing the same strong capacity for survival. Yet, though he still belonged to one of these ancient institutional sanctums – the club of his profession, the Athenaeum – it was with clubs of a different kind that I learned to associate him in the days when he was writing *The Great Duke* and *Jackets of Green*. Obsessed as he was with his work, the only kind of club he now had time for was one which he could attend for a couple of hours' occasional relaxation over a dining table where he could be certain, without giving notice of his coming, of meeting and enjoying congenial and stimulating company and conversation.

He belonged to three such clubs. One of them, Pratt's, which had once paid him the rare honour of making him an honorary member until his turn for election came up, he was now seldom, if ever, owing to the pressure on his time, able to visit. But he still managed, once every three or four weeks, somewhat like a small boy playing truant, to steal off to the Beefsteak of which he had been a member for the past thirty years. Here he could relax as nowhere else, finding, like

Dr. Johnson, a club chair where he could talk and listen at ease 'the height of human felicity'. Here he was able to forget his preoccupation with the past and, as it were, tune himself effortlessly into the present.

To the third of these clubs, Grillion's, he felt a special responsibility and obligation. Having been a member of this historic dining club since 1951, when I came to work for him he had become one of its two joint secretaries, taking on the more social side of the task. How much he put into it I realised when one of its members asked me to give him a message on the telephone, adding, just before he rang off, 'And please tell him how much we all enjoyed the last Grillion's evening, thanks to him. I don't know what we should do without him.'

A.B. did his best never to miss any of the fortnightly dinners at Grillion's. One of the features of the club is that no notice is ever required of attendance, so that no one can ever know whom he will meet or sit next to. On several occasions during its near two centuries' history, one member only turned up. Gladstone, finding himself the sole diner at its usually sociable table, consoled himself by drinking a bottle of champagne and recording the event in Latin verse in the Minute Book. Balfour had the same experience.

Although primarily a political dining club – founded in 1812 at a time when Party feeling was running exceptionally high – by a group of Oxford friends who wanted to preserve their friendship after they entered Parliament and so bring opponents into cheerful, regular, social intercourse on neutral ground, political distinction has never been its only title to membership. The club's first historian, Lord Houghton, wrote of it in 1880, 'Many of the leaders in both Houses of Parliament would not have found admission and many comparatively obscure have been our cherished comrades.' Part of Grillion's charm has always lain in the diversity of experience and opinion of those attending its dinners: eminent ecclesiastics and legal luminaries, senior civil servants, diplomats and Service chiefs, bankers, industrialists, and members of the T.U.C., writers and scientists. In Lord Houghton's words, 'any form of society that tends to combine political and intellectual life is an acquisition not to be neglected. . . . A statesman will willingly pass from the torpor or even the excitement of the House of Commons to the conversation of science, literature or art with a sense of relief, and may be of profit.' Or, as an 18th century jingle put it,

'When the long hours of public are past
We meet with champagne and a chicken at last.'

Some notes on its history record that

'during the great parliamentary epoch between the middle ⟨
Victoria's reign and the first World War, every British Prim
Minister, Lord Chancellor and Foreign Secretary was a membe
Gladstone attended its dinners for more than half a century
Disraeli said in the House that it possessed the only perfe⟨
constitution he knew. The 7th Earl of Derby – the "Rupert ⟨
Debate" and the first of its members to become Prime Minister
praised it for its "generous and courteous comprehension ⟨
diversities of political views". . . . Since 1919 eleven Prin
Ministers and former Prime Ministers have been members. . .
Churchill was a member from 1921 till his death in 1965 an
Asquith from 1893 till 1928; Macmillan has been one since 1937
So were Alec Douglas-Home and Edward Heath and the last tw⟨
Labour Prime Ministers.

Contrary to what many people have sometimes assumed, A.B. ha⟨
for a very long time been extraordinarily politically unbiased, an
this characteristic exemplification of British democracy at work – or
of those indefinable and inexplicable institutions never to be foun
anywhere but in this country – naturally appealed strongly to
historian who had spent a lifetime writing about the very qualities i
our national make-up which could produce such a phenomenon.

In his Prelude to *The Story of England* A.B. enlarged upon those force
which have all contributed to make us what we are: climate, geograph⟨
(that precious twenty miles of salt water which for nine centuries pa⟨
has protected us from invasion) and race. Before England began to us⟨
this sea barrier effectively she was invaded by Iberians, Romans, Jute⟨
Angles, Saxons, Danes, Norwegians and Normans. 'It was not,' he wrot⟨

'the island's first inhabitants – solitary, shambling, unaspiring
sheltering among the rocks of the Cheddar Gorge or Gow⟨
peninsula, who set the course of her history. It was those wh⟨
reaching the ocean's shores put out in frail boats across uncharte⟨
seas. . . . The ancestors of the British people were fighters, seame⟨

and pioneers. . . . Left to themselves the Anglo-Saxons of a thousand years ago . . . might have settled down into a sluggish complacency. But they were harried by the Danes and Norsemen, and later conquered by the clear-minded, ruthless Normans . . . The incessant challenging warfare of the races . . . probably accounted for the intermixture in the British blood of the matter-of-fact with the poetic; of love of home with the itch to adventure; of business aptitude with fantasy, speculation and idealism. English literature is full of examples of this conflict in the national make-up; of books like *Alice in Wonderland* written by a professor of mathematics, of *Songs of a Shropshire Lad* by a clerk in the Patent Office who became a master of Latin philology. . . . The British – and more particularly the English in whom the mingling of the races has been most marked – have often been charged with hypocrisy, with serving God and Mammon, with trying to eat their cake and have it. Since they have so many sides to their nature, there has been truth in this charge; yet in a world in which spirit and matter are inextricably mingled, it has not served them badly. . . . This clash of racial characteristics and cultures may have accounted, too, for the extraordinary range of British genius. . . .'

In A.B., this clash of racial characteristics was unusually marked. I have rarely seen anyone exhibit so many different sides to his nature within the course of a single day. One minute his poetic, dreamy side might be in the ascendant, inspiring him to quote a Miltonian sonnet; the next he would be like John Bull himself, fiercely laying down the law about the dangers of Britain joining the Common Market. With the arrival of the morning's post he might, with glee (especially if it came from a Government Department), find himself the recipient of an extra elastic band for the cherished hoard which he kept in a box on his desk; on opening the mid-day post and finding a friend in need, he would be whipping out his cheque-book. In many respects he reminded me of Sir George Sitwell, the father of Osbert, whom the latter portrayed so amusingly in his autobiography. When I once remarked on this to A.B., he agreed. 'I suppose I am a bit like Sir George,' he said. 'If I hadn't had my living to earn I daresay I would have busied myself rather as he did.'

But A.B. did have his living to earn and he earned it the hard way. Apart from his evenings at Grillion's or the Beefsteak and the more rare occasions when he entertained at home, dined out with friends or went to D'Oyly Carte productions of Gilbert and Sullivan or the annual festival of the English Folk Dance and Song Society, there seemed to be only one other engagement – except official ones – when he really indulged in taking time off. This was the annual Eton and Harrow match at Lord's. It was something he never missed, almost a ritual. Other than during the war years, when such an event was in abeyance, every July on two consecutive days he could be found in grey top hat and morning coat, with a posy of deep blue cornflowers in his buttonhole, taking a keen interest in the fortunes of his old school. 'It's amazing,' he said to me one afternoon in 1972, after returning from his annual pilgrimage on foot, 'a few years ago if I walked about London in these clothes I felt the proletariat looked slightly resentful. Nowadays, I believe they think I belong to another century or that I'm simply "doing my thing", as the modern generation puts it.'

Although such an expression coming from his lips seemed a little incongruous, A.B. invariably surprised me both by his subtle awareness of everyday trends and a seemingly complete unawareness of certain events or innovations. He never, for instance, studied the birth, marriage and death columns in the newspapers, although when such eventualities occurred amongst his friends or acquaintances, as most of them were already in the public eye, he usually read about them in another part of the paper. Likewise, he never looked at television and did not, in fact, possess a set, although he kept himself well-informed of the daily news through his portable radio or the Press. He read a fantastic amount or, rather, 'extracted the bones from' countless numbers of books: history, biography, autobiography and poetry, but rarely novels. The only time he felt justified in reading anything of a lighter kind was during the Christmas holiday season, when he would dash off to a second-hand bookshop on Christmas Eve and buy something to dip into during the course of the next few days.

He was also amazingly ignorant of, and bewildered by, anything mechanical or the latest type of consumer goods, so much so that an almost fool-proof modern gadget seemed to defeat him. If left alone to wrap up a parcel he became festooned and virtually paralysed by sticky tape and string, from which he had to be extricated. When I first began working for him in 1971 he had never seen colour television or heard of such things as contact lenses ('You mean people actually put them *in* their eyes?'); and, whenever I had to accompany him on a journey through London, especially by Underground, he kept up a delightful commentary on the posters therein, registering, with a kind of impish naïveté, astonishment, disapproval, and demanding in no uncertain terms an explanation of some of the more obscure and ingenious forms of advertising. He was possibly forced to take more notice of this kind of thing when I was with him, simply because I insisted on standing still on the escalators and refused to run up and down them, as he had hitherto done. Being thus thwarted, on seeing pictures of ladies in varying stages of dress and undress, he would get his own back by remarking quite audibly, 'What on earth does a spray a day mean?' or 'What would my mother have said?' and finally, as we panted down a passage to be confronted by closing doors and a train gliding away, 'There! I told you it makes all the difference between one train and the next if you don't waste time looking at those incredibly silly pictures.'

Train catching with him was invariably fraught. Although he was usually driven in London by Mr. Colin, a splendid driver with whom he had had a long and close association, I occasionally took A.B. to catch a train by taxi. Running up to the Kensington Road well in advance of schedule, I would flag one down, return with it to Rutland Gate and ask the driver to wait while the inevitable drama of lost papers, unexpected telephone calls, last minute instructions and undone shoe-laces was carried out. Eventually he would emerge from the house, accompanied by all his usual paraphernalia, and start to tell the taxi-man the best route to take. But, as often as not, after we had gone a little way he would decide that it would be quicker to change course. He would then open the sliding glass partition in the cab and remain, his large form crouched on one of the smaller seats, in a state of impatient and suspended animation, alternatively breathing down the driver's neck or confusing the poor man with interjections such as, 'I think it might be better to turn off here,' or 'Better turn round altogether and go back the way we came,' to which, with good-natured equanimity, he would receive such replies as, 'It's a one-way street, sir,' or, on one never-to-be-forgotten occasion, 'Well, sir, if I was driving this cab, I think that's the way I'd go, too.'

The extraordinary thing was that A.B. never did miss a train, except one. With a little acceleration round Hyde Park Corner and some strategic overtaking nearer Waterloo or King's Cross, everything usually came right in the end. Therefore I took it somewhat as a personal failure on my part that the only time he missed a train happened to be when I was seeing him off at Marylebone. The previous evening I had done some urgent typing for him at home which he had asked if I would bring to the station the following morning in order for him to set to work, as usual, on his journey. Knowing the importance of both the typing and the meeting near Aylesbury to which he was travelling, I arrived a good fifteen minutes before the train was due to leave. After buying myself a platform ticket (A.B.'s own ticket was always bought in advance by Mr. Chalkley), and waiting anxiously for twelve minutes, Mr. Colin drew his car up with a flourish and his passenger, complete with all his accoutrements, hastily extricated himself and I hurried after him across the station and through the barrier, waiting while he bundled himself into a carriage.

I then passed A.B. the typing through the window and received, in exchange, the morning's post with which he seemed to bristle, rather like a Christmas tree, and which he plucked from various places in and round his person, handing me each missive together with an instruction such as: 'Answer this,' 'Make a copy of that' and 'Hang on to those cheques till I get back.' When he appeared to have disgorged the lot I glanced along the platform and noticed the front part of the train was moving off. Unfortunately, two trains had been double-banked and the one for Aylesbury in which A.B. should have been sitting had, in fact, now departed without him.

After I had managed, after a frenzied dash to Baker Street, to thrust him into a train for Amersham, I walked away to a call box. Somehow I felt it was incumbent on me to redeem the situation by ensuring that he was met by taxi at the other end to take him on to his destination. I put through a call to Amersham station. 'You mean,' said the obliging taxi-driver who came to the telephone at the request of the station-master, 'Sir Arthur Bryant, the historian?' 'That's right,' I answered. 'I'll certainly meet him,' came the reply. 'It'll be a pleasure. I've read a lot of his books. But I don't know what he looks like. Can you describe him?'

'Fairly large, broad-shouldered, grey hair,' I began, weakly, 'wearing an old fawn mackintosh and a green deer-stalker hat – carrying four bags, two black, one brown, and a whitish, plastic one full of books. don't think you can mistake him. He'll be in a hurry. . . .'

18

The Mill-Race

'I never fear for England in storm:
that is when she sees most clearly
and rides most secure.'

Illustrated London News,
21st November, 1970

If I were asked to name the thing which impressed me most while I was with A.B., I think it would be the contrast between the work he produced and the way in which he produced it; in other words, the end-product and the maelstrom of activity which went into achieving it. His writing – and I feel that countless others would agree with this – was invariably balanced, rhythmical, inspiring and flowed, seemingly without effort, as it imparted knowledge to its readers. I shall always think of him as both a great writer and a great historian. Yet witnessing the process of how this came about was a little like being caught up in a mill-race and then seeing the main stream flow serenely away, delighting all who came across it by its beauty, simplicity and tranquil sense of *continuity in time*.

Had a book such as, say, *English Saga*, been made available to me in my youth, history would have been far from the dry subject I invariably found it; for I could hardly fail to have appreciated the difference between an author writing on nineteenth century London who simply said it was rather countrified, and A.B.'s own description, after he had studied every conceivable piece of information on which he could lay his hands, including pictures and prints which he often found told more of forgotten detail than the written word.

'How rustic London still was could be seen from its summer greenery. The West End was full of trees and green squares and courts. The fields were half a mile away from Buckingham Palace and Grosvenor Square, and snipe were occasionally shot in the

Pimlico marshes. In St. James's Park long rough untrimmed grass ran down to the water's edge, and there were no railings to keep people from wandering on it. Sometimes on wintry evenings the scarlet of a huntsman's coat could be seen in the fading light ascending the slope of Piccadilly or entering the Albany courtyard. In Chelsea, where the old brown roofs and twisted high chimneys of the houses almost tumbled into the unembanked river, the sage Carlyle rode . . . to improve his indigestion. . . .'

In going back a hundred years, it seemed as if A.B., without coercion or even persuasion, had simply swept his readers up and taken them as travelling companions on a beautifully-conducted and entertaining journey with him.

This capacity for travelling in time as opposed to space was A.B.'s great forte. On his own admission, he often used it as an escape mechanism:

'I have few or no opportunities to enjoy the relaxation of holidays in space . . . but whenever the pressure of daily work becomes too great, I can always relax for an hour or two in a holiday taken, not in space, but in time. I leave, not England for the Continent, but 1950 for some other year or period. I do not, of course, choose a time on which I have been working as a historian, for that would be no holiday. . . . I take up some book which presents the past, with a touch of comprehensive genius in a nutshell: Aubrey's *Lives* or Pepys's *Diary* or Boswell or Lockhart, gossiping Creevey or nostalgic Kilvert, and in a moment am borne on a broomstick of imagination into another world, where I can enjoy my surroundings and my fellow-men without obligations or anxiety. . . . The best medium of all for such journeys in time are the bound volumes of *Punch* and *The Illustrated London News.* . . . Such a choice, it is true, limits one's opportunity of travel to the Victorian and Edwardian ages . . . yet, as anyone who tried my recipe will discover, for ample range of holiday the Victorian era offers escape enough. What an age of fullness and plenty it was!'

Often I felt that A.B. stood outside time. It was as if he was up in some aeroplane looking down on the mortals of the present century as they went about their business, making the same foolish mistakes as their predecessors of another era, an era which, in some extraordinary way, he was able to visualise at the same moment. Possibly this was what made conforming to everyday life, speed-conscious and ruled by the clock, so incredibly irksome to him. Although he was capable of impatiently expecting a thousand words of closely-written manuscript to be typed in a quarter of an hour, he was also capable of remaining completely unaware of the minutes ticking by when he was intent on writing but should, by rights, have been doing something else. When A.B. was writing, time, as the ordinary person reckons it, ceased to exist.

Yet although he could be bewildering, unreasonable, irrational, inconsiderate and sometimes extremely bad-tempered, underlying these temporary lapses there was an unfailing quality of – for want of a better word – lovableness. In a single unexpected gesture he could redeem a whole unfortunate harassing situation. At the end of a day's work which looked like never coming to an end, he would suddenly say, 'You've done enough. Pack it in. I've booked a table. A car is coming in a quarter of an hour to take us out to dinner.'

One thing A.B. never did, even at the end of an exceptionally trying day, was to revive himself with a drink. He would occasionally have a little wine or a rum and orange juice with his evening meal, but because he wished to remain alert in order to work later on, more often than not he stuck to water. Other than the times when he entertained or went out, he was amazingly abstemious, and I rarely saw him drink before a meal. Yet, paradoxically, he was something of a connoisseur of wine and a member of the Saintsbury Club.

When, in the summer of 1972, A.B. was working on a history of the Rifle Brigade, a book to be called *Jackets of Green*, realising that he was behind schedule, he began getting up regularly at 5 am and going into the secretary's room, where he put in a straight four hours' work until the distractions of the day intervened. Later on, he was sometimes obviously fighting off sleep. Yet his resilience was extraordinary. A cup of tea, a pause to feed the pigeons and the grey look would vanish. Back he would go to his desk, tracking Harry Smith[1] through the

---

[1] Lt-Gen. Sir Harry Smith, G.C.B.

Peninsula or Tom Pearson[1] through the Western Desert. It seemed all the more creditable when I knew that the writing of this particular book was the result of a promise to a dying friend, Danny Meighar-Lovett, and that the royalties on it were to go to the Rifle Brigade Association.

As I typed and retyped the history of the Rifle Brigade, with its wonderful philosophy of courage and cheerfulness in adversity, I was very aware of my own shortcomings. Yet it was somehow difficult to take a breather or ask to put one's feet up when typing about men dying of cholera during a heroic march through India, especially when the account had been written by a man who, one felt, would have taken such a march in the same way as he strode so purposefully through Hyde Park. It seemed tantamount to defecting and going over to the other side.

When the proofs of *Jackets of Green* arrived it was sometimes difficult to see or talk to A.B. at all. On arriving for work each day there would be no dissertation on priorities. One lived for and with the Rifle Brigade. A.B. sat at his desk with the galley-snakes, as I had come to think of them, coiling round him, slippery and writhing, waiting to bite back if not treated with proper care and respect. Each day, chapter by chapter, they arrived by Express Post from the printers in Glasgow. Each day, chapter by chapter, A.B., shoulders hunched, pencils well bitten and pens running dry, corrected meticulously. Often he would ask me to read a certain passage from a book which he had quoted, saying, 'Always check your references. That's something Winston always advocated.' Then he would get on the telephone and double-check whole galleys with his various other proof-readers before collating all the corrections on to one fair copy.

For this particular book, besides those who usually read for A.B., there were also members of the Rifle Brigade itself who had checked the manuscript at all its various stages. General Sir Richard Fyffe, at the time a very sick man, often came to Rutland Gate in person and he and A.B. would go through long extracts together, seemingly regardless of meals or the clock. Tragically, Colonel 'Vic' Turner, the Alamein V.C., who also assisted A.B., died just before the publication

---

[1] Gen. Sir Thomas Pearson, K.C.B., C.B.E., D.S.O.

of *Jackets of Green* and General Fyffe only a few days after it, a copy of the book, at the latter's special request, being buried with him.

Although A.B.'s target had shifted since his early youth when he had longed to be a soldier, he maintained a lifelong admiration for the fighting man, carrying on what might almost be described as a perpetual love affair with the Army. The 'Colonel Blimp' image with which its members had sometimes been invested between the wars, annoyed him intensely. Though untidy, unpunctual and temperamental himself, he was tremendously keen on all the soldierly qualities: discipline, courage and loyalty to others engendered by a good regiment. He deplored the slipshod lack of *esprit de corps* which he felt was so prevalent in present-day Britain. 'At this rather murky (but not wholly cheerless) stage of our development as a nation,' wrote A. G. Dickens, the Director of the Institute of Historical Research and author of *The English Reformation*, to A.B. after the publication of *Jackets of Green*, 'your book recalls us to the values in which our generation was brought up. . . . A book such as this comes at an opportune time: thanks to your power of recreating the past, and the *vital* nature of your writing, it will inevitably be much read, and do a great (if immeasurable) service. When we recover confidence and find our new role in the world, it must surely preserve continuity with the values you have so ably inculcated in your books.'

This country's loss of religious faith, patriotism and standards of personal honesty, A.B. considered to be a great potential danger, much as he sensed the peril in our inability to defend ourselves against a foreign power wishing to do injury by blockade, invasion, rocket or nuclear bombardment. 'Never,' he wrote in *The Illustrated London News* in 1969, 'has Britain been so vulnerable to attack from the sea.' The drastic reduction by our political representatives of the naval shield with which the country formerly protected itself, seemed to him little short of lunacy, while the abandonment of our links with our British kinsfolk overseas saddened him beyond measure. 'We need an Aidan to re-teach us our faith and a Pitt and a Drake to show us what courage and confidence can do,' he continued in the same article, so that 'we can become once more a source of strength and stability to ourselves and a beacon and guiding light to others.'

In this he was fully aware he was old-fashioned, that most people nowadays considered 'dominion over palm and pine', as he put it, 'a pompous hypocritical cover for bourgeois greed and exploitation; respect and chivalry towards the weaker sex a stupid and tyrannical denial of the pleasures of the flesh; our traditional respect for law and order a shabby trick to preserve the goods and privileges of the rich from the avenging and corrective wrath of the poor; our patriotism a dominant bully's conspiracy against the rest of the world and our religion an outworn and irrational superstition.' Yet despite the state into which he felt Britain had degenerated, despite a historian's acute awareness of the less obvious signs which usually preceded a nation's ultimate downfall throughout the ages, he still retained hopes – albeit sometimes seemingly dying ones – that our instinctive national response to necessity might help Britain to regain some semblance of her former greatness, if not in the physical sphere, in the spiritual.

Considering A.B.'s intense individuality, his strange solitariness and his marked aversion to any attempt at being made to conform, this reverence for group feeling and effort was a little surprising, especially after he had once said to me, 'All my life I've really been an onlooker. Of course, I enjoy the odd evening with friends but much of the time I feel as if I'm outside what's going on, simply taking it all in as a spectator on the sidelines.'

I knew what he meant. In spirit he was so often up there in his aeroplane, outside and oblivious of time, watching the world go round and seeing England as she was centuries ago, as she appeared today, and as he was almost willing her to be in the centuries to come. . . .

'By far and away the most important thing to conserve in this country is the character and health of its people. . . . Character matters more than theories. . . . Nothing can be achieved without courage, faith and hard work. . . . Love of, and pride in, one's country is a necessary foundation for a nation's social well-being. . . . I believe that any society that ceases to value and promote these old-fashioned virtues is bound in the long run either to collapse through internal weakness or be destroyed from without by others more realistic. . . . I continue to champion them, even though to many they must seem absurd, distasteful and even repulsive. . . .

'The greatest conundrum of our time is to find a purpose in which men can believe and for which they will give themselves gladly and freely. For the nature of man is such that only when he is giving himself freely and gladly is he contented. If he is not contented, he will naturally wish to denigrate and destroy the society of which he forms a part. And a society in which a majority of men are discontented for lack of purpose in which they believe and for which they can gladly give themselves, is like a ship with a large hole in it. The crew of such a ship will remain in a state of constant disturbance and anxiety so long as that leak exists. And unless they can master it their vessel will presently sink. . . . There lies, and has long lain, the central problem of our age.

'I should like to see a Government that regarded the character, moral, mental and physical health of the British people as its most sacred trust: that applied to every measure it brought before Parliament the test of "Will it tend to foster virtues and capacities in her sons that will make Britain not only richer and stronger, but "nobler", worthy, that is, of the ideals for which at her best she has tried to stand. . . ."

'Cohesive in conflict, insular when storms gather, we yet remain a people with a greater diversity of viewpoint than any on earth. The blood of all the world is in our veins and it comes out in the variety of our opinions. No human belief or prejudice is too absurd or too obscure for some Englishman to champion it. . . . With our long island immunity from invasion we have developed, for all our racial intermixture, a very strong, almost unshakeable, national consciousness and unity. . . . I should like to feel that I could cast a vote for England rather than for an ideology or for the political party most likely to favour my personal interests. . . . The justification of all privilege and power is the fulfilment of social duty. . . . The problem of government is, fundamentally, that of training human beings, who by nature and interest are so little constituted for it, to exercise power with wisdom, selflessness and impartiality. . . .'

The Timeless Moment

'Death still remains the greatest of man's
adventures. To be able to embark on it in
the same spirit of wonder as a child sets
out on his holiday by the sea . . . is what
we must all wish for ourselves and those
we love.'

Illustrated London News,
2nd August, 1969

After A.B. had put the final touches to *Jackets of Green* and there could
(unfortunately perhaps for him but fortunately for everyone else) be no
further urgent, triangular communication between author, publisher
and printer, he embarked on something which he informed me had not
taken place for almost thirty years. He decided to have a grand
'turn-out':

'One of the peculiarities of my profession is that it involves the
constant accumulation of ever-growing hoards of paper – manuscripts, notes, newspapers, cuttings and documents of every
description. Another is that, based on a multiplicity of employers,
it never seems to admit of a holiday. Yet, in a sense, the former
creates the latter, for every now and then the accumulation of
unsorted paper becomes so formidable that I am driven to lay my
work aside and spend hours and sometimes days with scissors,
pencil, paste and envelopes, and amid clouds of dust, reducing
the paper chaos to order and sorting the chaotic piles into carefully arranged drawers and cupboards. Then the accumulation
and disorder begin again, until the time arrives for a new spring-
cleaning, perhaps forced on me by the entreaties and protests of
womankind – "worse enemies," as Pepys said, "to papers than
rats and mice!"'

Belonging, as I did, to that vague suspect aggregate, womankind, I was overjoyed about the present proceedings, for ever since working for A.B. my fingers had itched to eliminate what I could only regard as impedimenta. Yet even if I had had time to do so, I knew that it was more than my life's – or, at any rate, my job's – worth to be found guilty of throwing away anything which, however valueless it might seem to me, might nevertheless be a treasured relic of the past, for which he had such a profound respect. 'If someone didn't preserve what you consider to be trivia,' he would sometimes say, 'how are future generations going to know what a two-penny halfpenny stamp once looked like?'

Therefore each day when I arrived at Rutland Gate I marvelled to find him burrowing away, humming to himself rather like a large, happy bear, as he went about this long-overdue task. Anxious not to interrupt or divert him in any way from his admirable intentions, I hopefully left him to it, apart from appearing now and then to take overflowing waste-paper baskets down to the kitchen where, with a clear conscience and an overwhelming sense of relief, I upended them into waiting sacks.

At the end of each day's purge, A.B. would usually produce a tray of assorted memorabilia which was fascinating in its diversity: a letter from Max Beerbohm written in 1952, another from De Gaulle in 1969; a copy of *Homes & Gardens* dated May 1932, containing photographs of the White House in Buckinghamshire; a postcard sent from Kipling to A.B.'s grandmother in 1909; a little cluster of old faded envelopes, all of which were stamped 6th April, 1939, and had been received in one morning's post containing, respectively, letters from the Prime Minister, the Foreign Secretary, the Minister for Co-ordination of Defence and the B.B.C.; a Christmas card from P. G. Wodehouse, who had once, to his amazement and delight, written him a fan letter out of the blue; a mass of important-looking government forms threatening the recipient with legal proceedings if unanswered by a date long since forgotten by all concerned, on which had been scrawled with obvious relish in A.B.'s own handwriting: 'Leave them alone and they'll come home, bringing their tails behind them!' And one evening there suddenly appeared a few yards of primrose satin which greatly pleased the finder and made his mind enthusiastically turn to upholstery, producing a veritable volley of ideas: 'This would make excellent cushion covers – or curtains perhaps? Will you see about it? And I suggest that sofa by the window should be recovered.'

The next day A.B. announced that he wanted to go shopping to look for some suitable furnishing material for the sofa. Excursions such as these were always undertaken with a kind of *gaieté de coeur* which was infectious, albeit they were educational as well. Seeing London under A.B.'s auspices was rather like being with a fast-walking, humorous encyclopaedia. In the museums or art galleries there was rarely the need for a catalogue; Westminster Abbey seemed to take on a new dimension; odd little corners of the capital which one had never thought existed, suddenly turned out to be full of the most fascinating architecture. And then there were the more intimate revelations, when A.B.'s own past caught up with him and evoked personal reminiscences such as the day when, half way down Sloane Street, he paused to remark, 'There's where I used to go for dancing lessons. I remember how delicious all the little girls looked in their frilly frocks.' Who was I with? Arthur Bryant or Maurice Chevalier? '*Thank heaven for little girls*' seemed so much in the air. And a little further on, the shades of Chevalier still appeared to hover when he said, 'Ah, here is the block of flats where M . . . . . used to live.' Was it said with a sigh? Certainly with great nostalgia. . . . '*Ah yes, I remember it well*. . . .' On one occasion we stood outside A.B.'s childhood home, No. 17, Lower Grosvenor Place, peering, as far as politeness permitted, through the windows: 'I wonder what it's like now . . . so long ago. . . . I've lived so *long*. . . .'

Yet the day he bought the sofa material A.B. seemed so *young*. Although he did not go shopping often, he was surprisingly good at it and, after visiting only two department stores, he found, in the second, more or less what he was looking for: a few yards of not-too-vivid red and white striped damask which he bore home triumphantly, full of plans, it seemed, for re-organising his whole life.

At that time, having given up farming, he went to his house in Buckinghamshire at ever-lengthening intervals. He wanted to sell it but, for a variety of reasons, had not got around to it, the chief of these being his utter dedication to his writing commitments. There was also, of course, his immutable inability to part with any of his *lares et penates* which always had to be reckoned with.

As yet I had never seen A.B.'s second home, but a week or so after our shopping expedition he took me to the South Pavilion for the first time, travelling to Wotton Underwood on a day's trip, complete with a picnic. It was, perhaps, strange, especially to those who did not know A.B. well, that he maintained both a fairly large London house, as his working headquarters, and a country home for his more cherished possessions, particularly as the latter remained unoccupied for most of the year. To all outward appearances it would suggest the well-organised life of an extremely rich man, something which he himself always maintained was not the case, notwithstanding that riches are always relative:

'I happen to be a member of what would now seem to be a fast-diminishing minority who earn their livelihood without any kind of protection. I am paid purely by results and after my work has been delivered, enjoy no pension or holiday rights and, so far as my tasks are of a regular kind, can be discharged at any time and without notice. I cannot even go sick and expect anyone else to do my work, for there is no one but myself to do it. . . .

'Probably not more than ten per cent of the books published in normal times bring a financial reward to their authors in any way comparable, even by the most modest reckoning, to the work which has gone into their writing. Unless an author can finance his unsuccessful books out of his successful, he cannot hope to support himself from his work over a term of years or to achieve any continuity in that work. The attitude of the Exchequer makes this impossible. . . .

'By a strange ruling of our fiscal authorities, the copyright of an author's books, even those he has written many years ago and thereupon subjected to death duties, is not allowed to be used by him as capital in his lifetime; should he attempt to encash it to provide for his old age or illness, it is subjected to income tax and surtax as though it was part of the earnings of the year in which it was sold. As a result an author, however successful, who had not achieved success and provided for his latter years in the period before confiscatory taxation of high incomes began in 1939, was under a necessity of either continuing to write for a livelihood until he died – that is, if anyone was prepared to buy the products of his age or senility – or of being left in his latter years without any livelihood at all. . . . I could name a dozen authors who a little while ago were, and in some cases still are, household words who, after contributing for years the bulk of their earnings to the State and having thereby earned as good a right of retirement as any man, are today having to go on scribbling as they did when they were young hacks at the outset of their careers, and with an ever-diminishing reward, not because they have any further urge to write but because they and their families would go hungry and homeless otherwise. From that injustice the future professional writer, like other professional men, was partly reprieved some years ago by the Government's enactment that now enables a professional man to set aside, free of tax, several hundred pounds a year to provide a modest retirement annuity for old age. Though I am one of those to whom this relief was granted a decade or more too late, I cannot help being grateful to the Government which accorded my profession this act of justice and to the man who was personally and primarily responsible for realising its need.'[1]

A.B. was not a business man. He was a writer, a successful one who had commanded a high, but therefore heavily taxed, income for a great many years. He was a man of very little inherited wealth and any money of his own making which he had managed to save was invested in house property ¬ which he did not own outright – and pictures and furniture. Therefore, although he gave the appearance of riches, this was counterbalanced by an unusually economical *modus vivendi* in which he hardly ever took a holiday, no longer owned a car, gave up travelling by first-class rail, entertained less and less, drank little, never smoked and rarely bought a new suit. His one extravagance was his lifelong love of living amongst beautiful and historical surroundings. Moreover, although his pictures and furniture had now appreciated in value, all had been acquired during a period when it was possible, with knowledge and the necessary trouble, to pick up a good bargain for comparatively little outlay. 'I rarely paid more than £20 for a piece,'

---

[1] Harold Macmillan, himself a publisher, when Chancellor of the Exchequer.

he once said. 'I stopped going to sales when the prices became too prohibitive.'

On reading Frances Donaldson's book on Evelyn Waugh, it struck me that there was a similarity between the latter's attitude to his financial state in later years and A.B.'s own. 'Evelyn was never a bore about income tax,' she wrote. 'He did not regard it as a topic for conversation. But . . . I have always believed, perhaps fancifully, that income tax spoiled the end of his life. . . .'

But there seemed nothing to spoil A.B.'s delight on seeing the South Pavilion again on the October day in 1972 when he first took me there. It was an unusual house, one of two pavilions flanking Wotton House itself, all dating from the late 17th or possibly the very early 18th century. It was tall, almost like a house on stilts, surrounded by a peaceful, well-kept walled garden. In fact, the peace and silence at Wotton was something which impressed me at first more than anything else, coming, as we had, straight from London. It made me realise how sincere were A.B.'s frequent remarks such as: 'The *noise* when I was waiting for a bus the other day was unbelievable. Motorists have no right to roar down Knightsbridge at that speed. If a fairy were to grant me one wish, I should ask for a little gun to point at the worst offenders and render them immobile for ever.'

But now, here in Buckinghamshire, it was like the back of beyond: no village, just a few smaller houses seemingly set down at random near the Big Three. It was a perfect day on which to see it all. The autumn sun was diamond bright and the South Pavilion seemed almost to be smiling, glad to see its owner at last and to be lived in, if only for a few hours. It was not, by any means, a family house, but then its owner had never made any pretence at being a family man. Inside, it was rather like a stage-set, especially the Big Room which really was big, with steps leading up to a gallery at one end, a room which A.B. felt had once been used for showing off 18th-century gilt and silver coach harnesss. But now it was transformed by this twentieth century historian's prize possessions, his pictures and family portraits on the high walls, a *tout ensemble* or 'final act', as it were, of years of indulging in his one great love: 'the house beautiful'.

Each picture, each piece, had a personal little saga attached to its acquisition: 'I remember picking up that tallboy for £5 when my first wife's family things were sold at Somerford,' – 'That punch-bowl I broke, unfortunately, when I was trying to place it on top of a bookcase. That's why it's riveted.' – 'That Louis XV Grandmother's chair I saw in an antique shop in Paddington on my way to the station one day. I remember it cost forty-five shillings.' The details were too much to take in at once, but the overall impression was enchanting. I went all over the house: the small dining-room with an old mahogany table bought at Blenheim just after the Second World War, on which there had been many an ink blot (now miraculously camouflaged by countless polishings) for which A.B. liked to think a young Winston Churchill might have been responsible; the two bedrooms on the first floor, each with its four-poster bed; and the larger attic floor, including the bedroom where A.B. slept, in which there was another four-poster and, of course, more antiques. It was all meticulously kept by a faithful cleaner who came regularly to look after the place in his absence.

To sell the South Pavilion and then be forced either to sell its contents or put them in store was something its owner could not bear to contemplate. The pieces were like children to him, a substitute – possibly even more than his books – for the ones he never had, nor, indeed, had ever wanted. He seemed to see in these antiques, made by individual craftsmen in that distant past of which he was so fond, a kind of perpetuity, a stake, perhaps, in the future. He could not endure the thought of them being separated or sold off to less loving or appreciative hands. What he would have liked would have been to have had all his possessions from both his houses in one, and that one somehow to be preserved after his death. His belongings were almost sacred, their value to him impossible to price.

We left the South Pavilion soon after lunch. The sun was not quite as bright now, and it saddened me to think of the treasure-house being left to itself once more, until such time as its owner felt able to pay it another visit. I did not like to think of the grandfather clocks and the framed ancestors waiting there so patiently. I wished A.B. would hurry up and amalgamate his two homes so that he could enjoy the one. I took one more look at the Big Room before we left. There was a curious timelessness about it as, indeed, I realised there was about its owner. Perhaps neither he, nor the portraits, nor the clocks were in all that hurry. They belonged, in some indefinable way, to eternity, something about which A.B. was always very conscious. He looked on life, I believe, as transitory and on death as an inevitability which he would accept quite philosophically, almost – or so I sometimes used to think – with relief, when all would be one. . . .

As we drove away through the Vale of Aylesbury, sometimes green, sometimes blue, full of light and shade and soft undulations, I thought for a long time about yet a further revelation of the life of this unusual man which I had just witnessed, a man with so many sides to his character it was almost impossible to paint a composite portrait. Who *was* Arthur Bryant? Puck, Peter Pan, portrayer of the past, political thinker, prophet, property-owner, poet or philosopher? It was like trying to capture the likeness of a restless sitter who, as soon as one began painting from one angle, would suddenly get up and turn round so that, on looking up, one was presented with a side one hadn't reckoned on at all. Often I felt A.B.'s preoccupation with his possessions, for all the aesthetic pleasure they gave him, seemed deplorably worldly. Even his concern over penal tax and inflation bordered on the obsessive. And yet . . . how could I think him materialistic, this man whose mind was so often preoccupied with another world:

'Here is the eternal consolation of old age: the divine answer to the harsh decree of Time and Fate that man must loose his hold on all he sets store by, relinquish all things material that he has won, see the road he was travelling fade into unattainable distance before him. For even as it fails, the past he wrought so eagerly will begin to take shape for the first time: and what was sought as future tense and quickly forgotten as past tense will, in an hour of tranquillity, become present and thus eternal tense. . . .

'To one whose task it is to study the brief records of our transient human years, who thinks in terms not of any particular generation or any individual life but of history, of the whole interminable march of the human race – and it sounds a very inhuman thing to do – it seems in the long run of comparatively little account whether a man falls in battle in youth or dies in old or middle-age. He dies so soon, in any case; his body returns to the elementals of earth.

'Unless a man thinks deeply and steadily about death he cannot be said to be thinking realistically about life at all. It is the weakness of our age that we tend to avoid and shun the thought of death and seldom allow ourselves to dwell on it. . . . To regard death as the ultimate evil, the thing to be avoided at all costs, is to be dead indeed: it is to walk the earth a corpse. . . . Only when we have thought deeply and rightly about death and have learnt not to fear it, shall we be able to live on rational terms with it: to fit its unavoidable necessity into the pattern of life as we would have it lived, and to live life in right proportion – in other words, morally. Christ, we are told, came into the world to teach men how to live by dying. Without His life the crucifixion is nothing; without the crucifixion His life on earth has no purpose. . . . Religion renews man's contact with his own roots, which lie alike beyond the womb and beyond the grave. It releases us from the blindness of the trivial and enables us to see outside the walls of life. . . . A world without religion is a world of sleep-walking.

'There is one thing in life even more important than death: there is love. Without readiness to face death nothing can be preserved: without love nothing can be made. . . . The key to life on earth – what Christ called the Kingdom of Heaven – is love, and the ultimate test of love is to give up everything, even life, for what one loves. . . . The heart to love and the courage to be true to love is instinct in every human being, even the humblest and most degraded. It was this, Christ saw – the divine in man, the spark he derived from God – which, lit and tended, could make a Heaven for him on earth and, through faith, an eternal one in life beyond the grave. . . . It seems to me that those who love one another can help one another most by taking death into their mutual calculations. We have got to die, and, however much we may love another person, we have got to undergo the separation imposed by death. It would seem almost like a game of "make-believe" to build love – by far the greatest thing in the world – on any other foundation but a frank recognition of this fact. To love and know one is loved may matter to one even more in death than it does in life. . . .

'It is the profoundest pessimism to suppose that our existence on this planet is an end in itself. It makes nonsense of all our fine talk of idealism, justice and liberty, patriotism or moral nobility. By such a measure a man who gives his life for a cause is a fool: the only virtue is to live as long as possible. . . .

'Both our reason and our conscience remind us, if we ever pause from our avocations to take thought, that there is something more important than mere living or than being young. We are born into a world where from the moment of our birth we start to undergo a process of never-ceasing physical change which culminates inevitably in decay and death. There is a clock, as it were, that starts ticking against us at the very hour of our nativity and which continues doing so until our eyelids close in death. Unless the ignoble and cowardly aim of keeping alive for the maximum possible period at all costs be regarded as our objective in life, the only triumph open to us is to achieve something during that time-ticking process that places us above and beyond time. That something, if it is to have any significance at all, cannot be an external or material achievement, for all such achievement is subject to exactly the same inevitable extinction by time as our own brief corporeal lives. It may possibly outlast them by a few centuries, but in the long chronicles of time even a thousand years is an infinitesimally minute measure. . . . Anything we do which possesses value must be something which transcends the limitations of time. There is only one way in which we can conceivably hope to do that: by a transformation or enhancement of a spiritual faculty within us that is independent of our bodies and of the time-decay to which they are subject. An instinct deep within us, strengthened by all experience, tells us that the whole purpose of what we call life, that is, of growing old – for all life is "growing old" – is to enable us to intensify the quality of our own inner spirit. . . . The process of growing old is, therefore, one which should be of profound interest, and, if rightly used, satisfaction. . . . During the process man is, or should be, adding to the best of his ability to his spiritual stature. . . . His body may become dust, but his spiritual heritage is inextinguishable. . . . It endures from generation to generation. . . .

'The greatest of all death's functions in man's restless consciousness is that it unifies for him, as nothing else can – not even love – the whole vast and diverse universe of time and space. It makes him a citizen of all worlds and all ages, above all of all that he has ever loved, to all eternity. . . . It is good to leave this greatest of all future events to the individual spirit as an adventure to be taken when it comes, as adventures should be taken, with courage and faith as staffs. It will be time enough to take one's bearings when the soul sets forth on its new voyage. . . .

'Only in his own silence can a man hear the music of the spheres. . . .'

Bibliography

History of the Harrow Mission – Privately printed   1921

Rupert Buxton – A Memoir – C.U.P.   1925

The Spirit of Conservatism – Methuen   1929

The Story of Ashridge – Privately printed   1929

KING CHARLES II – Longmans   (re-issued Collins)   1931

Macaulay – Peter Davies   1932

SAMUEL PEPYS: THE MAN IN THE MAKING – C.U.P.   (re-issued Collins)   1933

The National Character – Longmans   1934

The England of Charles II – Longmans   (re-issued as *Restoration England* – Collins)   1934

SAMUEL PEPYS: THE YEARS OF PERIL – C.U.P.   (re-issued Collins)   1935

The Letters & Speeches of Charles II – Cassell   1935

Postman's Horn – Longmans   1936

The American Ideal – Watson Foundation Lectures – Longmans   1936

King George V – Peter Davies   1937

Stanley Baldwin – Hamish Hamilton   1937

SAMUEL PEPYS: THE SAVIOUR OF THE NAVY – C.U.P.   (re-issued Collins)   1938

Humanity in Politics – National Book Association   1937

Peace in Our Time – Speeches of Neville Chamberlain – Longmans   1939

Unfinished Victory – Macmillan   1940

Britain Awake – Collins   1940

ENGLISH SAGA – Collins   1940

THE YEARS OF ENDURANCE – Collins   1942

The Summer of Dunkirk – Kemsley Press   1944

The Battle of Britain – Kemsley Press   1944

Trafalgar & Alamein – Kemsley Press   1944

YEARS OF VICTORY – Collins   1944

History as Literature – English Association Presidential Address   1946

Historian's Holiday – Dropmore Press – (re-issued Collins)   1946

A Historian's View of the War – Royal United Services Institution   1947

THE AGE OF ELEGANCE – Collins – Sunday Times £1,000 Prize and Gold Medal   1950

Literature and the Historian (10th Annual Lectures, National Book League) – C.U.P.   1952

THE STORY OF ENGLAND: MAKERS OF THE REALM – Collins 1953

THE TURN OF THE TIDE – Collins   1957

TRIUMPH IN THE WEST – Collins   1959

Jimmy, The Dog in My Life – Lutterworth Press   (re-issued Collins) 1960

A Choice for Destiny – Collins   1962

THE AGE OF CHIVALRY – Collins   1963

Only Yesterday – Collins   1965

The Fire and The Rose – Collins   1966

THE MEDIEVAL FOUNDATION – Collins   1967

Protestant Island – Collins   1968

A History of B.U.P.A. – Privately printed   1968

THE LION AND THE UNICORN – Collins   1969

Nelson – Collins   1970

THE GREAT DUKE – Collins   1971

JACKETS OF GREEN – Collins   1972

A THOUSAND YEARS OF BRITISH MONARCHY – Privately printed   (re-issued Collins)   1973

Acknowledgements

The passages from 'Our Notebook' on the undernoted pages – none of which has already been re-published in *The Lion and The Unicorn* – are reprinted here by the kind courtesy of Mr. James Bishop, the editor of *The Illustrated London News.*

Index